CARUSO

Carissimo amico Giuseppe
Giuseppe
Barzi
sinceramente affe
Enrico Caruso

Londra 1902

CARUSO

Stanley Jackson

STEIN AND DAY/*Publishers*/New York

First Stein and Day paperback edition, 1975
First published in 1972
Copyright © 1972 by Stanley Jackson
Library of Congress Catalog Card No. 77-187313
All rights reserved
Printed in the United States of America
Stein and Day/*Publishers*/Scarborough House
Briarcliff Manor, N. Y. 10510
ISBN 0-8128-1851-2

Contents

FOREWORD

ix

PART ONE

'Santa Lucia'

I

PART TWO

'Addio a Napoli'

47

PART THREE

'La Donna è Mobile'

121

PART FOUR

'Vesti la Giubba'

185

PART FIVE

'The Star-Spangled Banner'

243

BIBLIOGRAPHY

294

INDEX

297

Illustrations

Following Page 80

Caruso at 22

Ada Giachetti

The forecourt of the Savoy Hotel, London, flooded for the Gondola Dinner, 1905

Sketch by Caruso of Gatti-Casazza, director of La Scala

Self-caricature by Caruso

Sketch by Caruso of a scene from *Madame Butterfly*

Sketch by Caruso of Toscanini

As King Gustavo in *Un Ballo in Maschera*

As Canio in *I Pagliacci*

San Francisco after the earthquake, 1906

Following Page 208

Dame Nellie Melba

Caruso posing for a bust in Genoa

Caruso with Helen Keller

Pavlova and Chaliapin

Caruso with his baby daughter

Caruso and his wife sailing from New York, 1921

Tetrazzini in New York, 1907

Giacomo Puccini

Caruso with Antonio Scotti and Paolo Tosti

As Eléazar in *La Juive*

Caruso on the terrace of the Hotel Vittorio, Sorrento, 1921

Foreword

With traditional exceptions like politicians and luckless generals, centenary biographies tend to be flattering or uncritical to the point of adulation. In the case of a legendary idol like Enrico Caruso, whose mystique has remained potent through the medium of countless records, there is an even stronger temptation to repair any chips to the marble with an over-loving hand. Although he gave his last performance over half a century ago, memories of his incomparable voice and personality are jealously cherished by a small but dedicated corps of admirers who had the good fortune to see him in the flesh. They are sadly outnumbered by a less discriminating generation of film-goers who find it almost impossible to dissociate him from Mario Lanza.

I missed hearing him at Covent Garden and was not old enough to strop my razor to 'La donna è mobile', but the Caruso sob was as much part of my boyhood as Kitchener's recruiting poster. I can still recall the numbing shock of his death and the grief which almost prostrated his countrymen, who for weeks afterwards lit candles in St Patrick's, Soho Square, and other churches in London's 'Little Italy'.

Like most of my generation I came to know Caruso through records, progressing from the vintage Red Seal and HMV labels to the electrical re-recordings of later years. Operatically I am lower middle-brow and an unashamed devotee of Puccini and most of the other composers in Caruso's repertoire, although custom has staled the appeal of some of the over-cantered warhorses in less gifted hands.

My interest in Caruso's personality was first sparked by a prewar acquaintanceship with Gigli, who often suffered from unkind comparison with his predecessor but could still pay generous tribute to his lovable qualities ('he created life and warmth wherever he went'). It is with this aspect of Caruso's career that I am primarily concerned rather than with the technical aspects of his art, which musicologists, critics and voice experts will continue to analyse and assess whenever a new series of his records is issued or yet another 'second Caruso' makes his début.

He was a fertile source of picturesque legends in his lifetime. They have accumulated since his death. The biographical data are voluminous yet not wholly satisfactory, in part because of excessive reticence about the less amiable aspects of his character. The first biography, published in 1922, was written by Pierre Key and expanded from a series of long interviews with the tenor, supplemented by affectionate reminiscences from Bruno Zirato, his private secretary for four years. Mrs Caruso's own book quickly followed. It offers many fascinating glimpses of their courtship and brief marriage. Both of these authors are compulsory reading for all students of Caruso's career, but with obvious reservations. They make only passing reference to Ada Giachetti, who shared his life for eleven years and gave him two sons. In their anxiety to erect a monument, neither considered it appropriate to dwell on the Central Park episode, which caused him to be convicted of indecency and threatened to wreck him professionally. A man can sing like an angel and still tweak a comely behind!

Caruso encouraged such camouflage. He had many virtues but objectivity about himself was not among them: once he actually scribbled 'Liar!' across an unfavourable review. He was also over-inclined to sentimentalise his childhood and early struggles. He kept accounts but no diaries. His letters written to his wife and lovingly edited by her are quaint, touching and semi-literate. They are devoted mainly to his health symptoms, itineraries and local appreciation or otherwise of his performances.

Documentation becomes more reliable and objective from the turn of the century onwards, when he made his first spectacular successes at La Scala, Covent Garden and the Metropolitan. The histories of these celebrated opera houses, reinforced by a plethora of critical notices and almost daily press reports of his activities, both on and off the stage, have all helped to place him in focus.

I know Naples, where Caruso was born and died, and am also familiar with most of the cities in Europe and the United States where he enslaved audiences and became a cult for millions of opera-goers as well as those who could afford only a few of his records. In attempting a 'centenary portrait' which will neither denigrate nor re-embalm, I have benefited from the reminiscences of singers, musicians, impresarios and many other contemporaries who are listed in the bibliography. While engaged in researching my history of the Savoy Hotel, Caruso's headquarters during his Covent Garden seasons, I was also fortunate enough to discover much new information about his life in London with Chaliapin, McCormack, Melba, Tetrazzini, Tosti and others.

I owe a special debt to the British Museum Reading Room staff; the editor of *The Gramophone*; and the librarians of several London newspapers, who gave valuable help in checking and cross-checking records, several of which were inaccurate, out of date and at times contradictory.

Finally, grateful acknowledgement is made to the Archive Office, the Royal Opera House, Covent Garden, for generous help in many directions, particularly in tracing rare illustrations and photographs.

Acknowledgements

I should like to express my thanks to the following publishers for permission to quote from the works mentioned: Hurst & Blackett Ltd and Little, Brown and Company for extracts from *Enrico Caruso* by Pierre Key; T. Werner Laurie Ltd and Simon & Schuster, Inc. for material from *Enrico Caruso: His Life and Death* by Dorothy Caruso; The Cresset Press and Harcourt Brace Jovanovich, Inc. for extracts from *Caruso* by T. R. Ybarra; George Allen & Unwin Ltd for an extract from *Nights in London* by Thomas Burke; Macmillan London and Basingstoke for a short extract from *Puccini Among Friends* by Vincent Seligman; T. Werner Laurie Ltd and Charles Scribner's Sons for an extract from *Bedouins* by James Huneker; Houghton Mifflin Company for a quotation from *Men, Women and Tenors* by Frances Alda; Routledge & Kegan Paul Ltd for an extract from *Midway In My Song* by Lotte Lehmann; Cassell & Co. Ltd and Simon & Schuster, Inc. for material from *Puccini* by George R. Marek; Macmillan London and Basingstoke for extracts from *Great Morning* by Osbert Sitwell; The Bodley Head for an extract from *My Autobiography* by Charles Chaplin.

ILLUSTRATIONS

Acknowledgements are due to: Culver Pictures; Radio Times Hulton Picture Library; Tomas Jaski Ltd; Messrs Raymond Mander and Joe Mitchenson; Royal Opera House, Covent Garden; Life Magazine © Time Inc.; Stein & Day Publishers; U.S.I.S.; and the Savoy Hotel Ltd.

His immortality is secure, for every day, somewhere, somebody will hear his voice for the first time and say, 'This was a singer'.

COMPTON MACKENZIE

PART ONE

'Santa Lucia'

Chapter One

Enrico Caruso was born during the evening of 25 February 1873 in a smallish room with a balcony overlooking via San Giovannello agli Otto Calli—an impressive name for one of the many swollen veins in the gangrenous slumland of Naples. The two-storeyed house, flaky with peeling stucco, accommodated several families, who shared a solitary cold-water tap on the landing, and like every other dwelling in that locality it lacked indoor sanitation.

Caruso's first audience was the neighbourhood's busy midwife, when she briskly slapped his wrinkled buttocks and was rewarded with an anguished cry of protest.

She had already delivered seventeen of his brothers and sisters into an unwelcoming world, but each of the frail human parcels had succumbed in turn to the *febbre Napolitana*, some even before they were labelled in the church next door. There was little hope of survival for this wriggling infant. His tiny claws clutched the arm of an emaciated hollow-eyed woman who at last lay tranquilly on her back clasping a crucifix between sweat-soaked fingers. His father, Marcellino, a chunkily built, peppery man with no patience for the spasms and snortings of his temporary heir, escaped into church to light a candle before hurrying off to the *cantina* for a few glasses of *grappa*. His friends cracked their stale jokes about his virility and commiserated over the noisy nights ahead which would surely end with yet another small coffin being trundled to the nearby cemetery.

Anna Caruso was then thirty-five, two years older than her husband, though he was already balding and his beard showed several grey streaks. Both were now work-worn and heavily lined, very different from the laughing newly married couple who had come so hopefully from their valley in Piedmonte d'Alife to set up house in the fourth largest city in

3

Europe after London, Paris and St Petersburg. San Gennaro, the patron saint of Naples, had once commanded the flowing lava of Vesuvius to stop short at its very gates, but now he was enthroned in a shining dome he seemed indifferent to the human tide of misery that flowed below the magnificent cathedral built for him on the site of Apollo's temple.

The Carusos were among the half million existing in only eight square kilometres of cellars and tenements and vile sewers. Barring some miracle, they could expect to live and die in their corner of *Napoli senza sole*, a sunless squalor of rats and mosquitoes. Those who escaped malaria and typhoid would still suffer the effects of pellagra from years of a starchy and inadequate diet.

Caruso was born into a recently united nation, but two races remained very much apart under the flag; the few who ate white bread and a vast majority more than grateful for black. The Bourbons had departed without noticeably changing the harsh facts of life for the impoverished masses of Naples and Sicily. In G. M. Trevelyan's phrase, 'Victor Emmanuel had stitched the boot, but the toe and heel still pinched'. Lombardy had capital, industries, raw materials and a kinder climate, while the south remained sullen, backward, slothful and largely illiterate after centuries of misrule. Garibaldi's hopes of a bright future were soon dismissed with the Neapolitan's traditional mocking stare and sceptical forefinger when most of the promised reforms failed to materialise. Property speculators, aided by corrupt officials, simply patched up the old slum dwellings, or replaced them by tenements hurriedly erected with inferior materials. New public buildings and showy marble fountains, topped by imposing obelisks, dazzled foreign tourists on their way to the museums hung with old masters and rare tapestries glowing in the light of crystal chandeliers. The poor, meanwhile, continued to exist on rice, beans, black bread and pasta (Caruso often attributed his early loss of hair to a childhood lack of vitamins).

The slum-clearance programme briefly provided jobs and regular wages, but it was soon followed by unemployment, higher taxes and yet more ruthless exploitation by the hated Camorra. This Mafia-like secret society controlled the customs and excise and deployed almost unlimited political power through a network of grasping officials, many of whom were themselves members of the sinister brotherhood. Railway porters, carriage drivers, whores and even the wretched peasants bringing their farm produce into the city were all at the mercy of an organisation with its own laws, ceremonies and private courts to punish those unwise enough to defy or betray the code.

Caruso's father, a skilled mechanic, had worked for some years in a factory manufacturing cottonseed oil and purified cream of tartar. His tough constitution and a bullying manner had won him a foreman's status, the kind of key position normally exploited by the Camorra, but he was too outspoken in his cups to be considered reliable. Besides, his wife's excessive piety and her devotion to the parish priest were obvious risks.

Their baby was christened Errico, the formal 'Enrico' only emerging later to dignify theatre posters. He owed his survival into infancy to chance and his mother's devoutness. It so happened that an acquaintance, a woman of noble birth who had met her at church services and did welfare work among the local poor, had just lost a baby of her own. Hearing that Anna Caruso could not feed her son, and aware also of the family's distressing medical history, she volunteered as wet-nurse. The baby thrived. In later years he would often speak with emotion of this foster mother, whose abundant milk had not only saved his life and endowed him with abnormally strong teeth but, he felt sure, also nourished his exceptional voice. The Contessa maintained her interest long after he was weaned. She gave him his first lessons in reading and writing, apart from bringing many a welcome basket of provisions during Anna's frequent spells of illness.

Another son followed after a few months, soon to be laid in his coffin. But a baby boy, Giovanni, who arrived in January 1876, would outlive his brother by many years. Their father

5

was far less enchanted by the birth of his twenty-first child, Assunta, a sickly girl whose whimperings drove him even more regularly to the taverns. He was only consoled by being appointed superintendent at the factory. Although his pay was not increased, Signor Meuricoffre had provided rent-free accommodation in a property he owned in the Sant' Anna alle Paludi district. It was a little more spacious, but the street so narrow and unfragrant that tourists held their noses as they hurried to catch the train for Pompeii.

Errico was devoted to his mother, who had become almost bedridden after the birth of Assunta, mercifully her last child. He ran errands as soon as his short legs could carry him and would bring up pails of water to bathe her and himself every day when the *solleone*, the pitiless August sun-lion, clawed the last shred of vitality from tired ill-nourished bodies. She used to clear the wax from his ears with a long hairpin while he made little jokes to coax a smile from her. He would never forget her pain-rimmed eyes or the waxen face as serene as the terracotta Madonna over her bed. He used to dab her forehead and fight an unending battle with the dirt and flies while his brother crawled round the floor and Assunta suffered her breathless spasms.

Caruso's hypochondria and his lifelong obsession with clean clothes, linen sheets and perfume undoubtedly date back to early infancy in that cramped sick-room, but more particularly to the agonised months of 1884 when a thousand cholera victims were tossed nightly into a vast pit on the Campo Santo. Huge rats, maddened by the antiseptic sulphur fumes, rushed out of the sewers to bite anyone in their path, while human vermin ravaged the city to rape and loot, even penetrating the churches.

As many as forty cases of cholera were reported in a single day in the Caruso's street, but the family was miraculously spared. Anna credited their salvation to her own prayers and Errico's solo performances in the church choir. With his hair brushed and glossy, a shirt-front cut from clean white paper by his mother and a saint's medallion round his neck, he hurried

6

every evening into Sant'Anna to light a candle for the Madonna of Pompeii before taking his place among the choristers trained by Father Bronzetti.

At the good father's he received his only formal education from the age of eight, barely two years in all but long enough to earn the complimentary nickname of 'Carusiello' for his pure treble. Before long he was being excused classes by the school organist, who rehearsed him for church choirs in Naples and the surrounding district. He would be given sweets and even a lira or two for singing at fashionable weddings or funerals, sometimes as far off as Amalfi.

Carusiello also showed a precocious talent for sketching, and soon developed such a fine hand that one of his tutors set him to duplicating manuscripts. Squatting under the street lamps he began to earn pennies by making copies of songs for music students and composers of *romanzas* entered for local contests. Years later, when his own repertoire ran to sixty-four operas in half a dozen languages, he travelled everywhere with a notebook and never lost the habit of writing out phrases to master some difficult passage.

Anna Caruso had made sacrifices to scrape together the five lire (a dollar) a month for his school fees. According to him she even went without shoes and saved pennies from the housekeeping, but he tended afterwards to exaggerate his mother's role. In a short time Father Bronzetti waived his fee altogether, but Carusiello showed no intention of becoming a teacher's pet or a model for his schoolfellows. Sociable by nature, he often cut choir practice when the nights were starlit and the spring air heavy with perfume. On feast days he loved to sing to the tinkling guitars and mandolins and drain a glass of the *vino nuovo* while the crowds danced a tarantella. He was always hungry. He would spend his last coins on blue figs from Sorrento and thought nothing more satisfying than a slice of good melon, with which one could eat, drink and wash one's face at the same time. When he had spent the few soldi the fishermen at Gergellina threw him for helping to haul in their nets he would sometimes wheedle a free dish of snails, dressed with tomatoes, pepperoni and garlic, from the handcart of a kindly *maruzzaro*.

The waterfront fascinated him. It was fun to take a dawn dip at Santa Lucia or dive headlong from the Molo into a bay curving so invitingly under the violet-tinted green slopes of Vesuvius. Even as a child he could swim long distances, which may have helped to develop the barrel chest and lung capacity of his adult years. Overwhelmed by the sick-room stench and rebelling against the treadmill of choir practice, he sometimes thought wistfully of signing on as a cabin boy or even stowing away on one of the big liners bound for America or the Argentine, where so many southerners were making new lives.

Daydreaming was almost inevitable in that theatrical city dominated by glowing old Vesuvius, but one was preserved from becoming too solemn. It was no coincidence that *opera buffa* had originated and flowered in the local sense of parody. When Caruso made his first money in the theatre, he once went round his former haunts. A beggar boy, with a fiddle under his arm, turned a somersault, swept off a battered hat and held out his dirty hand for a coin.

'Suppose I gave you nothing?' teased the singer in the Neapolitan accent he would never lose.

'Why, then,' laughed the urchin, 'I'll still have the sunshine.'

Caruso could see himself in that grubby little waif whenever he rubbed his cleft chin, a legacy of jumping too hastily from a street car to avoid paying his fare. Only his mother and Father Bronzetti kept him from joining the gangs of young bootblacks, pickpockets and homosexuals who usually ended up in the San Francesco prison. He was quick-tempered and wilful at school, where he once knocked down a bigger boy who wanted revenge after being deposed as chief soloist in the choir. At the prize-giving Bronzetti rebuked Errico, who at once flung down his medal for singing. His father then boxed his ears and made him kiss the principal's feet. Crimson-faced, he complied, but he never returned to that school.

When he was barely eleven he went into the De Lucca Mechanical Laboratories as an apprentice for a few lire a week, often putting in a ten-hour day and humping heavy sacks. He handled tools well, but his neatness and a flair for draughtsmanship soon led to promotion to the drawing-office. All week, however, he looked forward to Sundays, when he could get into clean clothes and sing in the local church choir. More important, he returned to favour with one of the Bronzetti tutors, whose daughter gave him instruction some evenings, accompanying him on the piano. He had a good ear and quickly memorised the lyrics which street singers chanted outside the city's cafés. Now and then he joined in and was rewarded with a few coins and even a free meal from some good-natured member of the troupe. After a punishing day at the works he would sit at his mother's bedside and divert her with snatches of operatic arias and ballads. If his brother and baby sister were asleep or Marcellino in no mood for a recital, he diligently copied out a piece of music, humming quietly to himself.

His first qualified teacher was the sister of a Dr Niola, who attended his mother. According to one of Caruso's Italian biographers, Eugenio Gara, his mother could rarely afford medical fees and used to pay with gifts of mozzarella cheese, fruit and olives which her relatives occasionally brought in from the country. Errico would take the basket to the doctor's house and linger in the kitchen while Amelia Niola was running through scales with some pupil in the drawing-room; then, the moment he arrived home, he would repeat them like a parrot.

The signorina soon agreed to give him free lessons two or three evenings a week, but she was something of a martinet. She appreciated his sweet contralto but disliked his rather flashy café-singer gestures and, even more, the slangy Neapolitan dialect, which offended her spinsterish ear. She used to rap his knuckles with a heavy ruler and one evening impatiently slapped his face. That ended the month's tuition. For the next fortnight he stayed away from the doctor's house and played instead with his old school friends in the railway yards or tagged along with the strolling musicians. Dr Niola exposed him

9

by casually asking why he had given up his lessons. That night Marcellino gave him such a brutal strapping that his mother, sobbing hysterically, threw herself between them. Nevertheless, when his father fell sick from a protesting liver and feared he might lose both his position and the house that went with it, the boy took over some of his duties and did creditably enough to be offered a berth by Meuricoffre. He declined, however, to change one ill-paid routine job for another.

He was already soured by the long hours at the laboratory. Desperate to start singing lessons, he had asked for an increase in wages but been fobbed off because of his age. He walked out and promptly offered himself as an outrider on the Count of Bari's coach. Lacking in inches, he lasted only a few days but refused to take an alternative job in the stables. He then joined a manufacturer of street fountains and enjoyed going out to adjust and maintain Signor Palmieri's ornate creations, a number of which still survive. On his sentimental tours of Naples in later years he would often point out a fountain at the Bridge of Cerra that he had once helped to install.

Errico began to supplement his earnings by hiring himself out to serenade young maidens, and to his delight some café minstrels adopted him as a kind of mascot. Patrons seemed amused by the small merry-faced lad with the snapping black eyes and surprisingly pure voice. He was polite, but his quick urchin wit brought smiles as the hat was passed around. Not only was he eager to run errands for the whole troupe, but he would solemnly stand treat whenever he had any spare coins in his pocket, asking in return only the chance to sing and a little friendly coaching if he went off key or botched a phrase.

His peak moment of the week arrived on Sundays, when he stood up in church to deliver a solo, particularly if his mother was feeling strong enough to leave her bed. Even Marcellino, no church-goer himself, grudgingly admitted that this brought a certain local prestige, but still thought the street-singing disreputable and not to be compared with a steady job. As the demand for fountains was limited, he persuaded Meuricoffre to take his son on as a junior storekeeper. Errico was then fifteen and already in fair demand as a soloist at church festivals outside the parish.

In June 1888 he was engaged to sing for the feast of Corpus Christi with the choir at San Severino, a church noted for its sculptures and some of Corenzio's finest frescoes. For several days he thought of little but the chance of singing before the vast congregation. That evening, although he was already dressed and scrubbed clean, he had no heart to leave his mother, who had scarcely eaten during the past week and seemed so feeble that even the usually cheerful Dr Niola looked anxious. Errico only agreed to go because his mother insisted that his prayers would surely restore her to health.

He had barely finished his solo when a woman neighbour signalled to him. He left the church at once and ran blindly home. Anna lay at peace between a squadron of candles, her crucifix resting on the threadbare quilt. He knelt beside his father and wept with him. Some hours later, when the house was silent, he found a little pastel portrait and placed it carefully in his Bible. To the end of his days it stood framed on his bedside table on trains, on ships and in countless hotel rooms all over the world, and he would never go on stage without calling for his mother's help.

For some weeks Errico was tormented by grief and a desperate loneliness. He no longer joined his old companions outside the noisy cafés, and he even gave up choir singing on Sundays. He spent all his evenings with Giovanni and Assunta, who were cared for during the day by kindly neighbours. But it was only a matter of weeks before they were packed off to an orphanage.

Marcellino had grown gentler, but self-pity was already sucking him back into the taverns. He was almost at breaking point when Meuricoffre sent him to install new machinery at Aversa, some miles from Naples. There he lodged with a widow, Maria Castaldi, who that autumn agreed to marry him. Like Anna Caruso she was a woman of deep piety, but she enjoyed more robust health and also happened to be an admirable housekeeper.

11

She was gentle with Assunta but sometimes thrashed Giovanni when he became mischievous. Errico, however, could do no wrong in her eyes. He had the few titbits from the larder and his clothes were always lovingly darned. Like his mother, Maria was convinced that his voice had come from heaven and encouraged him to practise his scales and lyrics. Before the end of the year he was back with the café troupe and again taking solos in the church choir.

Errico had now begun to earn a little more money at the factory, where he was soon promoted from stores to clerical work. His handwriting had always been good and he impressed Signor Meuricoffre with his neatness and punctuality. Soon he developed an audit system to check pilfering. The thrifty Swiss showed his appreciation by allowing him to work fairly elastic hours in the off-peak season, which gave him more freedom to practise his singing at home and even accept occasional engagements.

He worked sometimes for a local manager who supplied choristers for festivals in country districts around Naples, taking an all-in sum from which he paid the boys and pouching a fat profit for himself. As soloist Errico was given the largest fee, averaging ten lire for an evening's performance. After singing for several hours in the church at Majori, he was once 'invited' by the local mayor, a Baron Zezza, to entertain guests in his home. Although tired, he was too timid to refuse and had to sing Neapolitan ballads for several hours with only a few scraps from the supper table to sustain him. At six the next morning, wrapped in the mayor's old shooting jacket to keep out the chill morning air, he was put aboard a coach for the fifteen-mile journey back to Naples. He passed the coat on to his father.

(Twenty years later, during his last prewar season at the Royal Opera House, Covent Garden, Caruso received a letter from the same Baron Zezza, who reminded him half seriously that he had never returned the shooting jacket. Caruso replied that he had lost it and would be pleased to repay its value, but on one condition: as he had sung almost the whole of that night

12

at Majori without payment, he was still owed his fee, which, at his present rate, would be £400.* 'My voice was the same then as it is today . . . Moreover, I expect you to add the interest for twenty years!' The baron wrote back offering to forget all about the jacket in exchange for an autograph. Caruso good-naturedly sent him a framed and signed photograph, together with an elegant silver hunting flask.)

Apart from church festivals he used to entertain sailors at the Caffé del Mole, but soon found it more profitable to sing for the queues waiting outside public swimming baths. At the Bagni del Risorgimento in via Caracciola he teamed up with a pianist, and the owner allowed them to keep anything they collected. This could amount to quite a respectable sum on fine days, though it was sometimes hardly worth sharing.

One summer, now eighteen and despondent about his voice, which had broken disappointingly into a light baritone instead of the full tenor then much preferred by admirers of Tamagno and other favourites of the day, Caruso was warmly complimented on his singing by an elegant young bather, Eduardo Missiano, himself an aspiring baritone, who urged him to take lessons. He was flattered but pointed out sadly that such a luxury was beyond his means. Their acquaintance ripened. Missiano, the son of wealthy parents, finally persuaded his own singing teacher, Guglielmo Vergine, to accept the youth as a free pupil, threatening to go elsewhere himself if he refused. The Maestro was unimpressed by the audition. 'His voice is like the wind whistling through a window,' he declared acidly, but Caruso was permitted to join sessions at which the pupils would attempt arias and then submit to criticism from Vergine as well as from their classmates. He used to sit in a corner, forlorn and ignored, while the others confidently reached notes which still eluded him. When he did venture a few phrases, the Maestro would scoff at his backstreet style and demand more restraint. Ill at ease among the budding tenors, already so enviably accomplished, he was either inclined to hold back his voice or

* During Caruso's working life, £1 was equivalent to about twenty-five lire or $5.

13

would aim desperately for a power which needed the most patient nursing. Lacking it, he usually cracked.

The Maestro was a sound enough teacher but often combined the manners of a bosun's mate with a purser's guile. He informed Missiano that his young friend's voice was 'like gold at the bottom of the Tiber and hardly worth digging for'. Nevertheless, in exchange for the free tuition, he insisted on twenty-five per cent of anything Caruso might earn over the next five years *of actual singing*, an iniquitous agreement which, if interpreted literally, meant almost a professional lifetime. Caruso remained very small fry indeed in Vergine's classes and suffered agonies of embarrassment whenever he joined his better-dressed companions who seemed to be heading straight for San Carlo or even La Scala.

His own black suit had turned so green with age that he used to dab it over with dye before setting out for the studio. He bought his first pair of shoes from a good week's takings at the baths, but the cardboard soles let in the rain and curled up when he dried them by the stove in Vergine's basement. He walked the several miles home in bare feet, but was soon patiently running through the day's exercises while his step-mother, Maria, hung up his clothes and prepared an evening meal.

Only her encouragement and Missiano's repeated pleas to persevere kept him from losing heart. It seemed hopeless to compete with a star pupil like Punzo, a brash and handsome youth who needed little enough coaxing to air his powerful voice in class. The Maestro predicted an outstanding career for him on the operatic stage and welcomed him as a future son-in-law.

Instead of becoming the world's greatest tenor, however, Punzo would end up as Caruso's under-valet, assistant wardrobe master and life pensioner.

Chapter Two

Conventional tenors like Punzo were almost as plentiful as olives in a land where grand opera had become a second religion, particularly in the *dolce far niente* south. Even after the cholera epidemic few Neapolitans had complained when, instead of gutting the slums and providing workable drains, the municipality gave priority to a vote of 300,000 lire a year for the Teatro San Carlo, the city's operatic shrine for a century and a half.

The language, rich in vowels, seemed to have been created for *bel canto*. By the mid-nineteenth century almost every provincial town had its own opera house dedicated to the works of Donizetti, Bellini, Rossini and the most towering giant of them all, Verdi. With the decay of the princely courts and a merchant élite, a new bourgeois audience, including a sprinkling of the proletariat hitherto satisfied with the crude knockabout fun of *opera buffa*, had steadily taken over as devoted theatre-goers. Touring companies now had to face critical and often cruel enthusiasts who would not tolerate mediocrity. Scene-shifters and carpenters would argue passionately over individual performances, while excitable patrons were quite capable of assaulting a singer who offered sour notes. Accustomed to the decorum and stately protocol of St Petersburg, Chaliapin would never quite forget his astonishment on first hearing Caruso sing at La Scala. He was sitting next to a rather shabbily dressed individual with pince-nez and a scrubby grey beard whom he took for a schoolmaster or obscure government clerk. Caruso had sung a charming aria and willingly given an encore, but the crowd clamoured for a third and yet a fourth. Chaliapin's neighbour jumped angrily to his feet, rushed into the aisle and yelled, 'Savages! Do you think he can go on singing time after time, like a cannon loading and firing? Shame on you! Enough, I say, enough!' He was cheered to the echo.

When some luckless baritone failed to strike a top note in Parma, Toscanini's native city, the gallery—many among them illiterate—spontaneously joined in chanting the whole aria as it should have been sung and whistled the sinner off stage. Hysteria was not limited to audiences. Toscanini, then nineteen, had gone to Milan to play second cello with the La Scala orchestra for the opening of *Otello*, Verdi's first opera in sixteen years. Arriving back in Parma in the small hours, he woke up his mother and shouted deliriously, '*Otello* is a masterpiece. Get down on your knees and say "Viva Verdi"!' He then knelt beside her to offer up thanks for the revelation of such divine musical genius.

Caruso had been born into Verdi's green and vigorous old age. He was still a babe in arms when *Aïda* was produced at San Carlo by the composer himself, a snub to Milan, which had also to submit to a designer and director sent from Parma on Verdi's instructions. Naples had shown its delight by circulating flattering lithographs by the thousand. From his boyhood Caruso had been familiar with the dramatic cloak and black felt hat, the white cloud of hair, and the beard which masked the pockmarked features. One of his own first crayon sketches was an affectionately idealised portrait of the immortal Maestro.

The Neapolitans adored Verdi. They chuckled when it was reported that a woman prominent in local society had approached him in the arcades of the Strada San Carlo to breathe ecstatic admiration for *Aïda*. 'Then buy a ticket and leave me alone,' he had growled, brushing off her gloved hand. He once entered the buffet at a railway station near Naples, looking very frail but, as always, stiffly erect. The crowd of waiting passengers stood up respectfully, several spreading cloaks to make a carpet for him when he was ready to board the train.

Garibaldi had sung Verdi's swinging choruses on the way to Sicily, and every Italian, nobleman and peasant alike, tingled patriotically at his riposte to the alien chords of Wagner and Debussy. National pride had exulted in the world acclamation for *Rigoletto*, *Il Trovatore* and the passionate lyricism of *La*

Traviata. He was almost canonised as his operas became synonymous with the powerful voice of resurgent Italy. When the revolutionary *Un Ballo in Maschera* was first produced in Naples, the Bourbon police had been powerless to stop audiences shouting 'Viva Verdi!' although aware that the letters in the composer's name also formed the initials of 'Vittorio Emmanuele Ré D'Italia'.

Even before Verdi's fame resounded in every capital city in Europe and the Americas, his countrymen were internationally renowned as singers or teachers. Luigi Lablache, the very first Don Pasquale, was engaged to teach the future Queen Victoria, while Paolo Tosti, later a dear friend of Caruso's, would become singing master to the British Royal Family.

Giovanni Matteo, Cavaliere di Candia, who sang under the name of Mario, was the idol of his day and had triumphed in London, Paris and St Petersburg long before Caruso was born. Rossini had written several parts specially for him. A member of a noble family, he retained a rare distinction in looks and style which tempted him to give a marathon series of 'farewell' performances when long past his best. His voice was sweet but lacking in passion and he would often sing listlessly before arriving at a favoured dramatic passage which always roused audiences to frenzy. Not until the romantic Polish tenor Jean de Reszke had made the ladies swoon at the Paris Opéra, Covent Garden and the Metropolitan Opera House, New York, would Italian critics even hint at any possible successor to their incomparable Mario.

Caruso's fledgeling years were overshadowed by the fame of this legendary Cavaliere. Among living singers Tamagno, Verdi's original Otello, reigned supreme. Tall, broad-shouldered and equipped with an iron throat, he was a *tenore robusto* who made the chandeliers rattle. In the last quarter of the century he and other operatic gods received the kind of adulation which Spain accorded her bravest matadors. Caruso, still over-disciplined by Vergine, who dismissed him as a 'windy tenor' and semi-baritone, could not hope to emulate the full-blooded singers then in vogue. He turned instead for inspiration to the less flamboyant Angelo Masini, who had sung the *Requiem* under Verdi's own baton. Masini was far more successful in lyrical roles than Tamagno, who almost blasted audiences from their seats even when he spoke his lines as Otello or Samson.

Another idol was Roberto Stagno, whose sudden death would later give Caruso his greatest opportunity. He always travelled in state with an admiring retinue led by his wife, Gemma Bellincioni, the original Santuzza of *Cavalleria Rusticana*. He suffered from a vanity remarkable even by contemporary tenor standards. When Isidore de Lara once invited him to nominate a worthy successor to himself, he thought hard and long before sighing, 'There is no one. Alas, poor Italy!' This view was not wholly shared in Naples, where audiences continued to show blatant partisanship for native sons like Fernando de Lucia, who made his début in *Faust* at the San Carlo when Caruso was a boy of ten. His all-round technique and range won him international fame, notably with English opera-goers. He had been honoured by an invitation from Queen Victoria to sing duets with Emma Calvé at Windsor Castle, with Tosti at the piano.

Legions of small-time impresarios, teachers and agents scouted feverishly for hidden talent throughout Italy, and particularly in impoverished Naples, where every street tenor who could unload a ballad *con amore* was all too apt to see himself holding the stage at La Scala, the national springboard for world fame and riches. Only a talented few, however, would secure bookings even on the ill-paid provincial circuits, where they had to face claques and insular local patrons.

Two leading Milanese houses, Ricordi and Sonzogno, printed copyright sheet music and also held the leases of opera houses in many towns. They subsidised composers, hired conductors and ran touring companies, naturally favouring their own published works and singers under exclusive contract to themselves.

As Verdi's publisher and owner of the Italian rights in Wagner's operas, Giulio Ricordi enjoyed a near-monopoly of available musical talent for many years. He was not threatened until Eduardo Sonzogno, heir to a newspaper and industrial empire in Milan and rather more easygoing than his ultra-conservative competitor, began buying up opera houses before venturing into publishing. Sonzogno owned the Mercadente Theatre in Naples, where, in the early nineties, his local representative, Nicola Daspuro, staged ballet and such a brilliant season of opera with Tamagno and other celebrities that even the San Carlo was temporarily forced to close down. In addition to controlling the Teatro Lirico in Milan he provided the first serious opera threat to Ricordi by renting La Scala for two years, during which not a single Verdi work was put on.

This rivalry would have far-reaching yet oddly paradoxical effects on Caruso's career. He made his first major appearance in theatres run by Sonzogno, whose early encouragement he never forgot, but he would owe such outstanding roles as des Grieux, Rodolfo, Cavaradossi and Pinkerton to the man who was, after Verdi, Ricordi's most popular composer.

Puccini, seventeen years older than Caruso, had also started his career in a church choir. He went on to study music at the Conservatoire in Milan and for a while shared lodgings with Mascagni, a baker's son. Although *La Bohème* was based on Henri Murger's novel, it also derived from Puccini's frugal but gay student days when he and his room-mate lived, like Rodolfo, on 'herrings and dreams'. He once pawned his over-coat to sup with a ballet dancer from La Scala and often hid in the wardrobe to avoid creditors or outraged husbands. The landlord used to open his letters and extract the thirty lire for his month's rent from Puccini's scholarship grant. He forbade all cooking on the premises, which meant that one of them would be frying eggs while the other thumped the piano to muffle the sound of the sizzling fat.

Verdi had been Puccini's god from the moment he heard a performance of *Aïda* in Pisa. After leaving the Conservatoire he began to compose and turned automatically to Ricordi, who kept him alive with a subsidy of 500 lire a month and must have regretted his generosity when Puccini's first opera, *Le Villi*, was hooted by a San Carlo audience with no liking for beginners, particularly presumptuous young aliens from the north.

Puccini had supplemented his slender subsidy by teaching. He soon eloped with one of his pupils, Elvira, the handsome wife of a wholesale grocer. They lived precariously during the difficult years when he was composing his next opera, *Manon Lescaut*. In 1890 he had an opportunity to repay Ricordi's kindness. Mascagni had written a one-act opera, *Cavalleria Rusticana*, a melodramatic vignette of Sicilian peasant life with a bold and powerful score. Puccini drew it to the attention of his publisher, who offhandedly turned it down. Mascagni then entered his one-act piece for a talent-finding competition organised by Sonzogno. It won first prize and enraptured audiences at the première in Rome.

Another young composer, Leoncavallo, had also thought of entering an opera for that same competition but was debarred as it was in two acts. Encouraged by Mascagni's coup, he submitted his *I Pagliacci* to Sonzogno, who staged it triumphantly in Milan. De Lucia was soon singing Canio at La Scala, Covent Garden and the Metropolitan in New York. Audiences everywhere greeted his impassioned 'Vesti la giubba' with almost hysterical excitement. Hundreds of young hopefuls now scrambled for a clown's costume, convinced that a sobbing Canio, together with the easily learned part of Turiddu, would make their fortunes. As '*Cav*' and '*Pag*' were both short operas they made an irresistible combined attraction for impresarios anxious to exploit the new vogue.

Puccini's *Manon Lescaut* opened in Turin in 1893. It did not bring him the overnight fame of Mascagni and Leoncavallo, but emphatically established his international reputation. Bernard Shaw was among leading critics who at once welcomed him as Verdi's natural heir. Symbolically, perhaps, the première of *Manon Lescaut* had coincided with Verdi's operatic farewell at La Scala with *Falstaff*.

Caruso had just then celebrated his twentieth birthday with no reason to hope that, within barely a decade, he would be acclaimed as successor to Tamagno and Jean de Reszke. He looked inconspicuous among taller and flashily dressed fellow pupils like Punzo, who was already being booked for small parts around Naples and in the theatres of Sicily. He had grown to his full height of a nudging five feet seven and was still as thin as an anchovy. His hair was plentiful but coarse and straight. By local standards he was only averagely good-looking, with a vigorous moustache, brilliant eyes and a smooth olive complexion, but his manner was vivacious and people forgot the patched clothes when he flashed his white teeth.

Even Vergine had to admire his docile acceptance of criticism and astonishing speed in mastering almost any score. 'You have no voice,' the black-jowled Maestro grunted after his end-of-year examination, 'but you have intelligence. You have learned something here.' With this grudging praise as testimonial, Caruso had to break off his studies to begin three years of military service.

Chapter Three

The frail-looking Caruso had expected to be turned down on medical grounds, as part of the forty per cent or so of conscripts from the Naples area, but having somehow escaped cholera, malaria and typhoid, he was passed fit. Assigned to the Thirteenth Artillery at Rieti, he mournfully surveyed the fertile acres of vineyards and olive groves as the train puffed northwards from Rome. He had taken sad leave of his family and spent his last evening at the deathbed of his old teacher, Father Bronzetti, who gave him his blessing and counselled him to continue with his singing. There seemed no prospect of that for some years, but in his kitbag, crammed with food prepared by his step-mother, he had packed the bulky notebook into which he had copied out songs and Vergine's exercises.

During his first days in the barracks he discovered that the drill hall was rarely used in the early evenings, when the sallow-faced conscripts sat about smoking, drinking and feeling sorry for themselves. He began rippling his scales and continually went through his repertoire of ballads. Before very long his comrades were demanding recitals, with no shortage of volunteers on mandolin and guitar. He was polishing his buttons one day, while attempting the 'Brindisi' from *Cavalleria Rusticana*, when the battery commander, a Major Nagliotti, ordered him to come and sing after the party which officers customarily gave for other ranks at Easter. The audience clamoured for so many encores that he was hoarse by the time his companions carried him shoulder-high back to their quarters.

Next morning he was summoned by the major, who warned him illogically against over-straining his voice. He listened with sympathy to Caruso's account of his interrupted training with Vergine and his ambition to become a professional singer after military service. Within a day or two he was excused further squad drill. The major then introduced him to one of his friends in Rieti, an opera-loving nobleman who invited him to his house and corrected some obvious mistakes which Vergine had either missed or been too preoccupied with Punzo and other pets to notice. With the baron at the piano, Caruso went through the score of *Cavalleria Rusticana*. It took him only five days to memorise the role of Turiddu.

Three weeks later, after secret meetings between Nagliotti and his friend and, no doubt, some energetic wire-pulling in official quarters, Caruso was gruffly informed that he would be replaced by his brother, Giovanni. He had served less than two months. On the train back to Naples, still finding it hard to credit his good fortune, he made up his mind never to return to Meuricoffre's accounts office. He would take his chance with a singing career. Nothing else could justify the major's faith in him and, above all, Giovanni's self-sacrifice.

Vergine welcomed him back with unusual warmth. This almost incredible reprieve seemed to him both a good augury and a chance to recoup himself for all those free lessons. The operas of Mascagni, Leoncavallo and Puccini were now electrifying audiences everywhere, their lush and catchy melodies offering ready-made chances to young singers intimidated by Verdi's scores or too long overpowered by the aura of Tamagno, Masini and Stagno. These favoured veterans were still in splendid voice, but they were now in their fifties and content with familiar showpieces. With the part of Turiddu already under his belt, Caruso began to spend days and nights pouring out Canio's pitiful despair or warbling des Grieux's tender 'Donna non vidi mai'.

Throughout the hot summer months of 1894 he was again singing outside the municipal baths and cafés, but he had begun to miss his regular factory wages. After contributing even the modest few lire for his keep, he rarely had enough left for a cigarette or a sociable glass of wine with his old friends. He would go hungry all day but was often too tired and dispirited by nightfall to swallow Maria's ample bowl of macaroni and beans. He gave up long hours to practising his songs, or crouched over the inseparable notebook with its neatly arranged scales and arpeggios. He haunted the studio and implored Vergine to find him work, if only in some chorus, but preferably as a tenor on one of the country circuits.

Worn out by this persistence and still hopeful of making a commission, Vergine began to canvass his talents, and finally persuaded his friend Nicola Daspuro to grant them an audition at the Mercadente. This famous old theatre, known as Il Fondo, had seated generations of discriminating patrons in its five tiers of boxes and enjoyed a prestige second only to that of San Carlo. It was rather too awesome a setting for Caruso, who had never before sung in any theatre, but his excellent diction and lyrical warmth in the chosen excerpt from Ambrose Thomas's *Mignon* seemed to please Daspuro and a poker-faced conductor, but he was not helped by an unofficial jury of bored stagehands and members of the chorus who lounged about smoking cigarettes or sniggering behind their hands. He soon grew so dry-mouthed that he cracked his top notes and failed altogether to notice Vergine's agitated signals. They slunk out of the theatre without even the face-saving hint of possibly being recalled. Daspuro was politely sympathetic, but the conductor did not hide his annoyance at having his time wasted by an amateur.

Consolation came within a few days and quite unexpectedly. A rich young dilettante, Mario Morelli, had composed a four-act opera, *L'Amico Francesco*, and planned to put it on at his own expense for the critics and a few indulgent friends. He had booked the Teatro Nuovo off the Toledo for four performances and was seeking suitable but inexpensive talent. Caruso, then all of twenty-one, was engaged to play the role of father to the baritone, a sixty-year-old warhorse. His opportunity, quaint but most welcome, was probably due to Eduardo Missiano, who had continued to praise him lavishly in the salons which Morelli also frequented. The terms were modest enough: fifteen lire a performance, with no payment for weeks of rehearsal but a small advance to cover the outlay on a scarf, shoes and stockings needed for the part—which, to Morelli's fury, Caruso promptly spent on food.

The production opened on 16 November 1894 and lasted only two nights. But Caruso's operatic début, despite an attack of stage fright which caused him to fluff a number of lines, showed enough vocal sparkle to please the composer, who paid up for the scheduled four performances and even added a bonus of fifty lire. A visiting impresario also felt justified in offering him a short season in Caserta, an ancient hill town some twenty miles north of Naples and once a favoured seat of the Bourbon kings. Moreover, a well-known local agent of Sicilian origin, Francesco Zucchi, had warmly congratulated him and promised to look out for possible bookings.

While anxiously running through *Cavalleria Rusticana* before leaving for Caserta, he joined Zucchi's coterie at the noisy Caffé dei Fiori in via del Municipio. The burly Sicilian, a fantasy figure with his dyed moustache and frantic halo of hair, used the place as an office, rather like an Antwerp kerbside dealer in diamonds. He made bookings, signed contracts and kept a shrewd day-to-day watch on supply and demand, maintaining an almost non-stop and simultaneous dialogue with out-of-work singers and minor booking agents while he dispensed food and drink. Blessed with a card-index memory, he seemed to know the opening dates and costs for every production in Naples, Rome, Milan and Venice, as well as the budgets of the humbler provincial managers whom he cajoled or bullied with equal success. He took to Caruso at once and fed him with praise and very welcome free spaghetti and wine, continually dropping his name as a most promising young tenor—the equal at least of de Lucia!—and still available at bargain rates.

The season at Caserta was rich in experience only. Caruso had accepted a niggardly ten lire for a performance of *Cavalleria Rusticana* but felt more than compensated by the Cimarosa Theatre with its twelve Corinthian columns from the Serapeum of Puteoli. To his heated imagination the forty tiered boxes seemed to out-dazzle La Scala itself. His Turiddu proved unworthy of such a setting. The phrases, perhaps over-rehearsed, were often out of tempo and his acting amateurish. He followed with the title role in Gounod's *Faust*, which was also beyond his technical range and over the heads of a superstitious peasant audience. They might have overlooked his wobbly high notes, but they grew so scandalised by Mephisto's depravity that the curtain came down to chilled disapproval.

Caruso retreated from Caserta with hardly a lira but felt exultant at having given two standard operas in public for the first time without completely disgracing himself. He was quickly invited to sing solo for High Mass in the beautiful cathedral of Cotrone in Calabria and, on his return, decided to smooth out the very ragged edges of his Faust. It was a happy inspiration. He was playing cards one afternoon in a tavern near his home when a messenger summoned him to report at once to the manager of the Bellini. The tenor who was booked there for a benefit performance of *Faust* that very night had lost his voice. Zucchi briskly nominated Caruso as a last-minute substitute for a fee of 25 lire. After the agent's commission and a quarter share for the relentless Vergine, the singer was left with just enough to pay for a pair of white silk trousers and the matching kid shoes he had coveted for weeks past.

The sophisticated Sunday-evening audience, infiltrated by a claque from the Caffè dei Fiori, was far more sympathetic than Caserta's homespuns. By the time Caruso reached the ringing apostrophe in Act Three, 'Salve dimora casta e pura', the theatre was already buzzing. When the curtain fell with the Easter hymn he felt that, like Marguerite, he was being borne up to heaven.

The Bellini manager at once engaged him to play the Duke in *Rigoletto* and also arranged for him to appear in both that opera and *Faust* in the autumn. Zucchi had meantime exploited his client's triumph by slotting him into a company booked for a month at the Ezbekieh Theatre in Cairo—his fee a stupendous 600 lire.

They sailed in an English steamer and Caruso soon became a

favourite with some convivial army officers on their way out to the Sudan. Late one night he was shanghaied in the bar and ordered to sing; otherwise, they threatened playfully, they would toss him overboard. Fortified by several glasses, he sang 'Funiculí, funiculà' and 'Torno a Surrento', together with arias from his expanding repertoire. The Englishmen then passed round the hat and presented him with what seemed a fortune: close on £100 in banknotes. (Memory, reinforced by wishful thinking, can play strange tricks. Many years later, one of the Englishmen at this shipboard party recalled that he had encouraged 'an Italian waiter in the officers' mess in Cairo' to have his voice trained and also given him financial help to do so. 'His name was Enrico Caruso.')

During that Cairo season Caruso often sang seven nights a week plus one or two matinées, earning praise for his performances as Turiddu and the Duke of Mantua, apart from his first attempt at *La Gioconda* by Puccini's teacher, Ponchielli. However, with less than a week to rehearse the demanding tenor role in *Manon Lescaut* he was far from word-perfect. He became so terrified of drying up altogether that he begged the soprano, an amiable ex-pupil of Vergine's, to allow him to strap the score to her back while she expired in Act Four. Even so, he introduced a number of improvisations that would have startled Puccini.

The £100 soon melted away in the hot August sun. He and the baritone had found congenial society in two young actresses from a local music hall. During one of their excursions he toppled into the Nile and returned on the back of a donkey to Cairo, covered in mud but still gaily warbling 'Funiculí, funiculà'. He stayed on for a few days with his girl and sailed back in the steerage of an Italian boat. Although penniless, he stepped jauntily ashore to embrace Zucchi, who announced a month's booking at the Mercadente Theatre, the scene of his disastrous first audition. This was to follow his appearances at the Bellini, where he began to rehearse the very next day.

Not yet recovered from his strenuous season in Cairo, he now paid the penalty for Zucchi's over-enthusiastic promotion

27

during his absence. When he advanced to the footlights for the opening of *Rigoletto*, the front stalls seemed to be solidly monopolised by envious young tenors from Vergine's studio. His tonsils froze. He recovered slightly for his next appearance as Faust, but the critics, recalling the superlative Mario and, more recently, mighty Tamagno himself on that very stage, thought little of this strutting café singer with the precarious top register.

His morale was boosted on first seeing the name 'Errico Caruso' on posters outside the Mercadente, announcing *La Traviata* for 29 November 1895. Certain passages were somewhat forced, but one beautiful woman in the stalls had been startled by the exceptional purity and resonance of his voice. She was Emma Calvé, the French prima donna and the most exciting Carmen of her generation. She pinched the arm of her companion and kept repeating 'Amazing!'

'In Naples beautiful voices are as common as pebbles on the beach,' he reminded her with a laugh.

'This is no pebble,' she insisted, 'but a diamond of the first water. Who is he?' The man shrugged and glanced idly at his programme. 'Caruso.' Others in the audience shared Calvé's view. A newspaper rated his performance high enough to send its photographer to his home next morning. As his only shirt was then being washed by Maria, he had to pose with a bedspread over his shoulders.

The engagement at the Mercadente lasted until mid-February. He often made two appearances a day, doubling such strenuous roles as Alfredo in *La Traviata* and the Duke of Mantua. Unfortunately, the season ended with a rare misjudgement by Zucchi, who had rashly organised another company to brave Caserta once again with *Faust*. Caruso accepted the challenge with more confidence, but soon discovered that local taste had failed to mellow since the previous fiasco. This time the audience would not even sit through the five acts. Before the end of Act Two they surged towards the stage with the plain intention of lynching Mephisto and running the others out of town. The curtain was hastily rung down and the terrified artists fled to the station without stopping to collect their pay.

After a calmer season at the Bellini that April, Caruso prepared to go on tour in Zucchi's native Sicily. There was no hint of the coming disaster. The first booking was for Trapani, a walled seaside town where between rehearsals he swam and bought coral beads for his adored stepmother. Then he heard that Giovanni was now with his regiment at Massawa fighting the Abyssinians, and self-reproach and remorse led to one of his very few drinking bouts.

The first baritone, a jolly youth of his own age who came from Trapani, had insisted on Caruso lodging with his parents, who hospitably welcomed him with a bottle of the heady local wine. Caruso was merry by the time they reached the theatre for the dress rehearsal of Donizetti's *Lucia di Lammermoor*, an opera he had not so far attempted. He downed another glass or two in the manager's office before departing for his dressing-room, where he was soon fast asleep. A good half-hour after the scheduled curtain-rise, with the public now understandably irritable, he went on with spaghetti legs. He scrambled through until the tongue-twisting 'Le Sorti [Fate] della Scozia' which somehow became garbled into 'Le Volpi [Foxes] della Scozia'. The audience, stiff with local gentry, hissed its derision. The curtain had to be hauled down in mid-performance.

He was dismissed without pay and could not even show himself in the streets without being catcalled by urchins who kept yelling 'Volpi', until he had to run for it. A day or so later, without his return fare to Naples, he borrowed 8 lire from the baritone and bribed a sailor to conceal him aboard a small coasting vessel forbidden to carry passengers. They were about to sail when a messenger arrived from the theatre begging him to return and stop a threatened riot. The replacement tenor had failed to please the audience, which, surprisingly, was demanding its money back unless 'the Scottish Fox' resumed his role as Edgardo, Master of Ravenswood. He now gave such a splendid performance that the manager invited him to return for another season. He declined very firmly. Years later he

29

would still make a pair of horns with his first and fourth fingers, to ward off the evil eye, whenever anyone mentioned Trapani in his presence.

In Naples Caruso rocked the Caffé dei Fiori with an account of his misadventures but soon began brushing up *Rigoletto* for what promised to be a routine weekend engagement in Salerno. Zucchi had arranged for him to sing the Duke in a performance to celebrate Italy's Independence Day.

It was a momentous booking. A Salerno audience first heard him as the tragic clown in *I Pagliacci*; and there also he met Vincenzo Lombardi, who was to transform his voice.

Chapter Four

Salerno was in gala mood. Led by a euphoric mayor, fanatical Verdians welcomed Caruso's *Rigoletto*, hummed the lilting 'La donna è mobile' and were not too critical of his occasionally broken B flats. He was cheered on leaving the stage door and shadowed throughout his stay by a local young *aficionado*, Enrico Lorello, who had led noisy support for the second performance and went about town eulogising the tenor as 'the new and greatest voice in all Italy'. Caruso promised gaily to appoint him his secretary one day.

He was also flattered by an invitation to take a glass of wine in the office of Vincenzo Lombardi, the conductor, who quizzed him about his career and asked if he had ever attempted Bellini's *I Puritani*. Caruso shook his head, and confessed that his voice was too short for the difficult tenor role. 'Then I will make it longer,' promised Lombardi, who planned to open his August season with the Bellini opera but explained that his modest budget would not stretch beyond 700 lire for the ten weeks. However, he volunteered a bonus in the form of free singing lessons. Caruso stammered his thanks and promised to consult Zucchi, who took a long-term view, although a summer engagement in Salerno seemed unlikely to advance his client's reputation. He pointed out, however, that Lombardi was a most respected singing teacher and had coached, among others, the Neapolitan baritone, Scotti, later to achieve fame as a peerless Scarpia. Salerno would also be honoured by guest appearances from the composer-conductor Leopoldo Mugnone, who had directed the world premières of *Cavalleria Rusticana* and *Falstaff*. He was rated the greatest of all Italian conductors until the advent of Toscanini.

Lombardi was a musical grandee with the handsome beard and manner of a feudal seigneur, but he could be brutally frank. Caruso's first aria disclosed that he would have to unlearn much that Vergine had taught him; above all, a tendency to hold back his voice. He was now commanded to open his lungs and release the full tone. Lombardi had inspected his exceptionally wide larynx with the thoroughness of a throat specialist. He noted the long, thick vocal chords, admirably suited to deep and sustained breathing, and started him on a course of exercises to smooth his phrasing. There would also have to be a drastic change in stance. Caruso was made to hold himself like a toreador by keeping his head up and his spine taut against a wall. With his lower jaw loose and one foot extended, he now gave out freely on the high notes which had previously been smothered at birth or more often ended in the unlovely roughness of a backstreet fruit-vendor in full cry.

It was a slow and often painful process but Lombardi never lost confidence. He once turned to Mugnone and predicted that his protégé would soon be earning a thousand lire a night at La Scala. 'If that ever happens,' scoffed his colleague, 'I'll be crowned Pope!' The fat and very irritable theatre manager, Signor Grassi, agreed with him. He seethed at rehearsals and almost cancelled *Carmen* after Caruso's lamentable attempts at a top register.

Maestro Lombardi would not be discouraged. He was delighted by his pupil's *mezza voce*, whose soft, velvety timbre was already superior to that of Fernando de Lucia, whom he considered flashy and overrated. Caruso's natural spontaneity of phrasing seemed to him little short of a miracle, but he was careful not to be too lavish in his praise, for the volatile young Neapolitan tended to oscillate too violently between overconfidence and the blackest despair.

Sometimes when Caruso was almost at breaking point and resigned to remaining 'a windy tenor' for life, Lombardi would suddenly call off classes and take him for a carriage drive round the sunny bay. One unforgettable treat was a day's visit to the Greek temples of Paestum, poised in golden majesty between mountains and sea. Caruso almost shrieked with ecstasy. On the way back he recalled his many hours in the museums of Naples, where he had gaped at bronzes from Pompeii and

Herculaneum. He also babbled about the Farnese collection and confided that he had made several sketches of a cup belonging to Lorenzo the Magnificent.

This aesthetic discrimination on the part of an almost illiterate, slum-bred youth was not the only oddity about him that struck Lombardi. His knowledge of Italian history and literature was practically nil, and he had not read a book, even a novel, since leaving Father Bronzetti's. His roles must often have seemed to him like the figures in a child's garishly coloured volume of fairy tales, yet somehow he moved with smiling ease from Civil War England, in *I Puritani*, to Verdi's sixteenth-century Mantua. Above all, even when he made rough notes, his handwriting would not have disgraced any man of education. By contrast, some gutter mud splashed through his coarse Neapolitan dialect, and he used too many Sicilian obscenities picked up at Zucchi's table.

He was not a graceful eater and wolfed his food whenever his finances stretched to a square meal. The admiring Lorello often arranged invitations for him to sing in the mayor's house and at private parties for the chance of a good dinner. This was hard on tonsils already taxed by rehearsals and the treadmill of classes, but Lombardi could not stop it or wean him from cigarettes.

Hour after hour, page after page, they went through the score of *I Puritani* until the conductor was satisfied. Caruso's high notes had again splintered in *Cavalleria Rusticana* and his Don José was a near-disaster, but nothing could diminish the glory of his opening night in *I Puritani*. Now he could almost take his pick of supper parties, but preferred to spend most of his evenings with Signor Grassi's charming daughter, who was also studying opera under Lombardi. It was a sweet but difficult courtship. Out of class they would only meet in the presence of a duenna, who apparently distrusted all Neapolitans except *castrati*.

Grassi's smiles grew more benign as his box-office takings mounted and distinguished folk began arriving in Salerno to

33

hear the new tenor. The celebrated Fernando de Lucia travelled specially from his summer retreat in La Cava for the second performance of *I Puritani*. Afterwards he visited Caruso's tiny dressing-room to congratulate him, but added rather loftily, 'You must of course continue with your studies. There is much to learn.'

Caruso was by now inhaling rather too much incense for his own good. He had not forgotten his humiliating first audition at the Mercadente and was in a teasing mood when Daspuro arrived with Zucchi and hinted condescendingly at future engagements in Naples and perhaps even Milan, if Eduardo Sonzogno approved. When he went on to advise him not to sing at too many private receptions, Caruso winked at his Sicilian friend and replied airily, 'I have enough voice for the whole world.'

Nevertheless he was most nervous at having to make an unscheduled and unrehearsed début in *I Pagliacci*. One evening he had sung in a mediocre short opera, to be followed by Leoncavallo's now reliable standby. But the tenor engaged for Canio was in such poor voice that the audience began catcalling him almost from the opening of Act One. Grassi intercepted Caruso as he was about to leave the theatre and begged him to go on. He refused to miss his dinner and agreed to deputise only when Lombardi threatened to break off his classes. A messenger ran to a nearby restaurant for pork chops and spaghetti, which Caruso devoured before putting on the clown's costume.

He was applauded sympathetically when he came on stage for the first of many hundred Canios. Although his acting was wooden and not to be compared with de Lucia's, he sang the Lament with such intensity of feeling that many were in tears, while others cheered so loud and long that the house lights had to be switched off to make them leave. Next day scouts were on their way from half a dozen managements. They were forestalled by Leopoldo Mugnone, who had changed his mind about Caruso and speedily made contact with a friend in charge of the new Massimo Theatre in Palermo. He tele-

34

graphed back with an irresistible guarantee of 2750 lire for six weeks to follow Caruso's next season in Salerno.

This exciting news stimulated him to propose to Signorina Grassi. His infatuation had flowered under blue skies, but the manager remained unenthusiastic about a penniless young singer without family background. However, after this stupendous offer from Sicily, baptised with still more tears from his lovesick daughter, he could no longer oppose Maestro Lombardi and the mayor himself, who also spoke up for Caruso. The engagement was announced at an after-theatre supper crowned by a romantic duet from the blissful couple. They would be married at the end of the following season, for which Caruso's fee had been increased to 1000 lire by his future father-in-law.

After a joyful reunion with his family—Giovanni had survived the Massawa campaign and was out of uniform—he had two short seasons at the Bellini and the Mercadente. All the critics now united to praise his improved vocal range. While in Naples he picked up a copy of Puccini's *La Bohème* and was captivated by its sparkling score. His romantic imagination was so inflamed by the tubercular little sempstress in her chilly garret that he could not rest until he had copied the whole tenor part into his notebooks, although scarcely daring to hope that some impresario might entrust him with the role of Rodolfo.

The opera had now fully recovered from its very shaky première at the Teatro Regio in Turin on 1 February 1896, with the young musical director Arturo Toscanini on the rostrum. Although the composer had openly expressed his preference for Mugnone, a close friend, Toscanini extracted a memorable performance from his orchestra despite the poor acoustics. Nevertheless, he irritated Puccini by brusquely disallowing all encores, even for 'Che gelida manina', one of the few arias to spark any reaction on that lukewarm night. One critic had savaged the piece as 'empty and puerile', while others thought it much inferior to *Manon Lescaut*. A whispering campaign soon opened against Puccini, who was accused of filching his theme from Leoncavallo. It was predicted that the latter's own *La Bohème*, now nearing completion, would surely put him in his place.

However, the public and, equally important, many leading tenors and sopranos took a very different view. A company was soon preparing to give the Puccini opera in Buenos Aires while de Lucia planned to sing Rodolfo in London. Italian audiences also ignored the Turin critics and cheered the piece everywhere. A few weeks after the première it had been put on in Palermo under the direction of Mugnone, who, for once, defied his own superstition and opened on Friday, 13 April. As the audience was still screaming for encores at 1 a.m. he had to repeat the whole of the last scene after most of the orchestra had gone home and the principals were already changed into their day clothes. The tenor was inconspicuous but bouquets were thrust into the arms of the soprano who played Mimi. The name of Ada Giachetti had not registered in Caruso's mind; she departed soon afterwards for South America and, on her return, failed to be booked for Naples in her tour of the Sonzogno theatre circuit.

Caruso arrived back in Salerno in February 1897, well before the opening of the season. He was eager to see his fiancée and report his intoxicating discovery of Rodolfo. Lombardi, however, cautioned him severely to concentrate on the more reliable and well-tried *Manon Lescaut*, which the management had chosen as their main attraction. He submitted with fairly good grace and even made the painful sacrifice of shaving off his wax-ended moustache, instead of soaping it down and dabbing it over with white powder, to play des Grieux. But he continued to copy out and annotate difficult parts of *La Bohème* and practised the arias in the privacy of his hotel room or on any quiet beach.

He slapped his thighs on hearing that the Palermo season would open with the new Puccini opera, following its success there the previous year. In his mind's eye he already saw himself as Rodolfo on the stage of the Massimo. It became such an obsession that Lombardi again reminded him very sharply that he was giving far too much thought to a role which Salerno would not see. No doubt the Maestro already knew or had guessed that the shrewd Sicilian management would also demand a far better known tenor for the gala opening of their theatre. He tried to hint as much, but by this time Caruso could hear nothing but bubbles.

His second season in Salerno, even without *La Bohème* and *I Pagliacci*, proved such a draw that people stayed away if he were not singing and formed long queues when 'Enrico Caruso', as he was now formally named, appeared on the posters. This was gratifying, but it also demanded the bull-like stamina of a Tamagno, as Signor Grassi insisted on packing fifty performances into two months. It did not endear him to his future father-in-law. Besides, the romance had steadily lost its bloom for Caruso, who found the relay of watchful aunts irksome and almost impregnable. After Lorello had passed on tender messages from several local girls he began to think more and more wistfully about his adorable vaudeville artiste in Cairo. A warm-blooded man in his early twenties could not live on this snatched diet of chaperoned kisses. He had also developed an almost frantic, superstitious belief that Signor Grassi had the 'evil eye', and refused to allow him to attend rehearsals. This very naturally upset his unhappy fiancée.

One evening, while watching *La Gioconda*, he became fascinated by a graceful ballerina in 'The Dance of the Hours'. He soon discovered that she had traded her deliciously acrobatic body to Mugnone, who had promised to advance her career but was so possessively jealous that, according to frivolous talk, she had to wear a chastity belt in his absence. Caruso decided to put this tantalising rumour to the test.

It was not too difficult, while Mugnone was away visiting Puccini at his lakeside villa in Torre del Lago, to persuade her to join a crowd of younger folk for wine and spaghetti in the picturesque old quarter. Before long they were plotting release from the dual tyranny of a testy protector, nearly twenty years her senior, and Caruso's over-domesticated virgin. When the company broke up at the end of the season he thanked Lombardi fervently for giving him a top to his voice and, after an unnerving scene with the Grassis, skipped off with his bewitching ballet girl.

The 'honeymoon' in Naples was violent but brief. A grimy *pensione* lacked charm after their moonlit ecstasies on the beach at Salerno. Even before their combined cash had run out Caruso was already chafing to escape to Palermo for rehearsals, while the girl, unable to find work in Naples, fretted for her old companions in the *corps de ballet*. Although they wept and made love up to the last minute, vowing soon to be reunited, both were relieved when she left for a chance engagement in Rome.

In any event it had become quite impossible for them to go to Sicily together. By an ironic twist of fate, Leopoldo Mugnone would be directing the season in Palermo. Although normally a good sailor, Caruso was nervously seasick while crossing the Straits of Messina, and dreaded what could only be a most uncomfortable meeting with the outraged conductor.

Chapter Five

He had anticipated a frosty reception from Mugnone, but did not suspect that he would be denied his chance to sing Rodolfo. He soon learned that the ornate new Massimo Theatre would open with Verdi's *Falstaff*. This he took philosophically, but felt crushed and humiliated when rehearsals started for *La Bohème* without himself in the tenor role. But he already knew better than to argue with Mugnone, whose bullying intimidated the whole company. Everyone had heard about Leoncavallo's younger brother, who had once played violin under Mugnone and thought his name entitled him to special respect. He was quickly disabused. 'To me you are neither *leone* [lion] nor *cavallo* [horse], but only a donkey,' the Maestro had informed him.

La Gioconda, chosen for Caruso's début, could only have painful memories for Mugnone, who had neither forgiven nor forgotten the loss of his flighty little ballerina. To the delight of a Sicilian tenor who had been passed over, Caruso was summoned to rehearsals at nine in the morning and ignored until the conductor appeared hours later and promptly singled him out for sarcastic criticism. Without Lombardi on the rostrum and mercilessly baited by one or two fellow singers, he amputated his high notes and feared the management might soon cancel his engagement.

However, just before the opening on 15 May 1897, he suddenly found his voice and sang the aria, 'Cielo e mar', with all the poignancy which Lombardi had extracted during the Salerno season. Mugnone rapped his baton and exclaimed, '*Bravissimo!*' Caruso would never again be called for early rehearsal, and Mugnone directed with such sympathetic verve that *La Gioconda* was voted the success of that season, completely outshining Puccini's opera. But although each of his dozen appearances was warmly approved, that month in

39

Palermo had been disquieting. The company, even more hostile and envious after Mugnone's change of heart, began to spread malicious gossip. Caruso's previous misadventure in Trapani was recalled and hints dropped to the management that he might again walk tipsily on stage or even fail to appear at all if some girl took his fancy. Excuses were soon found to keep him in the theatre for hours before a performance; this made him so nervously hungry that he used to have wine and packets of sardine and cream cheese sandwiches sent in to his dressing-room from a neighbouring *osteria*. It did not prevent him from downing his usual huge bowl of spaghetti, followed by ice cream, after the show. His waist and buttocks were already rounding, while in costumed parts calling for breeches or pantaloons his calves seemed to bulge like Indian clubs.

He looked spruce enough, however, in his new frock coat with a pair of lavender gloves when he arrived back in Naples. He emptied his pockets of several hundred lire while his brother and Assunta watched goggle-eyed. Their father accepted a wad of notes, which he ruefully passed to his wife. She tucked it briskly into her bosom, but seemed far more excited by her stepson's news. Nicola Daspuro of the Mercadente Theatre, encouraged by reports from Sicily, had urged his principal, Sonzogno, to engage Caruso for an autumn season at the Lirico, Milan. A few days later, in a cubicle at the little sub-post office near the San Carlo, Daspuro signed the contract for 500 lire a month with Caruso and his old teacher, Vergine, who was at last justifying his commission, although baffled that the 'windy tenor' could be more in demand than his son-in-law, Punzo.

The Lirico could not be compared with La Scala or the San Carlo (the latter had so far shown no interest at all in its native son), but it was Sonzogno's showpiece theatre in Milan. While hugging himself over this opportunity, Caruso was suddenly offered an engagement to sing in Livorno (Leghorn) during the month of August. This had come about through Mugnone, who had praised him to the local impresario. He also nominated him enthusiastically as the ideal Rodolfo for *La Bohème*, which was to be the star production.

The impresario was not convinced. As his theatre was controlled by the Ricordis, who owned the copyright on Puccini's opera, he could not afford to take chances on this little-known tenor who would shortly be singing under the rival colours of Sonzogno. He therefore reserved judgement until Caruso had sung brilliantly in *La Traviata*, when he himself suggested him for Rodolfo.

While letters were flying between Livorno and Milan, Caruso received strong support from Ada Giachetti, who had been engaged to repeat her Mimi. She was a handsome and voluptuous woman with beautiful, small teeth and an unlined magnolia skin that gave her more than a touch of a Delacroix gypsy. Her enormous, smouldering eyes, heavy with mascara, were set off by a mass of black curls always elegantly coiffed. Now in her early thirties and long separated from her husband, she had enjoyed a succession of admirers during her professional career with second-rank companies throughout Italy and South America.

Shortly after Caruso's arrival in Livorno, where she had a small villa, Ada became his mistress or, perhaps more accurately, took him as her lover. He was ten years her junior and still piquantly innocent despite his few casual affairs. She seemed amused rather than offended by his occasional vulgarity and enjoyed his carefree laughter. He was also scrupulous over hygiene, scented himself freely, and kept his breath garlic-free by incessantly munching cachous. But he soon became more than a healthy and vigorous playmate for this sophisticated woman of highly developed sexuality. Herself a gifted pianist with considerable musical taste, she had thrilled to his Alfredo in *La Traviata* and shared Mugnone's view that he would make an exceptionally effective Rodolfo. She began rehearsing with him in private while the management still dithered over the tenor lead and auditioned several other candidates.

As the opening night approached he became desperate

enough to volunteer to play Rodolfo for his living expenses alone, a mere fifteen lire a day. The manager blinked but continued to hedge, pending final clearance from Ricordi. Soon afterwards one of Ada's local acquaintances happened to mention that he knew Puccini and might arrange an audition which would resolve the dilemma one way or the other. Caruso accepted without hesitation.

Within a few days he was heading for Lucca, only an hour's journey away by way of Pisa. He was enchanted by the green rolling hills of Tuscany and goggled at the white hump-backed cattle as the train followed the winding river through swamps before reaching Puccini's native city. But either Ada's friend had failed to finalise the necessary arrangements or the composer, then busy on the first draft of *Tosca*, had overlooked or perhaps simply ignored the message. The young tenor had some difficulty in persuading Puccini's handyman, Manfredi, to admit him to the villa at nearby Torre del Lago.

'Who is he? Who is this Caruso?' demanded the composer, looking up impatiently from a small table covered with scores and notebooks. Although it was mid-summer he wore his soft wide-brimmed hat indoors, and logs burned fiercely in a large open fireplace before which three gundogs were dozing. They answered surlily to the names of Lea, Schaunard and Nello.

'He speaks like a Neapolitan and calls himself a singer,' growled Manfredi with a flutter of white eyelashes. 'A short runt of a fellow with a bit of a moustache. Wears a hat to one side.'

'Another urchin from Naples!' Puccini snorted. 'Tell him I'm busy.'

Manfredi looked doubtful. 'I've told him, but he won't leave.'

Puccini went to the door of his studio and snapped, '*Chi è lei?*' ('Who are you?') Caruso laughed nervously and answered in Rodolfo's words: '*Chi son? Sono un poeta.*' ('Who am I? I am a poet.')

Puccini let out a roar of laughter and escorted him into the studio. Caruso found the room overpowering with its log fire and abundance of shrubs and palms, and longed to strip off his jacket and bow tie, but dared not ask permission.

The composer was at this time approaching forty: tall, handsome, and strongly built, with a bushy moustache and a mop of chestnut curls. He had a very prominent nose and sleepily sensual eyes with a drooping left lid. It was easy enough to accept his description of himself as 'a mighty hunter of wildfowl, beautiful women, and good libretti'. He sat down at his Förster upright piano with its special damper for night work, and asked Caruso to attempt 'Che gelida manina'. When it was over he swivelled in his chair and murmured in amazement, 'Who has sent you to me? God?' After a few staccato questions he volunteered to write at once to the impresario at Livorno, approving him for the part of Rodolfo. The tenor, although overwhelmed with relief, could not help mentioning that the high C at the end of the aria still gave him difficulty. Puccini shrugged it off with a smile. 'That note is not compulsory. Too many sing the whole aria badly just to hold themselves for the C. Take it half a note lower if you wish rather than ruin the song.'

He led Caruso to the window overlooking the shallow blue lake on which he rowed every day, often slipping out at dawn to shoot wild duck, pheasant and moorhens. He also showed him over the gun room and presented him to his resident mistress and future wife, Elvira, who invited him, though none too warmly, to stay for dinner. He declined politely, begging an opportunity to return once the opera was launched.

He was agog to report his triumph. At the station in Livorno he bought a bouquet of roses as red and full as Ada's lips. She embraced him almost hysterically, but he was soon flattened by the manager. 'That settles it then,' he grunted with a click of yellow teeth. 'You may play Rodolfo but, naturally, for fifteen lire a night, as we agreed.'

Caruso felt too elated to argue that his offer had preceded Puccini's blessing, which surely placed him above all other candidates. Ada, however, stormed into the manager's office and reminded him that he had offered 1000 lire a performance to the tenor originally chosen for *La Bohème*, and was taking advantage of a boy's impulse. He replied blandly that the house of Ricordi might still not thank him for entrusting the role to a young unknown. She flounced out, resolved to take a firmer grip on her lover's haphazard financial affairs, and above all to cancel his infamous arrangement with Vergine. The latter, on learning that Caruso would be appearing for a contemptible *cachet* of fifteen lire, had written back heatedly, urging him to leave Livorno at once and take a fill-in engagement in Naples before starting his season at the Lirico.

Fortunately Caruso ignored this advice, which would have denied him his long-awaited chance to play Rodolfo, quite apart from forfeiting Puccini's goodwill. Moreover, nothing would induce him to leave Ada Giachetti. They started rehearsing together with fanatical dedication, ignoring the protests of the orchestra and the other singers, who already resented Ada's prima donna airs.

Puccini's judgement was vindicated on the first night, a spectacular triumph for both tenor and soprano. Those who had heard Giachetti's Mimi the year before were astonished by the passion and vivacity she now gave to the role, while Caruso, no longer in terror of his high C, sang 'Che gelida manina' as if it were La Scala with the King of Italy himself in his box. They merged lovingly in the duets, and only a very sharp ear might have detected that now and then his voice was gallantly reduced to allow for his beloved's lesser volume. *La Bohème* was often repeated, more than once in the presence of Puccini, who usually brought appreciative friends over with him from Lucca.

Caruso and Ada would sometimes visit the composer's villa on Sundays to feast on spicy Tuscan dishes, beef swimming in olive oil and peppers or perhaps a brace of freshly shot birds roasting over a charcoal fire. Elvira seemed excessively formal towards Ada, as if to discourage familiarity or any hint of sharing a dubious marital status. With her hair piled high in plaits she looked so much the stately chatelaine that Ada could not resist responding a little too coquettishly to the compliments which her host bounced around like a well-trained dolphin. Caruso, however, was still far too naïve to notice this by-play or resent Puccini's cruel prankishness. Early one morning, while the host punted away with Manfredi, he was lured out to the marshes and left there for hours, shivering knee-deep in bog. Even Elvira had to smile when he squelched back with his total bag of a single tiny and mud-bespattered quail.

Puccini remained irreproachable in his eyes. 'He treats me like a brother,' he reported to Vergine. 'I have been pushed two years ahead in my career through having been chosen by him.' With such a patron and a bewitching mistress to comfort him, he seemed quite indifferent to being shamelessly exploited. The local manager, dizzy with his cut-price Rodolfo, greedily extended the season by a month at the same fee. It was a mistake. After Caruso had sung 'Che gelida manina' for the twenty-eighth time in six weeks, the tiny box-office was all but frozen.

He had hardly a coin in his pocket at the end of the season and there were seven hungry weeks to fill before the Lirico engagement. There was nothing for him in Naples, now operatically between seasons, and he could not bring himself to return home penniless after his exultant last visit. He decided instead to make his way to Milan with the vague hope of finding work there or, failing that, persuading Sonzogno to advance him something on his contract. Ada would stay behind in Livorno while waiting for her next booking, either in the provinces or possibly in South America, a nightmarish alternative. He hated being parted from her; he had become jealously possessive, and would sulk for hours if she glanced twice at another man.

With some difficulty he managed to borrow fifty lire from an acquaintance to cover the single railway fare to Milan. Ada's own resources were limited and had to last until her next engagement, but it might not have been too impossible, one imagines, for her to have sold or pawned one of her many rings. Against this, however, was the practical logic of an experienced and mature woman very much involved with her own precarious career. She believed in Caruso's future, but she had known him only two months in all. He was stimulating and refreshingly unsophisticated, but with rather too much of Rodolfo in his outlook to encourage any thoughts of a permanent liaison. Moreover, her love of creature comforts did not tempt her to play a real-life Mimi in some draughty garret.

PART TWO

'Addio a Napoli'

Chapter Six

In Milan he rented a back room in a modest *pensione*. After paying a week's board and lodging in advance he made at once for the Galleria, that glittering glass-covered arcade of restaurants and cafés where claques were hired and singers, impresarios, critics, and theatrical agents traditionally met for shop talk. He tried to catch the eye of Sonzogno, whom he recognised from photographs, but the publisher seemed permanently corralled by friends. Another crowded table was headed by Verdi's librettist, Arrigo Boito, a dandyish bachelor with a silky beard and cold eyes behind his flashing pince-nez. Sitting by themselves were a newly married couple, Arturo Toscanini and his bride, Carla de Martini, daughter of a Milanese banker. The little maestro was still mild-looking despite his fiercely waxed moustache and rakish, broad-brimmed felt hat. It seemed difficult to believe that someone —probably an artist curtly dismissed—had recently thrown a bomb at him while he was directing *Otello* in Pisa.

It was off-season and few singers were about, the lordly ones like Tamagno and de Lucia having gone off to their summer villas, but Caruso felt a stab of envy at the deference paid to the diminutive Alessandro Bonci, an up-and-coming tenor only three years his senior. Strutting on high heels and with an enormous moustache curling across baby-plump cheeks, he looked an unlikely choice for Rodolfo, still less a passionate Canio, but he had made a brilliant début at La Scala, the critics unanimously praising his luscious voice in both roles. Some even compared him with the immortal Mario, which made Livorno's recent approval of Caruso seem almost insignificant.

He wandered disconsolately past the Galleria's inviting shop-windows and café tables. Now and then he would be greeted by a fellow singer from Naples or some friend whom he had entertained during his flush days in Salerno. They seemed amiable enough but unimpressed by his chatter about the coming season at the Lirico. He was never asked to join Sonzogno's table and made lame excuses not to accept dinner invitations, usually sneaking off after an apéritif. Once or twice, still reluctant to ask Sonzogno's help, he had diffidently approached acquaintances for a loan, but most of them pleaded poverty or recommended him to moneylenders who demanded fifty per cent interest.

His arrival in Milan coincided with a period of slump. The humiliating defeat in Abyssinia had been followed by unrest and riots in the industrial north with repercussions far beyond the factories. That very month a wave of municipal retrenchment had closed the doors of La Scala for the first time in over a century. Economies had previously whittled down badly rehearsed orchestras and led to such sloppy productions that even Verdi's operas played to half-empty houses. When the local council withdrew its subsidy, the aristocratic Duke Visconti di Modrone, a direct descendant of Charlemagne, had sadly ended his family's long patronage.

Passing the silent theatre, Caruso stared at the mottled posters advertising its last production, *Cavalleria Rusticana*. Some afternoons, when his room at the *pensione* became too stuffy and he yearned helplessly for Ada, he would spend hours in the cool silence of the cathedral, thinking back to his choir days in Naples and often shedding a tear for his dead mother.

Not until his first week was almost over and he had stopped haunting the Galleria, without even a lira for a glass of wine, could he nerve himself to approach Sonzogno. The latter listened sympathetically and at once agreed to advance him the whole of his month's fees but thought he might fill in time with one or two performances of Leoncavallo's *La Bohème* at his theatre in Fiume. Caruso mumbled polite thanks and tried to conceal his dismay. Everyone knew that the piece had opened in Venice that May to a very lukewarm reception. Although dramatic in treatment, it lacked the lyricism and melodiousness of Puccini's opera, now filling houses everywhere under the auspices of Sonzogno's more powerful competitor, Giulio Ricordi. Mercifully, the manager in Fiume decided in favour of Puccini's *La Bohème*.

On his return, however, Caruso was peremptorily summoned to Sonzogno's office. Normally a man of courtly manners, Sonzogno now ordered him snappishly to prepare for the Leoncavallo opera, although Vergine had pleaded that the role was 'too strong' for his ex-pupil's voice. The publisher, rightly guessing that they were playing for time until the new *La Bohème* had found some favour, grew even more determined to have his way. He already half regretted engaging Caruso, who had become the victim of a whispering campaign. Rival singers had dismissed him as an upstart baritone masquerading as a tenor and quite unworthy to sing at the Lirico, the city's leading opera house now that La Scala was shuttered indefinitely.

He was sent off, none too politely, to learn the role of Marcello, the painter-hero in Leoncavallo's version. Soon afterwards Sonzogno's deputy also ordered him to rehearse Massenet's *La Navarraise*, which was to be staged five days hence. Helped by Ada, who had joined him between her own engagements, he somehow memorised the score but still had to endure a hostile conductor, who objected viciously to one of his friends having been passed over for the lead. Only Ada's sympathy, both in and out of bed, enabled him to survive a daily round of humiliations. At one rehearsal the soprano angrily knocked off his hat, which he had absent-mindedly kept on during their duet. Yet his was the only performance to please the critics. They dismissed all the other singers with stinging contempt and judged the opera unworthy of Massenet, despite a noisy claque, known locally as 'the thieves with yellow gloves', who had been given dozens of free tickets and their usual cash payments.

Sonzogno now felt encouraged to take up the option on his contract, but remained stubborn over Leoncavallo's *La Bohème*. However, he had second thoughts about challenging a Milanese audience which had already approved the Puccini opera and was notoriously prejudiced in favour of home-town singers. He therefore compromised by engaging Caruso for a ten-week season at the elegant Carlo Felice Theatre in Genoa. He would sing Bizet's *Les Pêcheurs de Perles* and the Leoncavallo opera, now doggedly mastered with the help of a most patient accompanist. His fee for the season was 5000 lire, enough to rent a parlour and bedroom in a more comfortable *pensione*, where Ada would often warm his sheets.

They had become more than casual lovers. To him she was already both wife and a most exciting mistress, with the additional attraction of being an experienced singer whose opinions he valued. When her mouth softened and she comforted him with almost a mother's gentleness, his head swam in ecstasy. But there were times when she became tense and irritable. He could not guess that she was already torn between physical passion and an ambition that nagged at her like an incipient cancer. He had mellowed a little and grown less coarse since Livorno, but he was still far too naïve and happy-go-lucky to notice her sulky glances when he talked too exuberantly of his own plans or paid her younger sister some artless compliment. Sensitive to the passing years, Ada had become neurotically jealous of Rina, whose superior voice was now winning her engagements at San Carlo and other leading opera houses. She was too good an actress to betray her feelings, but must have had moments of acute irritation when Rina chattered about her hopes of soon singing at La Scala and even London's Covent Garden. Although Ada had begun to turn down bookings which would separate her too long from her lover, she was missing her usual injections of applause and particularly the devotion of the faithful and not over-critical South American public.

Unaware of these inner tensions, Caruso blossomed in Genoa. In Ada's absence he enjoyed eating and drinking with other members of the company, who were far more agreeable than the backbiters at the Lirico. After the theatre they usually set off together for a favoured restaurant and sang gay choruses into the small hours while he made lightning crayon sketches of his friends and other diners on the menu cards. On mild Sundays they would often take picnic hampers out to the Ligurian hills and run races in which he always finished last, cheerfully paying up for the wine. He was tubbier and had also developed a weakness in an Achilles tendon, but the others laughingly blamed his poor condition on the demands of his voluptuous *signora*. He still flirted with every pretty girl in sight but, nervous of gossip which might reach Ada's ears, never went beyond the kissing stage.

That season at the Carlo Felice was congenial and profitable. He did creditably enough in Leoncavallo's opera, thanks to rigorous rehearsals and ultra-care over his phrasing, but failed to approach anything like his warm interpretation of Puccini's Rodolfo. Back in Milan he handed Sonzogno the money he had earned over and above his retainer, but the publisher generously refused it. With this very welcome bonus he rented an apartment in via Velasca and persuaded Ada, who had just confided that she was pregnant, to move in with him. It had not been easy. She dreaded her enforced absence from the theatre almost as much as the scandal that would inevitably surround their illicit ménage.

He was not perhaps too displeased at the prospect of removing her, even temporarily, from richer and worldlier men who, he suspected, comforted her when she went off on distant engagements. Now that she was safely anchored, however, he had to find work quickly. Money had become so tight that he was in no position to pick and choose. He even overcame his dislike of the manager in Livorno and signed a contract to sing there in *I Pagliacci* during the summer months—this time, however, for 500 lire a performance—while Ada waited for their baby. They stayed at her villa until she returned to Milan to be near her own doctor, and Rina, who had moved into the apartment. Caruso counted the hours until the season ended.

He was now so well known in Livorno that his Canio played to full houses, usually with a sprinkling of professionals in the audience. One night he heard that Umberto Giordano, whose work Sonzogno published, was in the stalls. Gratified that the author of *Andrea Chénier*, a recent success in Milan, should have come to hear him, he gave an exceptionally vibrant performance, but Giordano rather curtly declined to visit his dressing-room afterwards for a glass of wine. However he had been impressed enough to urge the celebrated prima donna Gemma Bellincioni to drive down from her nearby villa for *I Pagliacci*.

Caruso knew nothing of this flattering interest in him. In any event he was far too excited by the birth of his son, Rodolfo (quickly nicknamed 'Fofò'), on 2 July 1898. He hurried off to Milan on his first free Sunday, overjoyed that Ada and the baby were both thriving. That weekend he heard in the Galleria that La Scala would shortly reopen. This could only mean severe competition and perhaps disaster for the Lirico. Duke Visconti and the composer-librettist, Boito, had together formed a new directorship and, to restore La Scala to its old grandeur, hired two formidable people: Giulio Gatti-Casazza, as business manager, and Arturo Toscanini as his artistic director and conductor.

The former, although not yet thirty, was already a bulky and rather forbidding figure with his hooded eyes, jet-black Assyrian beard and tightly buttoned lips. Trained as a naval architect, he had succeeded his father as director of the Municipal Theatre at Ferrara after rescuing several provincial mocpanies from insolvency. He combined taste with a healthy respect for the box-office and often quoted Verdi's cynical aside to Boito: 'When the public does not run to a new production, it is already unsuccessful.' It became his lifelong credo.

Toscanini had a very different artistic approach, which would split him and Gatti-Casazza for many years, but not before they had made operatic history together on two continents. The son of a tailor, he had won a scholarship to the Conservatoire in Parma and left at eighteen with the highest possible marks. He soon graduated as a child prodigy conductor at the Teatro Regio in Turin, where he first introduced *Götterdämmerung* and Puccini's *La Bohème*, already displaying the irascibility and fiery independence which would terrorise

54

singers, musicians and even audiences whenever he picked up his baton.

He began his historic régime in Milan by dismissing forty singers as too inferior even for secondary roles. After a dress rehearsal of Bellini's *Norma* he cancelled the entire production because the soprano was still below standard. He drove orchestras and singers almost beyond their limits and used to stand on the podium like a predatory eagle with claws outstretched, ready to swoop on the smallest flaw. Not even the mighty Tamagno was spared. During a performance of *Otello*, Toscanini repeatedly called him to order over one particular passage. 'Maestro,' he had growled in his thick Piedmontese accent, 'Verdi himself taught me how this was to be sung, and at the première in this very theatre.'

'There is only *one* tempo, the correct one,' snapped Toscanini. 'And I too was at the première—in the orchestra pit.' The issue had been settled by Verdi in favour of the conductor, who continued to roast Tamagno for dragging his phrases.

La Scala's resurrection soon attracted back its leading singers, as well as newcomers like Antonio Scotti, a baritone outstanding in *Falstaff*. After a superb performance, Verdi sent Toscanini a telegram of congratulation, 'GRAZIE. GRAZIE. GRAZIE.' Toscanini, however, refused to play safe. He overruled Gatti-Casazza by bringing Wagner to La Scala and also made Debussy palatable to audiences who could never have too much of Verdi or Puccini.

Gatti's financial shrewdness and his conductor's perfectionism reduced the Lirico management to near-panic. Caruso had given seven polished performances of Leoncavallo's *La Bohème* which so delighted the composer that he once rushed on stage and kissed him passionately, almost choking him with his luxuriant Wilhelm II moustache. But these routine productions could not compete with La Scala's new décor or with an array of singing talents headed by Alessandro Bonci, Giuseppe Borgatti and de Lucia. Moreover they had the pick of Ricordi's copyrights to ensure a vast popular repertoire.

Sonzogno refused to accept defeat. His master card was the

world première of Giordano's new opera, *Fedora*. It would be mounted lavishly and with an augmented orchestra under the composer's baton. Based on a Sardou melodrama and set in St Petersburg, Paris and a Swiss mountain village, it offered spectacle together with star parts for Roberto Stagno and his wife, Bellincioni, both long-established favourites.

Heavy advance bookings had already been taken when Stagno had a heart attack and fell dead. Several replacement tenors were hastily rounded up but soon discarded as unsuitable. Gemma Bellincioni suddenly recalled Caruso's Canio in Livorno that summer and nominated him. Giordano agreed and poor Sonzogno, faced with the unthinkable option of cancelling the whole production, ordered rehearsals to start at once.

It was obviously a gamble. The tenor part called for a style which would have been within Stagno's powers even at sixty. But could the twenty-five-year-old and relatively inexperienced Neapolitan, although a passionate Canio, cut a more dignified and far subtler figure as Count Loris? Plump and shortish, he did not remotely suggest a Russian aristocrat, but nobody noticed that when he began singing arias like 'Amor ti vieta', which had something of the Puccini magic. Backed also by a dramatic soprano of Bellincioni's quality and directed with almost desperate inspiration by the composer himself, Caruso produced a gleaming golden timbre even at rehearsals without any forcing of the top register. The voice rang out so warmly that his fellow-artists often broke into spontaneous applause. After the final dress rehearsal on 16 November 1898, a theatrical agent, busily scouting for certain South American managements, hurried backstage and offered him 12,000 lire to appear in Buenos Aires the following May.

Fedora had a satisfactory reception, but it was the newcomer's night of triumph. An audience of very blasé opera-goers was moved to near-delirium. Caruso took several calls hand in hand with Bellincioni, who wept as she plucked a flower from her bouquet and pinned it to his lapel before nudging him to take the final curtain alone. Giordano and the orchestra clapped as loudly as any in the auditorium. Backstage there was bedlam as scene-shifters toasted Caruso's health in tumblers of bubbling Asti. At an emotional supper afterwards, Sonzogno presented him with a signed copy of every score he had published.

The wildly eulogistic press started a swarm of offers. Raoul Gunsbourg proposed an engagement at the Monte Carlo Casino but, to his lasting regret, had to leave Milan before making the final arrangements. Caruso also received a flattering invitation to join La Scala for a season the following year, but this too had to be shelved indefinitely. He had already been booked for St Petersburg, after which there was his solemn promise to repeat *Fedora* at the Lirico. He would then be committed for nearly six months in Buenos Aires, an engagement he was determined to fulfil although a wily lawyer opened an escape hatch. Several of his Galleria cronies also thought he had signed too quickly and for ridiculously low terms which might easily be 'adjusted,' but he refused to back out.

He grew dizzily excited by the prospect of joining the distinguished company that would be going to Russia. His only regret was that Ada would not be accompanying him. As Puccini's *La Bohème* was among the productions ahead, he had hoped until almost the last minute that she might also be engaged with him. But only a devoted lover could seriously have expected the impresario to replace such internationally known sopranos as Sigrid Arnoldson or Luisa Tetrazzini with a second-circuit singer in her late thirties.

Their imminent separation called for extreme tact on his part. As soon as Fofò was born Ada had made it quite clear that she would welcome neither middle-aged domesticity nor repeated pregnancies. By diet and massage she had shed superfluous inches and soon began exercising her voice again. She had been overwhelmed by Caruso's triumph in *Fedora*, but it had also stimulated her own ambitions. Fortunately for them both, an agent chanced to offer her a short tour in South America. She sailed a few days before Caruso's departure, leaving her six-months-old baby in the care of his Aunt Rina.

Chapter Seven

Caruso's fee for his eight-week engagement in St Petersburg was 6000 lire a month. This was gratifying, but it was less significant than the privilege of singing for the first time with artists from the top drawer of Italian *bel canto*. It was both a challenge and a valued opportunity to improve his technique since they all seemed well disposed towards him. After one rehearsal his boyhood idol, Angelo Masini, had presented him with a signed photograph, which he at once framed in silver and would always treasure.

The giant basso Vittorio Arimondi, no newcomer to St Petersburg, also eased him through the early days. Understanding neither Russian nor the elegant French which the impresario and his stage manager always used in the theatre, Caruso clung almost pathetically to his more sophisticated countryman. Mme Arimondi, a former mezzo-soprano of repute, took him shopping for warm clothes as he had rashly equipped himself with an outfit more suited to the Galleria in Milan than fashionable St Petersburg in sub-zero temperatures.

But the wife of baritone Mattia Battistini was far less approachable. This haughty and devout Spaniard allowed nobody to forget that her cousin was the celebrated Cardinal Merry del Val. She showed tight-lipped disapproval as soon as Caruso overcame his diffidence and became rather too boisterous for her taste. She thought his caricatures of the company vulgar and amateurish and particularly disliked his trick of marking time at rehearsals by shooting his ears up and down, which seemed to amuse everyone else.

Battistini gave himself no airs, although he was of noble birth and had a dazzling array of decorations from the King of Italy, Tsar Alexander III and other monarchs. He had sung at Covent Garden as long ago as 1878 and was now an adored veteran with Russian audiences, especially the ladies, who were

fascinated by his sensual Negro-dark looks. In his hotel bedroom he held what was almost a Court *levée* for an hour before
noon, handing out compliments and sly asides in fluent Russian
or French; but he always had a warming smile for Caruso, who,
perched on a chair in the corner, was quickly made to feel at
home.

He would often be allowed to stay while the baritone dressed
and reminisced, once confiding that he had refused all offers to
sing in New York because he was terrified of the sea. 'It's not
the sea you're afraid of,' Caruso said teasingly, 'it's all those
Indian savages in war paint and feathers sitting in the boxes of
the Metropolitan, ready to jump on the stage and kill you with
their hatchets if you break a top note!' Battistini, roaring with
laughter, had whirled him round the room and gleefully repeated the joke to the others. His haughty *signora* was not
amused. She had no time at all for the fat little tenor from
the Neapolitan slums, and even less for Luisa Tetrazzini from
whom he was already inseparable.

The vivacious soprano, then twenty-eight, was the daughter
of a Florentine military tailor. Her elder sister, Eva, once a
renowned Marguérite and Desdemona, had married the conductor Cleofonte Campanini, but continued to coach Luisa,
who quickly reached the top rank. She had played with leading
companies in Italy before and after touring Latin America,
where her superb coloratura with a range of nearly three
octaves, backed by a sparkling stage presence, made her a star
attraction in every theatre from Mexico City to Buenos Aires.
She had earned as much as £5000 a month at the age of twenty
but soon cultivated an extravagance which would end in a
pauper's grave.

By the time she arrived in St Petersburg on her first visit
she had had many lovers, among them President Peña of the
Argentine, and was already creating a legend with her furs,
rich collection of jewels and a private menagerie of pets,
including a parrot who was trained to sing E in alto. But she
remained so jolly and warm-hearted that Caruso had lost his
heart to her from the moment they embraced on the train.

Plump, with shining black eyes, a huge corkscrew of yellow curls and her button nose peeping over the sable collar, it was at first difficult for Russian opera-goers to picture her as a fragile Violetta in *La Traviata*. One journalist hinted that she looked as if she had dropsy instead of tuberculosis.

She ignored criticism and dressed up bravely in her sables and diamonds as if St Petersburg were no different from Buenos Aires, but nevertheless grew even more anxious than Caruso over her début. Before one dress rehearsal when, as usual, he had prayed to the Madonna of Pompeii and invoked his mother's help, he ventured into her dressing-room and was startled to see a jewelled dagger quivering in the carpet. Tetrazzini explained with an embarrassed giggle that in moments of crisis she always flung it to the floor three times. If it stuck upright, all would go well. She grew expert enough to cure her stage-fright but never abandoned this odd safe-guard.

They concealed their nervousness behind ceaseless private jokes and quite enormous meals. Her one regret was that she had lacked the courage and foresight to bring with her a stock of spaghetti, as Verdi had done when he visited the Russian capital to direct the first performance of *La Forza del Destino* nearly forty years ago.

The coming ordeal was daunting enough even for those who had previously sung in the blue and gold Grand Théâtre du Conservatoire. Without the comfort of a claque, nothing but an immaculate *Bohème* on the opening night would win approval from one of the most elegant and discriminating audiences in Europe, still less the hoped-for accolade of a command performance before the Tsar.

Rehearsals went smoothly enough. Arimondi, singing Colline, considerately avoided Tamagno's habit of drowning Tetrazzini's incomparable trill, while Masini coached Caruso for Rodolfo without a hint of patronage. He thought highly of his voice but tried to correct an obvious stiffness of move-ment on the stage.

The production won enthusiastic rounds of applause for

both Caruso and Tetrazzini. Her dressing-room was henceforth filled, night after night, with bouquets and invitations to sup in palaces or at the fashionable Restaurant Cuba. She flirted outrageously with all the grandees who continued to replenish her jewel box. Whenever she could evade admirers at the stage-door she would join Caruso for supper, always scolding him for smoking too many cigarettes, but more often he went sleigh-riding round the city with Arimondi, vainly seeking restaurants that served macaroni and usually ending with rather too much vodka.

His Rodolfo was followed by a spectacular Canio, but audiences were even more charmed by his duets in *La Traviata* with Tetrazzini, whose high Es lifted his own Alfredo to lyrical perfection. When the curtain fell he kissed her fervently and whispered, '*Carissima*, you must soon go to London and be recognised as the soprano of the world.'

His advice, well meant but ignored, was inspired by reports that Nellie Melba had recently been welcomed at Torre del Lago by Puccini, who had coached her, bar by bar, and even annotated her score for the first London production of *La Bohème* in Italian. He was reported to have called her 'the Mimi of my dreams,' which Caruso, intoxicated by Tetrazzini, thought absurd. However he was too modest to quarrel with Puccini's choice of de Lucia for Rodolfo.

It had come as something of a shock to him to see life-size portraits of Melba and Jean de Reszke displayed in the foyer of the theatre in St Petersburg. Apparently they had taken the capital by storm eight years before, when admiring young gallants had spread their capes over the snow for the Australian *diva* and crammed her carriage with orchids. Caruso had barely heard of them, except by name.

Battistini, who had sung abroad with them both, enlightened him. They were idolised in London, Paris, New York and Monte Carlo, earning quite staggering fees, although far less well know in Italy. De Reszke excelled in Wagnerian roles, long unpopular with Italian audiences, and Melba would not soon forget her La Scala ordeal as Lucia, when she had to overcome gallery hisses and even threats of poisoning from a chauvinistic claque of fanatics. Nevertheless, Leoncavallo had been enthralled at Covent Garden by her Nedda, while Verdi himself, sitting at his piano in Sant' 'Agata, had gone through the Desdemona scenes with her for a forthcoming London production of *Otello*.

Although gratified by his own success in St Petersburg, Caruso was dampened by Battistini's enthusiastic praise of de Reszke. He was said to be so tall, graceful and magnetic that box-office prices went up for all his appearances and women swooned helplessly over his Romeo, Don José, Tristan and Siegfried. Caruso had more or less resigned himself to being disparaged at home by comparison with Tamagno, de Lucia and even Bonci. Already sensitive to his own portly and squat figure, he saw no hope of competing in the world's opera houses with the romantic Polish tenor and was comforted only when Masini reminded him that de Reszke was now fifty, no longer slender and rarely able to reach the high C.

De Reszke was quickly forgotten when the company received a command to give a gala concert before the Tsar, though without the Empress, who was again pregnant and spent most evenings cloistered in her mauve boudoir reading *War and Peace*. For years afterwards Caruso would still rub his eyes in recalling that scene in the Imperial Palace. They had faced tiers of ambassadorial sashes and white and gold army dress uniforms, the light from numerous massive chandeliers sparkling on the Imperial Guard's silver breastplates. After the performance, without understanding more than a word or two of the complimentary remarks showered on him, Caruso had picked his way through the supper room, his plate piled high with sturgeon and caviar, while flunkeys circled between the marble columns like a drilled *corps de ballet* with their trays of crystal wine goblets. However, despite the gift of a pair of diamond-studded gold cuff-links, he had been disappointed in Nicholas II. In his mind's eye, suffused since childhood with crude picture-book images, kings were invariably magnificent and at least eight feet tall. But the Tsar of All the Russias, as he would sadly report to Ada, was 'only a small, insignificant-looking man with an anxious face'.

His homecoming was jubilant, although the change in temperature had given him a chill, which temporarily affected his voice. Ada spoon-fed him and was delighted with her own gifts and the carved wooden toys which had made Fofò squeal with glee. Buenos Aires had obviously fortified her morale. Although still inclined to fret over Caruso's absences, she was mollified by his solemn promise to take her with him on his next visit to St Petersburg, the following year.

With only two months before his South American engagement, he busied himself with a repertory which would include Mascagni's *Iris*, an opera new to him that had a Japanese setting. He also found time to sample the latest Galleria gossip. He now sat at Sonzogno's right hand, shooting out his cuffs to display the Tsar's gold links for the benefit of passing acquaintances who drank his wine and often borrowed money. Others, however, spread hurtful reports that his sore throat was nothing but an alibi for a decline in vocal quality and volume. He soon reassured Sonzogno, who had become demoralised by La Scala's unbroken run of successes and was looking forward to Caruso's month at the Lirico.

The tenor called at Puccini's flat, but the composer had locked himself away in his mountain fortress at Monsagrati, north of Lucca, where he was absorbed in the second act of his next opera, *Tosca*, based on the violent melodrama by Sardou. Everyone predicted a masterpiece, and Caruso already glowed with anticipation at playing Cavaradossi, another painter hero but apparently a far more rewarding and dramatic role even than Rodolfo.

Meantime, he had to apply himself to routine. He surpassed himself in eight performances of *Fedora* and was elated when Maurice Grau of the Metropolitan stopped in the Galleria to congratulate him, hinting at an engagement in New York. He suggested $200 a week, which seemed modest for one of the world's leading opera houses, but Caruso thought the opportunity too good to miss. Unhappily, Grau had not been enthusiastic enough to confirm the offer before leaving Milan to take a cure in Carlsbad for his gout. One or two half-hearted letters arrived from New York, followed by a rather patronising approach from Grau's Italian agent. Nothing definite emerged and Caruso put the matter out of his mind while he relaxed and prepared for his South American engagement. He would be partnered by Gemma Bellincioni, which pleased him and, equally important, helped to console Ada for their coming months of separation. The prima donna was an older woman and no temptation to Caruso, who, since his return from Russia had tactlessly rhapsodised over Tetrazzini's voice and sparkle.

His relationship with Ada had ripened with affluence and social acceptance by the bohemian-minded circles in which they moved. Both were hospitable and enjoyed entertaining in their flat, where guests, mainly from the theatre, were welcomed at dinner and indeed at all hours. Caruso revelled in shop talk over a bottle of wine and a game of cards. Among them was a big-nosed baritone from La Scala with a mop of lustrous black hair, Antonio Scotti.

Then thirty-three, Scotti had gone backstage one night at the Lirico to compliment his fellow Neapolitan. A tall, easygoing and elegant batchelor, he was fastidious in dress and had the air of a well-bred pelican. His main pastime outside the theatre seemed to be hunting women, on whom he squandered his pay, though not always successfully. One of his failures in Milan was a florist's salesgirl in the Galleria. He and his friendly rival, Fritz Kreisler, newly arrived from Vienna, used to entertain her on alternate nights, borrowing the same opera cape and silk hat from the property department at La Scala. They soon discovered that she was playing one against the other while being kept by a Polish count, who shot himself on discovering her infidelity. Scotti went about broken-hearted for some days, but revived on being offered a Covent Garden début in *Don Giovanni*, to be followed that December by his first engagement at the Metropolitan Opera House in the

64

same opera. He went off to London just before Caruso sailed for South America at the end of April 1899.

The sea voyage—'my ozone tonic', he assured the captain—cleared his throat and lungs miraculously. When *Fedora* opened in Buenos Aires he gave such a superlative performance that the local impresario offered him a contract for the next three seasons at an average of £160 a month, almost treble his present fee. The engagement was both a box-office and an artistic success, but it had been a long and rather solitary four months. He missed Ada and often thought wistfully of the gay camaraderie in St Petersburg. He admired Bellincioni, who helped him over his acting weaknesses and offered valuable hints on stage make-up, but she was still mourning her husband and was not the gayest of companions at their after-theatre suppers. As there were few other kindred spirits in the company and he lacked enough Spanish to mix easily with the local opera patrons who sometimes invited him into their homes, Caruso withdrew more and more to his hotel room, chain-smoking and playing solitaire. He would also spend hours copying out parts into his notebooks and trying to correct imperfections by singing phrases a dozen times over in different ways. He affected indifference but had been irritated by one or two critics who hinted sourly that his voice lacked the power of past Italian idols.

He enjoyed carriage rides around the city, particularly when any of his countrymen stopped to salute him. Thrown out of employment by an economic slump and the introduction of machinery, thousands had recently emigrated to the Argentine. Few could afford opera, which, to most of them, was almost as necessary to life as spaghetti. Caruso bought and gave away batches of tickets, no doubt aware that it did no harm to have an appreciative band of compatriots in the gallery, but also handed out 'loans' on a scale which would have exasperated Ada.

He struck up a friendship with an immigrant Italian artist who offered to instruct him in sketching and modelling. Since his far-off days in Naples with the street-fountain manufacturer he had liked working in clay, and soon showed distinct promise at sculpture. He packed several of his pieces when he sailed home in midsummer with money jingling in his pocket and a contract to return the following June.

As soon as the ship docked at Naples he hastened to his old home. Maria smothered him with kisses and at once prepared macaroni and beans with his favourite sauce. He thought, perhaps a little wishfully, that she had grown astonishingly like his mother in build and looks. Both wore black at all times and had similar deep-set, melancholy eyes with thickly braided hair austerely parted in the middle. But Maria was even more devout, and he had hastily decided not to mention his liaison with Ada or show her the photograph of Fofò in his pocket-book. He confided instead in his father, swearing him to secrecy. Marcellino, now grizzled and with malaria-yellowed cheeks, had lost his former thrust and seemed almost terrified of his sharp-tongued wife. He recovered something of his old spirit only when they left the house to call on neighbours.

Time and again Caruso had to exhibit the Tsar's cuff-links and repeat his stories of St Petersburg and Buenos Aires, usually ending with an operatic aria or two until crowds choked the street. Whenever he appeared in public throughout that week he was greeted affectionately as 'Rico' or 'Carusiello'. He had an uproarious reunion with Zucchi in the Caffè dei Fiori and embraced old friends at the Mercadente, discreetly slipping a few bank-notes to stage-hands and others with large families to support. He cracked jokes nonstop in the Neapolitan dialect and proved that success had not gone to his head by remembering everyone's first name. Schoolfellows and several street musicians were quick to remind him of his hard-up days. He gave freely and with good humour but shook off one importunate sponger who seized his lapel to remove a hair from his gaudy new jacket. He roared out in mock anger, 'You can have my wallet, but kindly leave that hair exactly where it was.'

He had to brace himself for an uncomfortable interview with Vergine. The singing teacher had drawn twenty-five per cent of his earnings since 1893 for doing nothing, but stuck fiercely to the ambiguous clause, 'five years of *actual singing*', in the original agreement. Caruso had reluctantly taken proceedings to settle the dispute, but it was dragging on tediously, with no prospect ahead but bad publicity for himself and good pickings for the lawyers. After much argument he finally charmed the Maestro into having the contract annulled for an *ex gratia* payment of 20,000 lire. Although Ada chided him for his weakness, he would never utter a word against the rapacious old man and often gratefully recalled the many free lessons in his studio.

His stay ended in a haze of food, drink, flattery and sentimental nostalgia. He bathed at Santa Lucia, lit a candle for his mother and gave liberally to the church where he had first sung as a choir boy. For good luck he touched the street fountain at the Bridge of Cerra which he had once installed for Signor Palmieri. These would become ritual acts of pilgrimage on all his return visits. He also took Maria and his father, still working part time at the factory, on excursions to Pompeii or into the country, rejoicing to see a little colour creep back into the pale cheeks of his sister, Assunta. His wallet was much thinner after forcing his stepmother to accept a large sum to keep them from want over the next few months, but he had every reason to feel exuberant about the future as the train headed north. His one lingering regret was that nobody thought highly enough of his successes in Russia and South America to invite him to sing at San Carlo.

He was soon comforted by an offer to perform at the great Costanzi Theatre in Rome, where he was warmly greeted by Mugnone, who would be directing the orchestra. He would open in *Iris* and then make his first appearance in Boito's *Mefistofele*, rehearsed by the composer himself, but this aroused far less interest that the forthcoming première of Puccini's next opera. Everyone was already talking of *Tosca* as the most significant work since Verdi.

Caruso's season pleased his audiences. So many complimentary letters and requests for signed photographs poured in that he decided on impulse to send for Enrico Lorello, whom, long ago in Salerno, he had so gaily promised to take on as his secretary. Lorello appeared almost at once, but he was more ready than able and soon reduced the correspondence to a chaos which the tidy-minded Caruso abhorred yet charitably forgave. He made himself useful as a valet and also proved a sympathetic confidant during a far from easy engagement. *Mefistofele* had been an ordeal, but with help from Mugnone, Caruso had overcome his nerves and given a performance which Boito praised effusively at a luncheon next day.

Almost at once, however, he had to take a crushing blow. Puccini arrived from Lucca and embraced him like a brother but seemed unaware that he had set his heart on singing Cavaradossi in *Tosca*. The role would go instead to Emilio de Marchi, who had a solid record in Italy and South America but was rated by Mugnone and others as little more than competent. Toscanini had recently berated him for a mediocre appearance in *Les Huguenots* at La Scala and then scolded the engineers for some minor fault of lighting. De Marchi, who had been angrily chewing his nails in the wings, jumped forward and exclaimed, 'Bravo, Maestro! These ignorant electricians caused me to sing a bad note. It's an outrage.' Toscanini glared at him and soon proceeded to demolish his performance in the most scarifying detail until de Marchi crawled out of the theatre with a very red face.

Caruso failed to understand why he had been rejected without so much as a trial, and Puccini never enlightened him. He may well have decided that Cavaradossi called for superior acting talent and a bigger voice than Caruso had so far displayed as Rodolfo, much as he had admired him in that role. Possibly he was also influenced by Ricordi's son, Tito, who would be in charge of the production and had an almost fanatical prejudice against any Sonzogno artist. But the deciding factor in Puccini's mind was no doubt the strong rumour that a claque had been plotting to wreck the première. If true, nobody could blame a nervous composer for withholding the lead from a newcomer to Rome where de Marchi had a staunch following.

Whatever the reasons for his being overlooked, Caruso could in fact only have taken the part by cancelling his second Russian engagement. *Tosca* did not open until 14 January 1900, almost a month after he had arranged to leave for St Petersburg. He was wise enough to conceal his injured feelings from Puccini and Mugnone and departed apparently in the best of spirits, attended by his new secretary and wearing a handsome astrakhan-collared topcoat ordered from the best tailor in Rome.

That second Russian season was challenging enough to make him forget his chagrin over *Tosca*. He would open in *Aïda*, an opera new to him and intimidating. He had repeatedly sidestepped Radamès, a part on which such celebrated actor-singers as Tamagno and de Reszke had long set their seals. All his terror of the top C returned, together with an almost unbearable stage-fright from the moment he was fitted for his splendid costumes. He felt dwarfed by the grandeur of the sets and was soon being racked by his headaches. Ada would certainly have soothed him, but she was not due in Moscow until mid-March, while poor Lorello, with his ten thumbs and two left feet, had become a handicap. Understanding only Italian, he simply avoided answering the telephone or confused even the simplest message.

Caruso was, however, fortunate in again having his old friends, Arimondi and Battistini, with him. They steered him through rehearsals, while Luisa Tetrazzini used to massage his temples afterwards with eau-de-Cologne. 'The fat one', as he called her, never failed to make him laugh with her saucy imitations of the passionate young noblemen who threatened to blow out their brains unless she surrendered.

The audience was with him from the moment he sang the opening bars of 'Celeste Aïda'. He had excellent support from the prima donna Salomea Krusheniska (later a memorable Butterfly), who played the name part with all the assurance of a national favourite. Although still straining for the top C, Caruso's high B flat, vibrant and unforced, was encored throughout that first performance. It was impossible to resist the exaltation of his 'Pur ti riveggo, mia dolce Aïda' in the Nile

scene with its tremendous climax as he strode across the stage
to surrender his sword. In his dressing-room he was emotionally
kissed by a weeping Tetrazzini and bear-hugged in Arimondi's
huge arms. It was quickly announced that *Aïda* would be the
company's leading attraction at Moscow's Grand Théâtre
in March, but he modestly discounted the eulogies for his
Radamès. 'Don't praise me,' he told one critic. 'Praise Verdi.'

He now had other good reasons to thank his patron saint.
De Marchi, Puccini's chosen tenor, had suffered a nightmare
experience at the *Tosca* première in Rome. Inflamed by a hostile
claque, the audience had hissed the torture scene and other
brutalities in the libretto. The cast, already demoralised by
threats to assassinate Queen Margherita in her box, were
understandably too much on edge to give of their best. Tosca
had been sung by an actress who possessed striking beauty but
was no vocalist, while poor de Marchi fell below his usual
standard. Both were singled out for violent disapproval.

Caruso had felt deep sympathy for Puccini and even more
for Mugnone, who at one point dropped his baton and fled
backstage in terror. However, the opera was now playing to
packed and enthusiastic houses and would be staged later in
Buenos Aires by the impresario who had engaged Caruso. Any
hopes he might have had of singing Cavaradossi were quickly
dashed by an announcement that de Marchi had once again
been chosen. Scotti reported soon afterwards that he would
shortly be leaving for London to play Scarpia, with Fernando
de Lucia in the leading role. Caruso could not help feeling a
shade envious, but was certain that the opera's growing popularity must soon create a heavy demand for tenors. It stimulated
him to study the score whenever possible.

There were few opportunities. After *Aïda* his hotel suite
became the haunt of so many friendly critics and other well-
wishers that parties often seemed to develop automatically. He
was easily tempted to play cards until well past midnight,
though he was always punctual at the rehearsals for *Mefistofele*,
which would be performed for the first time in Russia. With
excellent support from Arimondi and Krusheniska there was

little to fear, but he began to grow edgy. The incessant demand for interviews and photographic sessions made him neurotically certain that the glittering first-night audience would expect a far more polished Faust than he had given in Rome. He was therefore almost frantic to be reunited with Ada, who never failed to steady his pre-opening nerves. She was due to reach St Petersburg with Mme Arimondi at eight o'clock on the morning of the première.

Lorello was sent off to meet them while his master, after being shaved, perfumed, and moustache-waxed by the hotel barber, restlessly paced his flower-filled suite, a maid standing by to attend Ada after her long journey. By eleven o'clock, when neither the ladies nor Lorello had yet appeared, he was chain-smoking and impatiently stamping about while Arimondi tried to calm him. Lorello returned soon afterwards, babbling incoherently that the train had still not arrived. The railway officials could offer no explanation and the confusion only deepened when a telegram was delivered, written in Russian and signed by Mme Arimondi. Caruso, hatless and without coat or overshoes, rushed out in a temperature of thirty below zero to have it translated. The message was so garbled that he drove by sleigh to the station, where he heard that the train had been derailed. Fortunately there had been no casualties, but the passengers were waiting for a relief engine to complete their journey. Still distraught, and aware that he was already late for afternoon rehearsal, he went back to his hotel, but refused to eat lunch or go to the theatre until Ada and Aurelia Arimondi arrived at about three o'clock, both half frozen and exhausted.

They went to the theatre together, looking none the worse, but Caruso's troubles were not yet over. A few minutes before curtain-time Ada was seated in her box, elegant and composed, while Mme Arimondi had a chair in the wings from which she habitually lent her husband moral support on opening nights. Caruso was on stage working out last-minute details. Arimondi had once again demonstrated exactly how he would pull the cord of Caruso's dressing-gown to reveal him in the costume of

71

the youthful Faust when his wife, craning for a better view, tilted back in her chair. It touched off a button and prematurely raised the curtain. Tenor and basso fled while the audience roared with laughter.

It did not affect a fine performance, but next day Caruso ran a high temperature. A sharp attack of broncho-pneumonia kept him in bed for almost a month. Lovingly nursed by Ada and swamped with flowers, delicacies and hundreds of tender messages, including several from the Romanovs, he made good use of his time. After the rest of the company had left St Petersburg, he occupied himself with his notebooks, patiently copying out phrases for the parts he hoped to perform in Moscow. He also went through the score of *Tosca*, which both he and Ada thought even more exciting than *La Bohème*. Before long they were singing duets, almost feverishly anticipating the chance of one day playing together again. Chambermaids and hotel guests would crowd the corridor outside Suite 88 to hear Cavaradossi's aria, 'E lucevan le stelle', which even in the convalescent tenor's half voice sounded unbearably poignant.

He completed the season in Moscow, repeating *Aïda* and *Mefistofele* with apparent ease but not without paying a heavy price, mainly psychological, for his recent illness. He now lived in terror of suddenly losing his voice. He gargled incessantly, inhaled and took snuff before every performance, although continuing to puff one cigarette after another between acts.

Caruso had not fully recovered by the time he arrived in Buenos Aires, only six weeks later, for his second season. His opening in *Mefistofele* was so indifferently received that he glumly decided to leave for home by the end of the week. Yet two nights later, in the same opera, he had an ovation and thereafter won consistent applause throughout that season, particularly for *Cavalleria Rusticana*. Nevertheless over-concern for his voice had made him sparing with encores, and this displeased audiences. During that season he heard de Marchi sing Cavaradossi and become even more convinced that the role was tailor-made for himself, although he praised his rival generously. When de Marchi suddenly developed throat trouble, Caruso replaced him in *Manon* and moved the house to frenzy. Before sailing for a three-week season in Montevideo en route for home, he sang hymns in the beautiful cathedral at a memorial service for King Humbert of Italy, who had been assassinated that July.

He docked in Genoa at the end of September 1900, but had time for only a brief convivial meeting with a few old friends at the Carlo Felice before hurrying on to Milan. He had intended to rest, but the Galleria cafés were, as usual, quite irresistible. To his great joy he was invited within a few days to sing in *Tosca*, with Ada in the title role, for a short season at the Sociale Theatre in Treviso. They had hoped to have Scotti with them as the Baron Scarpia, but he was still enchanting Covent Garden audiences. The part went instead to a reasonably competent baritone from La Scala.

This début in the exacting Puccini opera showed the fruits of their patient work together on the score. They had smoothed out difficult passages with an affectionate consideration for each other that recalled their first days in Livorno. Ada seemed to blossom throughout the dozen successive performances until she almost matched him in power and poise.

This almost idyllic relationship continued when they were offered another short season together in Bologna. They would sing in *Tosca* and *Iris*, neither of which offered any terrors, although Caruso quickly found himself under fire. Here in Bologna he would have to alternate with Bonci and Borgatti, both veterans of San Carlo and La Scala. It made him so nervous that he was constantly examining his throat, and began to spray his tonsils several times a day. Ada, however, helped by the soothing presence of Mugnone in the orchestra pit, was finally able to reassure him.

He dominated his rivals from his very first appearance as Cavaradossi. The passionate outburst of 'Vittoria! Vittoria!' seemed to take his audience by the throat. They had listened

73

almost hypnotised as the sombre drama unfolded, but roared delirious approval when he sobbed, 'E lucevan le stelle.' Mugnone collapsed at his desk from giving so many encores. The most cherished moment of all during that season was the arrival of Puccini, who had read reports of these astonishing scenes and suddenly jumped into a train at Lucca to see for himself. He embraced Caruso afterwards, declaring he had never heard Cavaradossi sung better, and gallantly remembered to present Ada with an enormous bouquet.

That brief season, only a month in all, set bigger wheels in motion. Boito had already spoken enthusiastically of Caruso's performances in his *Mefistofele*, while Scotti had long sung his friend's praises. But it was his decisive triumph over the better-known Bonci and Borgatti that brought him an invitation which had seemed unattainable.

A few days after his return from Bologna he was summoned to Gatti-Casazza's office in La Scala and offered a three-month contract at the vast fee of 50,000 lire (£2000). Rehearsals for *La Bohème* would begin at once, Toscanini informed him brusquely. He signed without any misgivings.

Chapter Eight

In a milieu notorious for 'temperament', backbiting and bitter vendettas, Caruso emerges as almost unique. He could be guilty of clowning or high-spirited prankishness but never of malice. Throughout his career he rarely disparaged a fellow artist or made unreasonable demands on impresarios. Loyalty and a respect for the sanctity of contracts would often cause him to overtax his voice rather than disappoint the public. Such dedication, and a geniality that endeared him to the humblest stage-hands, are not easily reconciled with his explosive début at La Scala in December 1900.

In retrospect one can imagine his pride and awe as he stepped for the first time on that stage to survey almost three thousand empty seats and the majestic tiers of boxes. He would now be appearing with Italy's most celebrated singers, supported by all the resources of the world's leading opera house; first-class costumes, lighting and scenery, perfect acoustics and, above all, an orchestra under Toscanini's meticulous beat. It was a fearsome challenge for a newcomer aware that every production would be scrutinised by talent scouts, agents and influential critics. Caruso was therefore more than thankful to learn that the season would open with a Wagner opera before his own *La Bohème*.

Toscanini, his lean body encased like a stiletto in the tight black jacket, had greeted him pleasantly enough, but that first rehearsal was almost disastrous. He had been unprepared for so many onlookers, including the two directors, Boito and Duke Visconti, as well as Gatti-Casazza and several Milanese editors. Nervous of singing the high C in 'Che gelida manina' until rehearsals were more advanced, he had decided to give it in falsetto. Toscanini frowned and curtly demanded the full tone, but Caruso pleaded that he wished to preserve his voice. He continued to have his way through successive sessions

75

attended by Puccini and his Buddha-like librettist, Giacosa, neither of whom objected. But the conductor grew more irritated and began to croak disapproval of the smallest errors.

Storm clouds gathered when he called a full rehearsal for nine o'clock one morning. It lasted several hours, due to frequent stops and starts from the relentless perfectionist, until singers and musicians alike were limp with exhaustion. To avoid friction Caruso had this time sung in full voice although tired and cross at not having a lunch break, which Toscanini had brusquely ignored. When he was about to leave for home in the late afternoon, a message was handed to him ordering yet another general rehearsal for that very evening. He at once conferred with his Mimi (Emma Carelli), who gladly made a pact to sing with him in 'half-voice'.

Still dyspeptic after his rushed dinner, he returned to a theatre already swarming with opera enthusiasts and journalists. Their presence apparently caused the soprano to forget her promise and use full volume while Caruso doggedly avoided his top notes. Act One ended in a vocal anti-climax which startled the audience and inflamed Toscanini to near apoplexy.

Caruso was resting between acts and munching figs when Gatti-Casazza entered his dressing-room to plead for more volume. The tenor protested that his throat was already strained through over rehearsal. When he went back on stage for the second act it was difficult to produce even the demi voice. Toscanini rapped on the desk and pointed his baton accusingly. 'If you refuse to sing with your full voice, I shall not continue,' he rasped. Caruso fingered his Adam's apple and mumbled something which was lost in the hubbub. The conductor then threw down his baton and stalked out. The rehearsal broke up in disorder, but the reporters, scenting a front-page sensation, declined to leave the theatre. Few of them had a kind word for this Neapolitan arriviste who had dared to flout authority on his very first appearance at La Scala.

Gatti-Casazza plucked his beard and went off to plead with

the conductor, while the Duke Visconti made for the tenor's dressing-room and tried to calm him. By this time, however, Caruso was angry enough to offer to return his first month's pay and abandon the whole contract. The Duke purred solace but gently reminded him of his duty both to the management and to the other performers. Caruso subsided at once and agreed to continue although still insisting that his throat must be protected. By now Toscanini had also simmered down and the rehearsal resumed without further disturbance. It did not end until 1 a.m.

Next morning Caruso awoke with a touch of laryngitis which could have been genuine, imaginary or psychosomatic in origin. He stayed in bed for a day or two, attended by his doctor. Ada was sympathetic but practical enough to warn him sharply against continuing to antagonise Toscanini. All seemed well until Gatti-Casazza suddenly announced that *Tristan* would have to be postponed because of Borgatti's indisposition. He proposed opening instead with *Bohème*. Caruso protested but finally went on, reeking of iodoform and with his tonsils sprayed to the very last second. Few critics showed more than politeness for his début, but patrons welcomed his every appearance after he had sung Rodolfo several times that month.

There was strong box-office support for the world première of Mascagni's new opera, *Le Maschere*, which had been heralded as the season's main attraction, but it turned out to be mediocre and only partially salvaged by Caruso's spirited singing. After only three performances 'the Padrone' had to find an urgent replacement. He and Toscanini were constantly to be seen with their heads together at the nearby Caffè Cova. Finally they decided to play safe with a revival of Donizetti's comic opera, *L'Elisir d'Amore*. This could be staged fairly quickly and offered few production problems. It was a light-hearted affair about a village bumpkin under the influence of a quack's love potion, but in his mind's eye Gatti-Casazza could clearly see the plump little tenor, often so merry off stage, as the lovelorn Nemorino. The opera also included a moving aria,

'Una furtiva lagrima', which never failed with audiences and might make a display piece for Caruso's voice. That very evening they approached him and were delighted by his willingness to cooperate. Apparently he already knew the aria and felt confident of memorising the whole score in a few days.

While rehearsals went smoothly ahead, with conductor and tenor now on the most affable terms, the nation was stunned by Verdi's death. A memorial concert was at once arranged, with Toscanini conducting and Tamagno, the original Otello, as leading vocalist. Caruso had the honour of singing the Duke in the Quartet from *Rigoletto* and was warmly complimented by Puccini, Leoncavallo and Mascagni among the many celebrities in the theatre.

He soon became anxious about his next appearance, however, The advance bookings for *L'Elisir* were disappointing. Already jaundiced by that season's moderate offerings, the critics had almost unanimously denounced the revival of a familiar piece of *opera buffa* as unworthy of La Scala's great tradition. They sneered even more openly on learning that a veteran basso, one Carbonetti, had been winkled out of semi-retirement to play the quack doctor. All Milan jeered when he arrived at the railway station without an overcoat and grasping a cardboard suitcase tied with string.

That opening performance, on 17 February 1901, saved the whole season from disaster. Carbonetti surprised everyone while Caruso's performance long remained, in the words of Gatti-Casazza, 'a sensation in the annals of the Teatro alla Scala'. His Nemorino exhibited both a natural sense of comedy and quite remarkable ease in moving from farce to pathos. The climax to an historic evening came with 'Una furtiva lagrima', which ended to applause not far short of that for *Otello* thirteen years earlier. Toscanini had made it almost a house rule to disallow encores but even he could not withstand such a furore. People stood up to clap and cheer until Caruso had to give the aria again and again. When the artists finally came before the curtain, Toscanini embraced him and whispered ecstatically to

Gatti-Casazza, '*Per Dio*! If this Neapolitan continues to sing like this, he will make the whole world talk about him.'

The opera was given a dozen times to crowded houses. Meantime Caruso was also busily rehearsing Boito's *Mefistofele* to climax that topsy-turvy season. It soon became clear, however, that this production was anything but a safe choice. 'Don Giulio', seeking novelty appeal, had enterprisingly invited a Russian basso, Fedor Chaliapin, to play the name part. Never having sung abroad and eager to make his bow in Milan, he had asked only 1000 lire (less than £50) a performance!

Even before his arrival the directors were already being upbraided for importing a Russian savage from the steppes when any of a dozen native bassos seemed admirably equipped for the role. The blond, blue-eyed giant was accompanied by his pretty young wife, an Italian ballerina. They made a charming couple and greeted everyone with friendliness and modesty, but were almost brutally cold-shouldered by the critics. Worse, Chaliapin had fallen out with La Scala's influential and quite ruthless claque. Their leader had soon called at his hotel to demand a considerable bribe, payable in advance, failing which he and his friends would wreck the opening performance. The huge basso picked him up like a rag doll and tossed him down the stairs.

Boito was understandably terrified of what the claque might do in retaliation. His nervousness even infected Toscanini, who usually disdained first-night threats. He now gave Chaliapin a repeat performance of what Caruso had so recently suffered. At rehearsals he insisted on the basso's giving full voice while the others were allowed to sing in lower tones. Chaliapin angrily threatened to return home, but Caruso calmed him. 'The Maestro knows what the rest of us can do,' he explained soothingly. 'You should not worry. He is like one of those dogs who bark and do not bite.'

Basso and tenor had become almost soul-mates on discovering several astonishing personal links. Both were born in the same month of the same year and shared a humble origin. Chaliapin, the son of a drunken cobbler, had also started his singing career in church choirs. He soon confided that, despite all his triumphs in Russia, he still suffered as acutely from stage-fright as Caruso. But perhaps the most remarkable coincidence of all was their talent for sketching; before long they were making lightning caricatures of each other, on and off stage.

The Chaliapins became frequent visitors to Caruso's flat in via Velasca, where they used to sit up late, laughing, drinking and chatting about mutual friends in St Petersburg. In later years Chaliapin would often speak affectionately of Caruso's 'face of goodness' and recall the excitement of listening to him for the first time in *L'Elisir*. 'It was the finest tenor voice I had ever heard.'

Mefistofele silenced the claque. Chaliapin's powerful tone and acting intoxicated audiences, although next day the critics handled Caruso's Faust with some roughness. It did not diminish his delight in his friend's triumph or his gratitude for the many hints which that master of stage make-up generously passed on to him. They parted almost in tears, pledging a friendship which remained unbroken for the rest of Caruso's life.

He was already preparing for his third season in Buenos Aires at the handsome *cachet* of 35,000 lire (£1400) a month. This time he would be working for a new impresario who had spared no expense to launch himself successfully. Mario Sammarco, a masterly baritone, was to partner him in *Rigoletto*, while Borgatti would alternate as leading tenor. Toscanini had also agreed to make his début before the South American public, but de Marchi, an established idol with Argentine opera-goers, was unavailable. This meant sacrificing a very popular Cavaradossi. It was hoped that Caruso might fill the gap, although La Scala had so far hesitated to entrust him with the part.

He appeared sublimely self-confident and enjoyed a month's relaxation before sailing time. The La Scala season had not only fattened his wallet but entrenched him firmly in the Galleria, where he now held court at his own regular table,

Caruso at 22, the first Press photograph. He posed in a bedspread as his only
shirt was being washed.

Ada Giachetti, the soprano, whom he first partnered in *La Bohème*.
Their ten-year liaison ended in tragedy.

Caruso was paid £450 by George A. Kessler, the American financier, to sing for his guests at the lavish Gondola Dinner in July 1905. The forecourt of the Savoy Hotel, London, was flooded and transformed into a replica of a Venetian canal.

A gifted draughtsman, Caruso often made lightning sketches on trains or while waiting for his cue. *Above left*: Gatti-Casazza, director of La Scala, Milan, and later the Metropolitan, New York. *Above right*: One of many self-caricatures. *Below*: Caruso as Pinkerton (*extreme left*) in a scene from *Madame Butterfly*. Geraldine Farrar sang the geisha role.

Toscanini in action.

As King Gustavo in Verdi's *Un Ballo in Maschèra*.

As Canio in Leoncavallo's *I Pagliacci*.

Caruso had a lucky escape when San Francisco was almost destroyed by an earthquake and fire in April 1906. He had barely time to dress and leave his hotel, clutching a silver-framed photograph autographed by President Theodore Roosevelt.

looking every inch the *divo* in well-tailored yet gaudy clothes, with his moustache waxed and a sparkling diamond on his wedding finger. He had been promised another engagement by Gatti-Casazza in March of the following year, possibly in a new opera, while Scotti continued to hint that the Covent Garden Syndicate might also be interested in booking him.

Meantime he had signed an agreement to sing at the Monte Carlo Casino that winter under the auspices of Raoul Guns-bourg, who had many patrons among the Russian nobility and was quick to exploit Caruso's success in St Petersburg. But this glamorous engagement, in which he would partner inter-national stars like Mme Melba and Maurice Renaud, leading baritone of the Paris Opéra, excited him far less than a long-awaited invitation to sing in his native city. He would open at the San Carlo on 30 December 1901 in *L'Elisir d'Amore*, the opera which had already brought him so much acclaim.

Caruso was perhaps rather too excited by his prospects to worry about Ada's changes of mood. She had enjoyed queening it briefly in her box at La Scala, wearing the necklace on which Caruso had spent most of his first month's pay. It was also flattering after the hard years of touring with second-grade companies to be greeted so respectfully by Gatti-Casazza and have her hand kissed by Boito and other notables. But she could not help missing the excitement of her own first nights, and yearned to be back on stage. She would never forget that ecstatic final curtain in Bologna when Puccini had thanked her for *Tosca* and driven her back to the hotel in a carriage piled with bouquets.

She could not easily reconcile herself to the near-certainty that her operatic career was over unless she left Caruso. She had already suffered one painful miscarriage and lost a son at birth, followed by the death of another in early infancy. Recurrent pregnancies would almost inevitably wreck her still shapely figure. Motherhood had so far proved no conso-lation. Fofò was an attractive child with golden curls, but he was sickly and demanded more attention than she was ready to give. Subconsciously, perhaps, she tended to resent him even more when her unattached sister, Rina, left so elatedly to sing in Rome or Naples. Caruso's batches of letters from women admirers also reminded her that she would soon be forty and increasingly vulnerable to competition. So far he had confined himself to harmless flirting, but she grew touchy whenever he set off on his long South American engagements.

He remained devoted to her and often talked wistfully of marriage when her exasperatingly robust husband died. But Ada's mouth used to harden if they were asked to some wedding or christening, and the most innocent reference to her own irregular status would bring on a flood of tears. In the dark moments he lavished gifts of perfume and jewellery on her or outlined exciting plans for their future. After one Sunday visit to Torre del Lago he could talk of nothing but his dream of buying a property in Tuscany, where they would grow vines and olives and breathe the sweet country air. He envied Puccini who had discovered the perfect *modus vivendi* with his spacious villa and a flat in via Giuseppe Verdi for his visits to Milan. Their own apartment was becoming uncomfortably cramped with Fofò and his nurse, and a separate room for Lorello, apart from all the clothes and household trinkets which they bought with each burst of prosperity.

His tidy nature hankered for space to keep his files, notebooks and music scores, and perhaps a quiet studio to practise new parts with an accompanist. He already saw himself presiding benevolently at his own farm-house table with his family and friends around him. He saw no reason why his father and Maria should not spend their declining years in rustic serenity, although so far he had failed to shift them even from their dilapidated dwelling in Naples to better quarters.

These rosy dreams faded in the harsh sunlight of Buenos Aires, where the heat and possibly his over-indulgence in cigarettes—a daily minimum of fifty strong Egyptians—had brought on severe attacks of migraine. He also started to suffer from a skin irritation which he attributed to the hotel's rough cotton sheets. He soon had them replaced with linen and rarely travelled again without a private stock. It was perhaps psychologically significant that this strange allergy to cotton, together with his sudden headaches, had developed in the first weeks of being separated from Ada. He dreaded the four long months ahead and declined to renew his contract for the following season, promising half-heartedly to return two years hence.

That engagement was memorable mainly for his Cavaradossi. He had been tepidly received until 'E lucevan le stelle', when the audience quite forgot de Marchi and roared hungrily for encores. *Tosca* was given ten times that season but Caruso's Duke of Mantua was equally welcomed. Critics praised his control of 'Questa o quella', but it was the lightness and abandon of 'La donna è mobile' that really brought the South Americans to their feet. They were still unappeased after four encores. Even Toscanini's stern face softened when a crowd of Italians in the gallery screamed 'Viva Caruso!' until the theatre attendants had to restore order by brute force. Unhappily this hysteria encouraged him to sing Lohengrin (in Italian) which demanded a physical nobility and vocal qualities beyond his range. He would never again attempt to emulate de Reszke in Wagner.

Back from Buenos Aires he gave two charity performances in Trieste of *L'Elisir d'Amore*, with which he would open his San Carlo season. He travelled down to Naples with Ada, who, to his relief, was politely received by his father and Maria. They seemed far too excited over his forthcoming début to think of much else. Ada went on shopping expeditions with her sister, Rina, who had also been engaged by San Carlo, while Caruso toured the cafés and hunted out old friends. They made him so welcome that he could not help contrasting his own good fortune with Titta Ruffo's very different experience.

Caruso had sung at the Costanzi in Rome with this handsome young baritone, who used to tell ribald stories in the ripe Tuscan dialect. But he always crossed himself nervously when recalling his terrifying début in Naples. He had only a small part and was amazed at being approached by a tough member of the Camorra who demanded a weekly cut from his modest salary. Ruffo had the presence of mind to fabricate a tale about having recently escaped from prison in Livorno. He also confided fictitiously that he was being blackmailed by the manager of the San Carlo, who had discovered his past.

On the very next night a noisy claque hissed off the first baritone and kept encoring Ruffo. Unfortunately for him, his new friends were so impressed by his 'criminal record' that he was handed a revolver and recruited for a bank raid. He left hurriedly for San Remo, where he played under another name for several months. Caruso had thought the anecdote amusing but without any relevance to himself. As a Neapolitan born and bred he seemed to have nothing to fear from the Camorra or anyone else. On the opening night he would also have the support of influential friends like Nicola Daspuro, who had given him his first big chance at the Lirico.

He had of course experienced claques in Milan and elsewhere but seemed oddly ignorant of San Carlo's quite exceptional hierarchy. Two rival bands of patrons, known locally as the *sicofanti*, were led by noblemen powerful enough to make or break any singer. Even giants like Tamagno and de Lucia had suffered at their hands and now took good care to placate either or both of these ruthless groups, particularly that ruled by an effete dandy, Prince Adolfo di Castagneto, whose retinue included several leading critics. His monocle, screwed into a supercilious eye or more often removed in disapproval, had all the authority of the imperial thumb.

As a native son who had conquered La Scala and been honoured by the Tsar of Russia himself, Caruso had naïvely expected something like a hero's welcome. He was a little hurt but not too alarmed when the critics failed to call on him for interviews. A good manager would have advised him to entertain them or at least leave his card at their newspaper offices. He tippled instead with back-slapping acquaintances and was deceived by the hypocritical politeness of some of his fellow artists at rehearsals.

He had taken an even greater risk in ignoring the *sicofanti* and failing to bend the knee to either Prince Adolfo or the

Cavaliere Monaco, ruler of the opposing claque. He was also handicapped by his previous début at La Scala, a theatre traditionally hated and envied by all good Neapolitan opera-goers. Moreover, instead of appearing in a new opera, which might have soothed local pride, he would open in *L'Elisir*, already blessed by Milan. San Carlo therefore decided to sit on its hands while this strutting expatriate and former street-singer demonstrated exactly why he now thought himself worth 3000 lire (£120) a night.

The result is now part of operatic history. On that night of terror the comic bumpkin, Nemorino, failed to raise a single chuckle. A spatter of welcome from Daspuro and other staunch friends was at once squelched by the *sicofanti*, who called ominously for silence. When the Cavaliere finally gave modest approval, his enemy's monocle was whipped out to signal a counterblast of hisses. Caruso struggled on with his stage clowning, but not even the normally fireproof 'Una furtiva lagrima' could survive such an audience. He had to be prodded to take a single curtain and went back to his hotel with a raging headache.

His subsequent appearances had a better hearing, but he sang Nemorino with more determination than pleasure. The visit ended with four excellent performances in *Manon*, in which he was partnered by Rina Giachetti, who had been spared his nightmare and was sympathetic. For her sake as much as his own he put all his skill into their duets and won bursts of applause, but could not conceal his impatience to get back to Milan. He refused to join the fickle critics at after-theatre suppers and preferred a bowl of soup with his father and stepmother.

Daspuro saw him off at the station and wished him success in Monte Carlo. He added consolingly that the tenor's next appearance at the San Carlo would no doubt be happier.

'I'll never sing again in Naples,' Caruso declared emphatic-ally. 'When I come here in the future it will be only to eat spaghetti.'

Chapter Nine

Caruso always considered 1902 his year of destiny. It was then that he began his career as a recording artist and soon afterwards made his début at Covent Garden. Although he could not hope to match Jean de Reszke's physical grace or emulate Tamagno as a *tenore robustissimo*, he also emerged as their most likely successor when, within months of each other, both retired from the operatic stage. This was no overnight conquest, however. For years to come every leading tenor in Europe and the United States would be exposed to nostalgic and often disparaging comparison with these former idols, who had reigned jointly for a quarter of a century.

Caruso's first test was severe: he would partner Melba, still inconsolable for 'darling Jean', with whom she had shared her most dazzling triumphs in grand opera. Raoul Gunsbourg, the impresario at Monte Carlo, had shrewdly weighed all the odds in deciding to open his season with the Australian prima donna in *La Bohème*. Whatever the shortcomings of Rodolfo, she would be ecstatically received by her English admirers, always in a majority at the Casino Theatre. He was sanguine about Caruso but did not make the mistake of heralding him as 'the new de Reszke'; instead, all the advance publicity was skilfully tuned to reports of his recent successes in St Petersburg and Milan, unimpeachable warrants of pedigree for this audience.

Gunsbourg had long been putting on French-language plays in Moscow when he paid his first winter visit to Monaco for his health. Camille Blanc, eager for more patrons to his gaming tables, had decided to tempt them with outstanding opera and ballet. Gunsbourg was offered an almost unlimited budget to engage the best musicians, scenic artists and choruses. He commissioned Massenet to write specially for him, and throughout the nineties he had signed artists like Calvé, Tamagno, de

Reszke and Maurice Renaud at enormous fees. All his presentations were noteworthy for artistic taste, though with a top-dressing of Byzantine extravagance. In his studios near the railway station, sets were designed and painted, often more original than those at the Paris Opéra. He rightly boasted of being able to stage almost any opera in a fortnight.

Gunsbourg was an ugly little man with a Cyrano-like nose and bright squirrel eyes that missed nothing. He camouflaged the pathos of a Velázquez dwarf by talking almost non-stop and often exaggerating madly. He had hardly known Caruso for ten minutes before he was displaying a scar on his groin, allegedly the relic of a bayonet wound suffered while serving with the Russian army against the Turks. He would have been fourteen at the time, but nobody pointed this out, least of all his artists. They adored him. He congratulated them on their successes, scoffed at any bad notices and entertained them regally; if they came from distant lands he had luxurious meals served at railway stations en route where a local reception committee would do the honours in his name.

Caruso was delighted with the crisp linen sheets at the Hôtel de Paris. An elegant suite, filled with baskets of fruit and flowers, also helped to sweeten his recent humiliation in Naples. On his very first visit to the Casino he had been greeted by the tall Grand Duke Nicholas and his brother, Michael, who both graciously recalled his St Petersburg appearances. But Melba seemed to him haughtier than any grand duchess as she sat at the roulette table, magnificent in diamonds and wearing a Worth gown of daring décolletage. She looked far too disdainful to recall the gay *femme fatale* whose romance with the French Pretender, Philippe d'Orléans, had once scandalised Europe, but Caruso noted and approved her splendid teeth when she gave a laugh of pure music. He saw a woman of forty, fully twelve years older than himself, but with a flawless skin and still unwrinkled neck.

Her excellent carriage made her seem taller than she was; nevertheless he seriously considered wearing high heels or built-up shoes, as Bonci always did when singing with her.

Gunsbourg, however, sensed that this might add to his nervousness and wisely dissuaded him. Melba would have top billing and be paid almost three times Caruso's fee, but the impresario was determined to protect him from the kind of humiliation which poor Bonci had recently endured in London. After singing Rodolfo admirably, Bonci's calls were severely restricted by Melba, who had made it a policy at Covent Garden to take all her curtains alone. That would not happen in *his* theatre, Gunsbourg decided. A rabbi's son with bitter experience of pogroms in his childhood, he refused to pander to a *prima donna assoluta* who behaved like a cossack towards anyone daring to dispute her exclusive claim to the limelight.

Caruso had no suspicion of her autocratic and capricious temperament. She seemed graciousness itself when he reported on time for rehearsals, a good mark in his favour, as she was fanatical about punctuality and travelled everywhere with several alarm clocks, all synchronised to the minute. She showed her appreciation by helping him to move less stiffly on stage. To Gunsbourg's relief, he did not seem to resent her little reminders that 'darling Jean always did it like this' and other tender references to the dear departed. In fact, Caruso was so respectful that she even forgave him his strong Egyptian cigarettes, which made her cough between acts—no singer at Covent Garden would have dared to smoke in her presence. To the surprise of those who had previously sung with her and experienced her unkind tongue, she expressed open delight in his voice. After the manly charm of de Reszke, who had so often partnered her in *La Bohème*, this chubby little Italian must have seemed almost a caricature of Rodolfo, but she soon found herself responding to his exceptional lyrical power in their love duets. Caruso marvelled in turn at her immaculate phrasing and a silvery timbre which, he had to admit, challenged his own Tetrazzini.

Melba recalled him at the time as 'a simple, lovable creature' but deplored his vulgar taste in clothes and found his coarse table manners offensive. She still sighed for the exquisite Pole who had deserted her to give singing lessons only a tantalisingly few miles away in Nice, but all this was blotted out at their very first rehearsal as they soared together into 'O soave fanciulla'. 'When I sang with Caruso in *La Bohème*,' she declared afterwards, 'I felt as if our two voices had merged into one.'

Monte Carlo gave them a clamorous reception but Caruso did not acclimatise too readily to the socialite atmosphere. He avoided the sugar-white Casino after bumping one night into Melba as she sailed out imperiously in an ermine cape, escorted by a brace of Russian nobility who made him feel even more provincial in his ill-cut tail-coat. Instead he liked to sun himself in the gardens overlooking the harbour or take a carriage drive into the hills with Lorello. He rarely ate in the luxurious hotel but used to recall one sumptuous dinner with the prima donna who introduced him to her favourite dish of plover's eggs stuffed with caviar. She also made him sample Pêche Melba, explaining coyly that the great Escoffier had created it in her honour and every chef thereafter served it *ad nauseum* on her travels. But Caruso much preferred to down an honest bowl of good spaghetti with a flask of Chianti in a small restaurant near the quay.

On stage he soon ceased to be overawed by Melba. One night, during Mimi's death scene, she had been startled by a sound of squeaking and discovered that he was pressing a little rubber doll in her ear. She managed somehow to expire with convincing pathos but was shaking with laughter as the curtain fell.

They shared the laurels for *La Bohème*, but *Rigoletto* was his personal triumph. That unforced voice, velvety and nimble by turns, almost miraculously transformed the stocky Neapolitan into a graceful Duke of Mantua. Among his audience was Henry B. Dazian, then the leading costumier of New York City, who urged Maurice Grau by cable to engage Caruso for the Metropolitan Opera House. Grau, however, still hesitated to commit himself. He was not easily moved to expenditure. 'He will give you a cigar but not the match to light it with,'

breathlessly, through a grinning interpreter, that they wished him to record a few arias.

Some of the tenor's entourage jeered and urged him not to waste his precious voice on this new toy, but Caruso took an instant liking to Fred Gaisberg's good-natured face and invited him to lunch at his flat next day. He thought a fee of £100 for ten songs more than generous and signed without hesitation when the Gaisbergs hinted astutely that the records could be on sale in London before his Covent Garden début, which was already making him feel nervous. Fortunately, he was kept in ignorance of a last-minute complication. Fred Gaisberg had gleefully forwarded details of his coup to the London office, which, to his dismay, wired back: 'FEE EXORBITANT. FORBID YOU TO RECORD.' He decided to go ahead anyway.

Caruso looked 'debonair and fresh', according to Gaisberg, when he arrived at their suite in the Grand Hotel, exactly above the suite in which Verdi had died. His first recording would be 'Questa o quella' from *Rigoletto*. It was a sunny and very warm afternoon and he complained ruefully of having to delay his lunch, but otherwise he seemed to be treating the whole affair as an amusing outing.

Accompanied by a pianist perched on a packing case, he sang for two hours into a bell-shaped tin horn hanging five feet from the floor. The programme, effortlessly delivered, included 'Una furtiva lagrima', 'E lucevan le stelle' and 'Celeste Aïda'. He then pocketed his cheque, shook hands with the Gaisbergs, embraced the accompanist and hurried off, whistling cheerfully, to join Ada for a late lunch. The waxes were rushed to Hanover and processed without a single failure. They would yield around £15,000 in net profits for the company.

The Gaisbergs had kept their word and the records were already selling fairly briskly by the time he arrived in London. Many of the Italian exiles could ill afford the high prices at Covent Garden and listened to their phonographs instead. Nevertheless queues gathered for the half-crown gallery seats from the early afternoon of 14 May 1902. Caruso sang two dozen times in that first season, making his début in *Rigoletto*, in which Melba's trills won the usual ovations. His Duke was smooth and the audience obviously appreciated the unforced high tones. However, their reception was still only mildly enthusiastic. The *Daily News* noted his 'delightful *mezza voce* of soft velvety timbre' but also pointed out certain 'vocal limitations, especially when he has any florid parts to sing'. The *Manchester Guardian*'s critic was more far-seeing in welcoming him as the finest Italian singer to be heard in London since Mario's peak. Although admirers of Tamagno missed that tenor's robust power, there was unanimous praise for *La Bohème*, a few nights later, when Caruso repeated his Monte Carlo triumph with Melba as his partner, both this time reinforced by Scotti's admirable baritone.

He began to be encored at each appearance, making a strong impact in *Cavalleria Rusticana* with Emma Calvé, whose pure soprano and accomplished acting made her an ideal Santuzza. She was then nearly forty-five, three years older than Melba, but more congenial and always vivacious. She urged him not to be discouraged by the London critics, who were good-natured at heart and far less venal than their Parisian colleagues. 'At least there is no tariff, as at the Opéra-Comique,' she reminded him. 'When I first began there, I had to pay one of the directors 30,000 francs before they would even allow me on stage!' She also helped Caruso to overlook Harry Higgins's offhand manner, which was a chilly awakening after Gunsbourg's warmth.

Melba had graciously allowed Caruso to go before the curtain with her after *La Bohème* and often praised his Rodolfo ('The higher he sings, the more easy it seems to him,' she told one of her retinue), but remained very much the queenly *diva*. She had the only permanent dressing-room, with a notice, 'Melba! Silence! Silence!' nailed to the door, which would be kept locked when she was away on tour, often for several months. During the season she ruled jointly and imperially with her friend Lady de Grey, supported by the most powerful in the land. Lord Northcliffe had once dismissed the drama

93

critic of the *Daily Mail* for daring to write unfavourably of her Juliette. However a more independent colleague braved life exile from Covent Garden by declaring sourly that she expressed her love for Romeo by raising one arm and used both arms only in moments of 'extreme passion or violent despair'.

She terrified the stage-hands, who had to creep about in tennis shoes at rehearsals. One of them finally hit back. A non-smoker herself, Melba chewed wattle-gum, which was deposited on a small glass shelf in the wings before she went on. After the last curtain for *La Bohème*, she once reached for her piece of gum, stuck it into her mouth and promptly spat it out in disgust. Someone had substituted a quid of powerful shag. Caruso joined so heartily in the laughter that she would never quite believe in his innocence. Henceforth the precious wad was guarded by one of her dressers, who later growled, 'I'd like to 'ave put something stronger than shag in its place, but she'd a' knew 'oo it were.'

Caruso had been stunned by his first view of the red-plush auditorium with its footmen in livery and endless tiers of jewelled gowns and white boiled shirts, but he was soon made to feel at home by the chirpy cockney stage-hands, who taught him bits of slang and chortled at his broken English. He would often stand in the wings with a stump of pencil and make sketches of his fellow artists on any handy piece of scenery or odd scraps of paper which he handed around with a merry smile. He once buttonholed Mr Webber, the chief engineer, near the prompt corner and exclaimed, 'Ah, you are the clevaire man who lights me up! Pliz, pliz, where do you make it from?' Wearing Radamès' heavy costume, he insisted on mounting a steep iron ladder to examine each of the switches in turn until Webber had to remind him that he might miss his cue. He went on breathlessly and with only seconds to spare.

But that first season would have been a severe trial without Scotti as guide, mentor and interpreter. Within a few days the baritone had firmly steered him to his own tailor in Savile Row to be measured for new suits and an overcoat. Caruso's tight-fitting flashy clothes had not only offended his eye but made Higgins and other front-office exquisites wince whenever he bounced through the stage door.

He thought London the most exciting but noisiest city on earth. He risked death many times under the wheels of hansom cabs while stopping to admire elegant ladies in the streets. He never missed the Sunday parades in Hyde Park and especially Rotten Row. New York would be just as exhilarating, Scotti assured him after his friend had been visited and complimented in his dressing-room by Maurice Grau of the Metropolitan Opera House. This time, impressed by Caruso's records and rather more perhaps by Covent Garden's seal of approval, Grau obviously meant business. A day or two later, accompanied by Scotti, Caruso called on the bald, bearded impresario. He seemed affable enough but kept him dangling while exchanging small-talk with the baritone, who took his cue and praised the Metropolitan's magnificent facilities to the skies. Grau, a former lawyer and brilliant poker-player, had long experience in handling Wall Street financiers and the most temperamental opera singers. He had Caruso almost drooling by the time he was ready to outline his proposition. He offered a five-year contract, dating from the winter of 1903, with a fee of $960 (£190) for each of forty performances in a season. He then jotted down the details on a sheet of notepaper and asked him to incorporate them in a formal letter of acceptance, together with copies for his own signature, explaining that he was at present heavily engaged in more urgent affairs.

Caruso had the documents drawn up and called with them at Grau's hotel three days later, only to learn that the impresario had departed for Wiesbaden, leaving instructions for his mail to be forwarded to his New York office. The singer was disappointed, but Scotti saw no complications ahead and kept reminding him that this engagement could prove even more profitable in the long run than Covent Garden.

During the last weeks of his London season he was often invited by Paolo Tosti to his home in Mandeville Place, where

95

almost every musical celebrity, including his former pupil, Melba, would gather for delicious food and the most entertaining gossip in London. After guests had admired a vast collection of china pigs of which he and his wife, Berthe, were very proud, the white-bearded, genial host would invariably be coaxed to the piano to sing his 'Serenata' in a voice still melodiously flutey at fifty-six. Caruso enjoyed his racy stories and would never forget the evening when 'Ciccio', as he was known to all his intimates, invited him along to a duchess's mansion in Eaton Square. Tosti sang his sentimental canzone, 'Marechiar', in Italian but introduced many ribald and outrageously obscene Neapolitan phrases for Caruso's special benefit. He had to stuff a handkerchief into his mouth to keep from laughing, while the audience cooed decorously without understanding a single word.

Wearing his romantic long black cape like Verdi, Tosti would often whisk Caruso and Scotti off to his favourite restaurant, Pagani's in Great Portland Street, after their performances. The head chef had formerly been in the service of the great tenor Mario, and his risotto, spaghetti, and cutlets *à la milanaise* attracted all the visiting Italian artists, as well as diverse celebrities like Bernhardt and Paderewski. The most popular patron was Carlo Pellegrini, a sprightly Neapolitan nobleman who ran up enormous bills and was always being hounded by creditors, including one unfortunate pharmacist who had recklessly supplied him with rosewater to the tune of £300. Caruso found him excellent company and admired the caricatures he drew for *Vanity Fair* under the pseudonym of 'Ape'.

Caruso revelled in the food and bohemian atmosphere at Pagani's, which became his haunt whenever he visited London. Here he first met Luigi Denza, the composer of 'Funiculí, funiculà', and was soon asked to add his own signature to the dozens of others on Pagani's walls. During every Covent Garden season the leading members of London's Italian colony and visiting celebrities like Puccini and Mascagni would meet there most nights under the chairmanship of Tosti ('the Master

Bandit') to consume huge meals and indulge in intricate practical jokes.

One of the more elaborate was performed when it became known that Tosti had a superstition about riding in any hansom drawn by a white horse, and the whole of Great Portland Street was mysteriously lined with them as he emerged late one night. Caruso, too, was soon victimised by a plot worked out in fine detail by Tosti and other conspirators. For days he had been receiving passionate letters followed by the photograph of a most beautiful young woman. Then, one evening, while he was dining at Pagani's, a telegram was handed to him. It seemed that the lady would throw herself under a train unless he met her at Victoria Station at eleven o'clock that very night. He made his excuses and hurried off by hansom. However, after waiting for nearly two hours on a very draughty platform, he drove sadly back to his hotel.

He took affectionate leave of Tosti and Scotti when the season closed at the end of July. Harry Higgins unbent enough to thank him almost amiably for his services and regretted that Caruso's South American engagements would prevent him from returning to Covent Garden the following year. He was assured of a most cordial welcome in the summer of 1904.

He arrived back in Milan with gifts for Fofò and a ring purchased for Ada in the Burlington Arcade, where he had also bought himself some stylish English cravats. That hot summer they spent a month at Salsomaggiore but also found time to tour the Tuscan countryside. Both were now eager to find a country house although they were aware that funds were still far too low to permit anything even as modest as Puccini's villa at Torre del Lago.

The Covent Garden engagement had been an artistic rather than a financial coup. They consoled themselves with an endless vista of dollars from the Metropolitan, although Grau seemed maddeningly dilatory in returning his signed copy of the agreement. This did not prevent them from excitedly planning their American trip. Caruso had temporarily eased Ada's frustration by promising that she should sail with him. He also felt confident enough about his future to repay Sonzogno's past kindness to him. That November he created the tenor role for a new Cilèa opera at the Lirico and insisted on taking only a nominal fee for his services, even providing his own costumes. He recorded again for the Gaisbergs at the Grand Hotel for the same modest fee, this time including 'Vesti la giubba', with Leoncavallo at the piano, an aria from Giordano's *Fedora*, also accompanied by the composer, and a Tosti canzone. By now the wax cylinder was slowly being ousted by the gramophone disc; the scratchy surface noises had still not been eliminated, but Caruso's strong voice helped to keep them to a minimum. These recordings would sell in vast numbers and could have earned him an early fortune had he possessed anything like Tamagno's business acumen. That shrewd veteran had quickly grasped the potential of Caruso's first issues and was already recording some arias for release the following year. He had negotiated a cash advance of £2800, plus a royalty of 4/- (20p) on every one-pound disc.

Caruso gave two charity performances in Trieste before singing a very popular month's season at the Costanzi in Rome. While appearing there he learned with horror that Grau had been taken ill and might not be continuing at the Metropolitan. He wrote in panic to Scotti, who promised to clarify the situation. The new director was to be Heinrich Conried, a Silesian-born former actor who had staged many plays for New York's large colony of German immigrants. He was a beetle-browed, saturnine man with a skinflint's reputation. It was strongly rumoured that he would look very closely indeed at all singers' contracts and might discontinue Grau's policy of importing costly talent from Europe.

Caruso became alarmed. He had been so keyed up by this New York engagement, exuberantly celebrated in advance, that the prospect of ridicule hit him almost as hard as his disappointment.

Meantime, however, he had an excellent reception in Lisbon, where he appeared for a month with Eva Tetrazzini under her husband's baton. There, too, he was saddened to read that Puccini had had a serious accident. The composer had been busily engaged at Torre on his new opera, *Madama Butterfly*, when he decided to consult a specialist for throat trouble. Driving at night on a frosty road in his new 'horseless carriage', he had overturned and nearly suffocated from the escaping fumes. He not only fractured a thigh, which left him with a disabling limp, but on medical examination was also discovered to be suffering from diabetes.

When Caruso visited him at Torre del Lago he was shocked to see his usually high-spirited friend looking so bloated and irritable in his wheelchair. The accident did not cure him of his passion for fast cars and speedboats, but it may have affected Caruso. In the years to come he would himself own many automobiles and loved to pose at the steering-wheel in beret and goggles, but he never learned to drive.

While visiting Puccini and still fretting for news from New York, he and Ada had at last found the property of their dreams. The Villa alle Panche, near Rifredi and only a few miles from Florence, was set in an idyllic corner of Tuscany. It had a large ball-room which would make a perfect studio, and a Moorish-style den where he could keep his racks of operatic scores and deal with the correspondence, which Lorello found hopelessly beyond him. Above all, the surrounding acres of tranquil olive groves were a delight to the eye.

He returned to Milan in a frenzy of impatience to buy the villa before sailing for his long South American season. He approached his bankers, but they refused to advance the purchase price unless and until his contract with the Metropolitan was finalised. From Monte Carlo, where he was giving five performances of *Tosca*, he sent feverish wires to Scotti and also to Pasquale Simonelli, President of the Italian Savings Bank in New York, urging them to try to convince the elusive Conried.

Simonelli was an opera lover, but this did not prevent him from insisting on a commission of three per cent to act as intermediary. He called on Conried, who had not yet moved into the Metropolitan and was still winding up his affairs at the

99

Irving Place Theatre. Conried gruffly reminded Simonelli that Grau had signed no formal contract with this Caruso, whose name meant nothing in America; furthermore, he had all but decided to engage the far better known Bonci. These tactics were obviously designed to secure Caruso at lower fees than Grau had settled on. Simonelli, according to his own version, had finally won him over by playing Caruso's recent recording of 'Vesti la giubba' on a phonograph which he had brought with him for precisely such an impasse. He also reminded Conried that New York Italians were raving over their country-man's records and would surely give him a tremendous wel-come at the Metropolitan. Conried grunted and finally agreed to engage him at Grau's original fee of $960 but for only ten performances instead of the forty stipulated. He also stubbornly refused to go beyond a year unless the box-office justified a renewal. Caruso then demanded a minimum of twenty-five appearances and, with his eye on the villa, also insisted on an advance of 25,000 lire ($5000) being immediately deposited at the Bank of Milan to cover the first five performances. As soon as Conried had cabled his consent to Monte Carlo, Caruso instructed his lawyers to buy the villa.

He could now leave for South America without Ada's usual last-minute recriminations and hysteria. She seemed reconciled to commuting between their flat in via Velasca and the villa, where extensive plans for furnishing and redecoration would help to divert her in his absence. Caruso sailed from Genoa in cheerful mood, additionally heartened by the presence of his old St Petersburg colleague Arimondi, in a distinguished company directed by Toscanini, who would be travelling with his wife. It was a gay voyage, although Toscanini disapproved of the all-night poker parties and admonished Caruso for smoking too much and missing his sleep.

Intoxicated by the prospect of New York, he sang like a bird and even won approval from Toscanini, except for one lapse. During L'Elisir he broke on a high note, which prompted the supporting baritone to make a premature entrance in a gallant attempt to cover up for him. Taken by surprise, Toscanini had

to drive his orchestra frenziedly to catch up. He gave the baritone a severe dressing-down and lectured the assembled company on the propriety of keeping to the score at *all* times.

They were fêted by audiences in Buenos Aires and Montevideo, but just before they were to leave for Rio the whole
tour came suddenly to the brink of collapse. The Toscaninis
were completely shattered by their four-year-old son's
death from diphtheria. Carla Toscanini became so distraught
that she decided to sail home at once, and her husband could
obviously not allow her to travel alone. Caruso sat with her for
hours, hand in hand, until she had calmed down. Next day she
bravely insisted on remaining with them until the end of the
season.

Caruso enjoyed some weeks of sunlit relaxation at his villa. He
put on overalls to whitewash the Moorish den, which he had
soon hung with portraits of Verdi, Angelo Masini and other
idols. He also arranged for a piano to be sent from Florence and
began practising for his American début with a thoroughness
that exhausted his accompanist. He would open in *Rigoletto*,
which had few terrors for him, but was more nervous of
following, only a week later, as Radamès before a fashionable
New York audience still praying that Jean de Reszke might
yet be enticed out of retirement.

He could not have foreseen that before long he would be
playing a major role in the Metropolitan's own battle for
survival.

Chapter Ten

New York's opera lovers had been served in the seventies by the Academy of Music at Fourteenth Street and Irving Place. The few boxes were monopolised by the Astors and their intimates, who continued to regard the Vanderbilts as Staten Island potato-pickers. When the governors refused William Henry Vanderbilt's $30,000 for a box for the 1880 season, he retaliated by forming a syndicate to buy a piece of land for $600,000 at Thirty-ninth Street and Broadway. Here they erected a new five-storeyed opera house with a seating capacity of three thousand, designed to put the Academy's nose permanently out of joint. The auditorium aimed to incorporate the best features of La Scala, the Paris Opéra and Covent Garden. The stage was over 100 feet wide and 125 high with a gilt triple band of boxes, five in the permanent ownership of the Vanderbilt clan.

The Metropolitan Opera House, contemptuously dismissed by its rival as 'the new yellow brewery on Broadway', opened with Gounod's *Faust* on 22 October 1883. Christine Nilsson, the Swedish soprano from the Paris Opéra, repeated her Marguérite with Italo Campanini and Roberto Stagno in support. Most patrons arrived in elegant carriages with Negro retainers in livery perched on the boxes. The men wore velvet-lined capes over tail-coats, the sables and diamonds of their ladies dazzling the onlookers massed four deep on the illuminated sidewalk. Two nights later the Polish prima donna, Marcella Sembrich, made her American début in *Lucia di Lammermoor*. M. Worth of Paris provided all the costumes and shoes, which helped to compensate for a somewhat ragged orchestra.

That first season ended in a financial loss, like many that followed, despite the acclaim for Adelina Patti and several lavish productions of Wagner. But the competition proved altogether too stiff for the Academy of Music, which had to close down. In August 1892 during a successful season graced by Emma Eames, a memorable Juliette to de Reszke's Roméo, the Metropolitan was destroyed by fire after a workman had tossed his cigarette into a can of paint-thinner. It reopened the following year with electric lighting and so many jewels in the thirty-five parterre boxes that this section was instantly re-named the Diamond Horseshoe. Each of the box-holders had subscribed $30,000 for stock and an equal sum towards the rebuilding fund.

Sharp at nine and well into the first act of *Faust*, the curtains of Box Seven parted for Mrs William B. Astor, who subsided into her seat with a swish of satin while dozens of pairs of diamond-studded Lemaire opera glasses were trained on her. The demise of the Academy of Music had made it imperative for the Astors to give their patronage to the new Metropolitan and declare an honourable peace treaty with the Vanderbilts. Caroline Astor, who had united her Schermerhorn blue blood with William's greenbacks, was the cornerstone of New York's ultra-snobbish Four Hundred, compiled by Ward McAllister ('Mr Make-a-Lister' to those excluded from his social Valhalla). The Diamond Horseshoe enabled matrons to display their gowns and jewels, although spectators were often regaled by a satin frieze of behinds bulging over the gilt seats. The boxes, each with a brass plate bearing its owner's name, were arranged to give the audience a good view of the occu-pants, who could survey each other and pay calls, but *never* until the second intermission.

Mrs Cornelius Vanderbilt presided over Box Three, entering ritually in the middle of the opening aria. She hummed off-key through most of the opera and always took her leave in the middle of the finale. Although she paid Caruso and others enor-mous fees to sing at her private musicales at 660 Fifth Avenue, she would never quite compete in magnificence with the Astor Monday Nights at the Metropolitan. These were dreaded by the artists, who opened to half-empty houses as few of the élite cared to arrive too far ahead of Mrs Astor.

That formidable hostess occasionally used the stage to entertain her friends. At one New Year's Ball she presided over a 'light' supper with sixteen hot and cold dishes, including grouse, terrapin and partridge. She and her fellow box-holders demanded similar lavish entertainment, operatically, if only to demonstrate that New York could more than match the best in Europe. Splendid Wagner productions were staged, soon to be reinforced by an exciting repertory of Verdi, Mascagni and Puccini. The board could preen itself on having imported performers like Tamagno, the de Reszke brothers, Eames, Scotti, Melba and Calvé.

Maurice Grau had begun to show a profit from 1898 onwards. When he retired five years later, as much as $100,000 was being offered and refused for a box in the Diamond Horseshoe, but the thriving balance-sheet had been achieved at some artistic cost. By the turn of the century the *New York Times* was lamenting 'bad scenery, a poor chorus, a wretched ballet, a mediocre orchestra and general laxity and carelessness in all departments'. Grau relied heavily on top stars, to whom he paid huge fees, but cheese-pared on most other departments to keep the price of his tickets down. He saw no reason to hire expensive conductors ('Nobody ever paid a nickel to see a man's back') and exposed artists to conditions that would have started riots in most provincial French and Italian houses. There was no running water backstage and even Jean and Edouard de Reszke had to fight for a dirty cupboard-sized dressing-room to themselves. But Grau's genius for talent-spotting, exemplified by his early engagement of new stars like Scotti and Caruso and a far-sighted option on the services of Geraldine Farrar, paved the way for his successors.

Caruso's engagement coincided with the opening of a new era at the Metropolitan. For the next five years it would be dominated by Heinrich Conried as general manager and his staunch ally Otto H. Kahn, the leading stockholder, who poured over $2 million of his private fortune into the opera house. The banker, blue-eyed and clipped of speech, was a silk-hatted dandy who wore a velvet-collared topcoat and pearl-grey cut-aways with a black pearl in his Ascot cravat. Like Joseph Chamberlain, he often sported an orchid in his buttonhole, and on Sunday mornings led a string of dachshunds along Fifth Avenue. But there was nothing of the dilettante about his passion for grand opera. He could play three instruments himself and encouraged performers and orchestras to respect the musical score scrupulously. He also helped to inaugurate early training schemes for promising young singers.

His taste and wealth made the Metropolitan a showplace for the finest operatic productions in 'the Golden Age of Song' but, ironically enough, this was paralleled by an efflorescence of snobbery which would long preclude him, as a Jew, from becoming an individual box-holder in his own opera house. He sat in the director's box even after becoming chairman of the board. (In 1917 he accepted one in the Diamond Horseshoe but, with an exquisite touch of contempt for the long years of anti-Semitism, never occupied it. Box Fourteen was made available to foreign visitors of distinction.)

His German–Jewish general manager was far more concerned with dollars than such fine social distinctions. It was characteristic of Conried that one of his early inventions, perfected during his boyhood in Vienna, had been a metal clasp for the old-fashioned pocket-book. Kahn agreed to pay him a salary of $20,000 a year and also allowed him the proceeds from annual benefits, for which Caruso and the other singers contributed their services without fee. Apart from being a major stockholder, he received a half share of profits after all expenses were met. He squeezed the rank and file mercilessly, paying members of the chorus only $15 a week, and also missed out on several top stars. He engaged Tetrazzini for the Metropolitan, but the deal collapsed when he failed to deposit the minimum guarantee she demanded. Similarly he let Maurice Renaud, the French baritone, slip through his fingers by scrapping Grau's contract, preferring to pay a penalty rather than add him to his payroll.

According to Herman Klein, the distinguished critic, Conried 'knew no more about opera than an ordinary chauffeur knows about aeroplanes'. He had a phobia about French composers and saw no percentage in buying up rights in the works of Massenet, Charpentier and Debussy. This blinded him to the promise of Mary Garden, who had been specially chosen by Debussy to create the soprano role for the première of *Pelléas et Mélisande* in Paris. However he had a stage director's eye for detail and sometimes even dressed up as one of the chorus to assure himself that costumes, lighting and other technical points were correct. But he could never forget his early stage training and used to infuriate singers by attempting to act out their parts for them. As his knowledge of both opera and music was limited and he could speak no Italian, he became a severe trial to most of his foreign artists.

Caruso had no suspicion of what lay ahead when he landed in New York on 11 November 1903. Conried had not thought him important enough to welcome personally, but otherwise the publicity arrangements were faultless. The tenor and Ada were besieged by reporters almost as soon as they booked in at the Hotel Majestic as 'Mr and Mrs Caruso'. This registration may have had some significance; it seemed to imply that Ada had not only reconciled herself to giving up her singing career but now saw her liaison with Caruso as permanent. She played the dutiful 'wife' to perfection and rarely hinted at her own operatic past, while he gaily answered the reporters' questions, with Simonelli acting at interpreter, and struck comic poses for the cameras. Accustomed to aristocratic stars like Jean de Reszke and European prima donnas who treated them like serfs, the reporters found his slapstick and down-to-earth style refreshing. He also made many press friends with his thumb-nail caricatures, which he handed round as souvenirs. He was besieged by dozens of countrymen who soon reminded him that New York's streets were not paved with gold. None departed without a few dollars or a ticket for his opening per-formance, although Simonelli warned him against spongers.

Caruso was unimpressed by his first meeting with Conried,

who strutted about his imposing office in high-heeled suede boots and then showed him into a small windowless dressing-room. He hid his feelings and was tactfully enthusiastic over the Metropolitan's recent face-lift. The auditorium now had a fresh maroon and gold décor and a mechanical apparatus for changing elaborate sets, designed by a technical director newly appointed from Munich. Caruso, cued by Scotti, gaped dutifully at the attendants, who would henceforth wear full evening-dress with silver badges, but he was more gratified to learn that the orchestra would be conducted by Arturo Vigna, whom he had met during his first Monte Carlo season with Melba.

Vigna and Scotti both helped him to acclimatise in the twelve frantic days before the scheduled opening of the season. He would have preferred more time, but Conried discouraged lengthy rehearsals. However, he was confident of his début in *Rigoletto*, with Marcella Sembrich playing Gilda and Scotti as the Jester. Through the lorgnettes lovingly focussed for so many years on de Reszke as the graceful Duke of Mantua, Caruso's well-rounded paunch must have struck a chill in the diamanté bosoms. Although scores of Italian immigrants cheered loyally, 'La donna è mobile' had only a single encore, a bleak disappointment after the minimum of three he had always given in South America.

The press next day was polite if fairly restrained. The *Tribune* praised the newcomer's vocal quality but objected to his 'Italian mannerisms'; the *Sun* liked his smooth voice; and the *Times* approved 'the intelligence and passion' of his performance, while noting the flexible *mezza voce*. But connoisseurs reserved judgement, and the Diamond Horseshoe could not help deploring his lack of height and style. Only his countrymen in the gallery failed to lament the absence of princely 'Jean'.

A week later and still suffering from a sudden attack of tonsillitis, he had to sing Radamès because Conried would not risk losing a few dollars at the box-office by putting on a substitute. Caruso spaced himself cautiously in the early acts, but his 'Celeste Aïda', which de Reszke had generally omitted as too banal, was so warmly received that he dared all before the finale and took several curtain calls. The critics began to praise his phrasing, although one or two considered his acting below standard until he finally won them over with an impassioned Cavaradossi. Three nights later, on 5 December, he confirmed his triumph with such an outstanding performance in *La Bohème* that Conried began to rub his hands. He became almost ecstatic when Caruso's Canio played to four full houses and the scalpers moved in to corner the ticket market.

Conried could not resist taking advantage of his unexpected bonanza. After a rehearsal for *La Traviata*, the next production, he buttonholed Scotti and urged him to inform his friend that the light part of Alfredo offered meagre value to patrons clamouring for seats. 'I think he might sing a few romanzas between Acts Three and Four,' suggested the wily impresario. Caruso went purple-faced. 'Tell him,' he spluttered, 'that if I don't sing enough to suit him, it's not my fault but that of Verdi, who wrote the opera.'

Conried stomped off angrily but found his usual solace in dollars and cents. The newcomer was already receiving several invitations to sing at fashionable soirées. Mrs W. Payne Whitney had started a vogue which was soon taken up by all the other leading hostesses. Caruso was gratified although he gained nothing financially from the handsome fees of $1500 and upwards. By the terms of his agreement he would be paid only the normal $960 for these 'concert' appearances, the balance going into the Metropolitan's coffers.

Caruso's success in New York and also Philadelphia, where he performed to raving audiences, had quickly come to the sharp ears of Calvin G. Child, chief recorder and artistic director of the Victor Company. He had heard his first discs for the Gaisbergs and was already in active negotiation to operate in association with the London company. He asked Caruso to record a few arias, offering him an outright cash payment of $4000 for the exclusive rights in ten discs. The recordings were made with piano accompaniment in a single afternoon in

Room 826 of Carnegie Hall, a small high-ceilinged studio facing Seventh Avenue. The first Victor record was 'Questa o quella', followed by 'La donna è mobile', 'Una furtiva lagrima', 'E lucevan le stelle' and, of course, 'Vesti la giubba', which thousands of amateur tenors would soon begin to sob while stropping their razors. These recordings were made with only one 'master' and showed hardly a join between phrases, the occasional surface scratches submerged by the brilliant climaxes of each aria. Child promptly guaranteed Caruso a retainer of $2000 per annum for the next five years. He then put out huge advertisements announcing that 'Caruso, the greatest tenor of all time, makes records only for Victor'.

Conried must have chewed his nails to the quick for not having included 'recording rights' in Caruso's agreement, but he was shrewd enough to sense their box-office potential. Now fully aware of Caruso's drawing power, he lost no time in signing him up for a further four years and even agreed to an increase of $200 a performance. That first season netted the tenor $30,000 for his Metropolitan appearances and concerts.

By now Caruso felt very much at home in New York, but found the Majestic Hotel too cold and impersonal. He liked to ride on the horse buses and was far more impressed by the new Elevated than by the fine carriages outside the brownstone mansions on Fifth Avenue, where he would often be asked to sing. The ferry-boats to Brooklyn and New Jersey delighted him, and he bought dozens of picture postcards of the East River Bridge to send to his family and various friends in Milan. He also spent happy hours in New York's barber shops, where he not only had his moustache perfectly trimmed and waxed but could even take a hot scented bath. This novelty never ceased to enchant him, although he still missed the gossip of his favourite saloon in Milan's Galleria. The Central Park Zoo, soon to bring him tragedy, was also an unfailing source of fascination, particularly the antics of the monkeys.

He and Ada disliked chop-house food, but there were new and unexpected discoveries like Dorlon's 'oyster saloon'. So far they had discovered only one Italian restaurant, the Café

Martin at Broadway and Twenty-fifth, where the oily spaghetti was exactly to his liking. It made them all the more impatient for a kitchen of their own, and they soon found and rented an apartment near Lexington Avenue, where he often cooked pasta for friends and entertained a host of callers, many of them priests from tenement parishes in 'Little Italy'. They never left empty-handed.

Ada seemed at home in this apartment where she loved arranging American Beauty roses in gilt bowls. She used to accompany Caruso on the hired Steinway grand when he wished to run over a passage or sing Neapolitan ballads for their friends. But her large dark-lashed eyes were melancholy as she nibbled away at boxes of Huyler's chocolates or closeted herself for hours in a darkened bedroom heavy with the scent of cologne.

She seemed vivacious enough, however, when they sailed for home in mid-February 1904. On the last night of the season, which closed with a sparkling performance of *Lucia di Lammermoor*, she cut a stylish figure in her long white kid gloves, with violets pinned to the waist of an oyster-coloured satin gown that set off her chestnut curls. She handled a diamond-encrusted fan with panache and now and then caressed her new gold-mesh bag stuffed so reassuringly with crisp $50 bills from Simonelli's bank.

Caruso had no suspicion of another pregnancy until she angrily announced the news one night. He had returned to their cabin, a little flushed and over-amorous after celebrating his thirty-first birthday with several fellow passengers. This time he could not comfort her by citing the Puccinis and other couples who had achieved happiness out of wedlock. The composer and Elvira, released at last by the death of her first husband, had been married the previous month at Torre del Lago.

Ada recovered her spirits in mid-Atlantic. Caruso was solicitous but too exuberant over his prospects to tolerate recrimination. Almost immediately after arriving back in Europe he would be heading for a short engagement with Raoul Gunsbourg at Monte Carlo, followed by appearances in Barcelona,

Prague and Dresden, before the opening of his second season at Covent Garden in mid-May. They planned to return together to New York in November, with several recording sessions already lined up for the Victor Company.

In Milan they learned with consternation that Puccini's new opera, *Madama Butterfly*, had opened and closed after one night. The La Scala claque had hissed, booed and catcalled, recalling Rome's boorish reception for *Tosca*. Puccini had limped out of the theatre almost broken-hearted, but resolved to extend the opera into three acts instead of the two lengthy ones. Caruso wrote to commiserate before departing, with some relief, for Monte Carlo. Ada was again sulking, a doctor having definitely confirmed that she could expect her baby at the end of the summer.

Gunsbourg gave Caruso a cordial welcome and disclosed that Melba had behaved quite disgracefully towards their mutual friend Titta Ruffo during the previous season at Covent Garden. After his excellent début in *Lucia* he had been invited to take over as Rigoletto from Scotti, who was indisposed. He sang so impeccably at the dress rehearsal that the orchestra stood up to applaud and the entire chorus had slapped him on the back. Melba, playing Gilda, was put out by this reception, which threatened her own supremacy. When Ruffo reported at the theatre next morning he was told that another baritone would replace him. Melba had suddenly decided that he was far too young to play her father. (Ruffo never returned to Covent Garden, and had to wait some years for his revenge. Passing through Naples en route for an Australian tour, Melba sat one night in the manager's box at San Carlo for a performance of Ambrose Thomas's *Hamlet*. She sent Ruffo a note of congratulation and graciously offered to sing Ophelia at his next performance. He would not receive her in his dressing-room and ordered the manager to inform her that she was *too old* for the part.)

Gunsbourg now introduced Caruso to a young soprano, Geraldine Farrar, who would be playing Mimi to his Rodolfo. She was then a slim curly-mopped girl of twenty-one with a carefree manner which he found refreshing after Melba's haughtiness. The only child of a National League baseball star, she had made a sensational European début after being auditioned by Jean Reszke, who encouraged her to continue her studies. Melba had agreed with him and told the young soprano, 'I hail you as the coming Jenny Lind of America,' but she cooled off noticeably after Farrar's triumph in Berlin and soon saw to it that she was not welcomed at Covent Garden.

Caruso flirted mildly with the American girl, who had left dozens of broken hearts behind her in Germany, including that of the Crown Prince, who made sheep's eyes at her whenever she appeared. She saw nothing romantic in Caruso but liked him for his merry laugh and kindliness. In later years she recalled his wild checkered waistcoats, a curly brimmed hat worn brigandishly over one eye and his gold-headed cane clasped in yellow gloves. She was at first disappointed in his singing after all the enthusiastic advance reports. As usual he had sung in half voice at rehearsals and seemed only a dumpy little man with absurdly waxed moustaches. He was also rather too apt to play for cheap laughs from the stage-hands. But all this changed when she heard his first aria at the opening performance; 'I was literally stricken dumb with amazement and admiration until the conductor, Vigna, rapped sharply with his baton to bring me back to my senses.'

While in Monte Carlo he was invited by Leoncavallo to create the leading role in his new work, *Rolando*, and promised to consider it. He was wise to hedge, as the opera proved no more successful than all the other sequels to *I Pagliacci*. But he could not decline an invitation from the Russian ambassador to France, then enjoying a brief holiday in Monaco. The diplomat called at his hotel and begged him to appear at a benefit performance in Paris on 27 April, only four days after his engagement in Barcelona. It would be in aid of a hospital train for the Japanese front and endowed by a grand duchess whose husband was president of the Russian Academy of Fine Arts. They had both been kind to him during his two visits to St Petersburg, and he gave in gracefully when reminded that Arimondi, Maurice Renaud and the conductor, Vigna, had all agreed to give their services.

He had barely time to record 'Mattinata' at the Hotel Continental in Milan before hurrying off to Spain. Leoncavallo had composed it specially for the gramophone and insisted on playing the piano accompaniment.

Caruso had arranged to give two performances of *Rigoletto* in Barcelona, demanding the same high fee as Gunsbourg was paying him. The Spanish impresario resented this and perhaps cut corners on the rest of the company and the production. Caruso's first arias were received well enough, but the audience, asked to pay increased prices for their tickets, seemed hard to please. A duet with the soprano (no Geraldine Farrar) was hissed by the gallery, some alleging that she was singing flat, while others accused Caruso. By the time he reached 'La donna è mobile' he felt angry enough to refuse encores. It was childish of him and tactless, but the impresario behaved even worse by demanding that he take half pay for his second performance. Caruso scoffed and went doggedly ahead, braving a storm of hisses when he ignored all appeals to encore his favourite aria. He vowed never to appear again in Spain and in later years refused every offer to sing in Barcelona and Madrid.

His hurt pride was soothed in Paris, where he sang the Duke in *Rigoletto* for a benefit performance at the Théâtre Sarah Bernhardt. Here he first met Gabriel Astruc, who was to become his agent and impresario for all his subsequent engagements in France. Astruc had busily spread reports about Caruso's 'divine' voice from the moment he agreed to appear. Seats were sold at dizzy prices, and queues for the cheaper parts of the house formed day after day, rough workers scraping together their sous and even holding lotteries to buy hundred-franc (£4) tickets to perch on the gallery aisles. The tenor was, of course, the main attraction, but many were almost as excited to see and hear Lina Cavalieri as Gilda. This dazzling soprano had been a flower-seller, programme girl and café singer before making her name on the Folies Bergère stage and finally in grand opera. It was the first of several exciting performances together, but no operatic partnership could rival two others which, oddly enough, had both started under Gunsbourg's wing in Monte Carlo. By pairing Caruso first with Melba and then with Geraldine Farrar he had created an imperishable legend on both sides of the Atlantic.

Caruso was reunited with Melba for his second season at Covent Garden after crowds had flocked to hear him in Prague and Dresden. In the two years since his London début he had become a world figure, partly because of his successful Metropolitan season but even more perhaps through the phenomenal sales of his records, which had now passed the quite unprecedented million mark. Tamagno, Bonci and de Lucia had also entered the profitable new field, and even Melba was slowly overcoming her early repugnance to what she still called the 'obnoxious little box'. Although continuing to protest that the rasp and scratchy buzz of 'the machine' destroyed her unique timbre, she soon insisted on having her first twelve-inch discs issued with specially autographed labels printed on regal-looking mauve paper. On discovering that Caruso's records were being sold at $3 (a sovereign in England) she at once stipulated that hers should cost a guinea.

These little vanities did not upset their reappearance together. Covent Garden was sold out weeks ahead. Bonci had sung sweetly enough in the preceding season, but he was not Caruso and could never be more than a junior partner to Melba at the top of her form. When the new season opened with *Rigoletto* on 17 May 1904, she had her ritual welcome from an audience which included the King and Queen and other members of the Royal Family, but a spontaneous burst of applause greeted Caruso even before he sang 'Questa o quella'. It came mainly from the Italian galleryites, many of whom had queued for seats from early that morning, and who yelled 'Viva! Viva!' as he ended each of his arias, and during the intervals, intoxicated by the heat and music, staggered out for air, laden with hampers of cheese, salami, fruit and flasks of Chianti.

Herman Klein, the London *Sunday Times* critic and a close friend of the de Reszke brothers, had earlier paid tribute to Caruso's 'facile art and beautiful voice' without concealing the view that 'his impersonations had none of the poetry and romance, the rare nobility of conception which made Jean de Reszke great in contrasted roles.' Now he and de Reszke himself were both won over. The Polish tenor visited Caruso in his dressing-room and whispered to his brother somewhat condescendingly, 'This boy will one day be my successor.' Caruso, receiving the accolade with becoming modesty, sighed, 'Ah, if that were only true.' Edouard, a basso with a Chaliapin-like frame but gentle manner, had been far less reserved in his praise. He later wrote to Caruso, 'I have never heard a more beautiful voice. You sing like a god. With these qualities you will be the master of the world.'

His conquest of London could not have been achieved without Melba, whose vocal purity contrasted with a harsh speaking voice. Even at its sweetest, however, it sometimes had the flavour of 'a frozen fondant', as Debussy once described Grieg's music. Her singing, according to Ernest Newman, could be 'uninterestingly perfect and perfectly uninteresting', yet an almost incredible alchemy began to work when her technical precision was wedded to Caruso's lyricism. Together they achieved a mellowness and warmth which she had never quite reached with Jean de Reszke, whose voice could bewitch audiences but without moving them to tears. Even Melba had to acknowledge that her idol always disliked rehearsals and the kind of sheer hard work which Caruso put into all his performances.

Their relationship off stage never became close. She rarely invited Caruso to her elegant soirées among the plaster cupids at Great Cumberland Place and did not present him with one of the platinum or gold tie-pins which qualified her men friends for 'Nellie's Order of Knighthood'. But sometimes she unbent enough to play dominoes with him in her dressing-room—an ordeal for both, as she abhorred his strong Egyptian cigarettes almost as much as he detested her habit of whistling during a game. He was also too inclined to horseplay. During *La Bohème* he once pressed a hot sausage into her hand and murmured innocently as she dropped it, 'Eengleesh lady no like sausage?' But she had to laugh during Act Two when he nudged her to point out Tosti, who was sitting in the front row of the stalls with a white handkerchief over his mouth that looked uncannily like a huge cavalry moustache. That day he had had all his front teeth extracted but made the pilgrimage to Covent Garden dentureless rather than miss the opera.

Over the years Caruso's native taste for *opera buffa* stimulated him to play vulgar pranks. Nobody was immune, and he took a special delight in baiting Melba, whose high-and-mighty attitude to Titta Ruffo and other of his friends invited reprisals. She would never forgive one episode when, as Mimi, she was expiring with dignity and in perfect pitch only to hear a sudden guffaw from the audience. Caruso had bribed a stage-hand to place a chamberpot by her bed. Two nights later he was killing time in the wings by doodling away, as usual, with his pencil and sketch pad when he accidentally dislodged a piece of scenery just as Melba came off. He hid behind a pillar rather than face her wrath while she picked herself up and glared furiously at the guiltless scene-shifters.

La Bohème became Caruso's favourite playground for high-jinks in low taste. His old friend Arimondi once delivered Colline's Overcoat Song to find his stovepipe hat half filled with water. Another Colline, this time Caruso's fellow Neapolitan Pasquale Amato, was preparing to go out into the cold night to buy medicine for Mimi when he found he could not put on his coat as the tenor had sewn up the sleeves. Frances Alda also had a most unnerving experience in Philadelphia. Instead of snowflakes, a shower of string, paper and old buttons descended on Mimi's deathbed. Her decanter was also filled with ink instead of water and two castors had been removed from the four-poster, so that the luckless soprano had to expire in a bed which rolled like a hammock in a storm.

At the Metropolitan, not long afterwards, he gave poor Alda another playful nightmare in the same opera. Stooping to pick up a key, she had the misfortune to unhook her white pantalettes, which collapsed like a concertina below her crinoline. She retrieved the situation by slipping out of them behind a sofa but Caruso, without interrupting his singing, scooped them up and laid them carefully on the sofa. The audience shrieked with laughter until Alda's blushes inflamed the pale cheeks of tubercular Mimi.

The baritone Eugenio Giraldoni also had a taste of unrehearsed slapstick at the Metropolitan. During an impassioned moment in *La Gioconda*, he had an egg pressed into his palm and was left to cope with the rest of the scene like a slightly demented conjuror. Caruso later convulsed the audience by 'milking' the tassels of the magnificent curtain when taking his final call.

Many of his antics were impromptu. He once brought the house down in *La Forza del Destino* in the scene where Don Alvaro throws away his pistol, which accidentally goes off and kills Leonora's father. That night, however, the sound effects failed completely. Caruso winked at the audience and solemnly called out, 'Bang! Bang!' He showed more serious initiative in the second act of *Martha*, in which the soprano, singing 'The Last Rose of Summer', is supposed to pluck a bloom from her corsage. On this occasion her unlucky dresser had forgotten to provide her with one. Caruso picked a rose from her floral hat and handed it to her instead, an improvisation which passed unnoticed.

One of his jokes misfired badly during his second season at the Garden. This time his intended victim was Louise Kirkby-Lunn, whose build and style admirably suited the Wagnerian roles in which she excelled. Caruso blew playfully into her ear as she began a solo in *Rigoletto*. Without hesitation she responded with a slap which sent him reeling. The audience chuckled, innocently taking it for part of the action. Caruso was quick-witted enough to play up to it, but Mme Kirkby-Lunn, with whom he often sang in *Aïda* and other operas, would never again be subjected to such familiarity.

*   *   *   *

117

That second Covent Garden season was rewarding in every sense. He had given twenty-seven performances to full houses and with such unanimous approval from the critics that the syndicate re-engaged him without hesitation for the following year. He supped almost every night either at the Tostis' or Pagani's, and a pile of flattering correspondence always awaited him at the Savoy Hotel, where he had a suite, complete with piano, overlooking the Thames. He was idolised by the Italian staff, who loved his new party trick of pretending to push the baby grand by inflating his barrel chest against it. On fine days he walked from the hotel to the opera house, hopping merrily between the piles of market garbage. Often he handed out picture postcards of himself to the porters, who crowded round and hailed him in cockney slang, incomprehensible to him but clearly good-natured.

He spent money lavishly in the Burlington Arcade at an establishment where, he heard, Mascagni always bought shirts and neckties by the dozen. He was fitted for several more suits at Scholte, Scotti's tailor, but insisted with a touching naïveté on being squeezed into sizes rather too small for his figure. He seemed fatally drawn to the loudest checks, usually in green, which he and his countrymen considered a lucky colour. He was not the best advertisement for the Savile Row cut after he added lurid waistcoat and socks to an ensemble invariably topped by a white curly brimmed fedora from Milan.

Caruso did not give all his time to frivolity. For some six hours a day he would be closeted in his hotel suite with Richard Barthélemy, an excellent musician whom he had engaged as his accompanist and *répétiteur*. Together they went over numerous scores, Caruso taking infinite care to improve his phrasing, at first in half voice and then with a full throat. He never missed his breathing exercises, carefully adapted and improved since those early days in Salerno with Maestro Lombardi. With Barthélemy riffling the keys he would march up and down the room, coffee-cup in hand, humming or whistling passages. They often argued long and vehemently over the interpretation of a single phrase, the tenor growing ever more nervous and irritable if he happened to be performing that night. He would examine and spray his tonsils every few minutes, but, illogically, kept puffing at his strong cigarettes, sometimes smoking as many as twenty before a demanding role.

Barthélemy had agreed to accompany him to New York for the new Metropolitan season. It was no sinecure, for Caruso became angry when he thought himself in the right and used to flourish his notebooks to prove a point. He could also accept criticism, however, particularly when the accompanist accused him of straining for too much volume. A scholarly, deeply read man, Barthélemy would tactfully explain the subtler undertones of characters like Radamès, and fill in the historical period and background of various operas. Caruso's interpretation benefited from these conversations. He took notes assiduously and applied himself with more care to his costumes and make-up.

In later years he used to say, half in jest, that a singer needed only 'a big chest, a big mouth, ninety per cent memory, ten per cent intelligence, lots of hard work and something in the heart'. He developed a chest expansion of nine inches, worthy of Eugene Sandow himself, but his resonance owed more perhaps to the depth and spaciousness of his mouth. According to his wife, he could put an egg in it and close his lips without even having to puff his cheeks. The superb phrasing and unforced breath control were the end-product of hours, months and years of perseverance. When he left London at the end of July 1904, few critics disagreed with the verdict of the *Musical Times*: 'To a fine voice he adds an excellent method; for though his voice is big, he can move it with the greatest agility'. But such praise, although pasted at once into his handsome leather-tooled press-cuttings book, did not make him complacent or try to play safe with established favourites. He was feverishly impatient to study Puccini's *Madama Butterfly*, which in its revised version had been vindicated in Brescia that May; the composer had taken ten curtain calls. Toscanini was already on his way to direct performances in Buenos Aires, although he thought the music 'sugary' and far below Puccini's best.

The Galleria in Milan was now aflutter with 'Butterfly' wings. It was rumoured that Puccini and his publisher's son, Tito Ricordi, were already negotiating with Covent Garden to stage it in London with Caruso as Pinkerton and Melba as Cio-Cio-San. This was quickly disproved. Melba went to Venice to read the part with Puccini at a friend's *palazzo* but soon found it beyond her dramatic range. Caruso had no such doubts about Pinkerton, but instead of becoming involved in Galleria gossip and speculation during those prickly summer days, he wisely went off to join Ada at the Villa alle Panche, where, on 7 September, she was delivered of another son. He was christened Enrico and at once nicknamed 'Mimmi'. Ada could not conceal her disappointment at having to miss a second trip to New York, but seemed mollified by Caruso's promise to give the two boys his name and make them his legal heirs.

He was diligently preparing for his Berlin début the following month when a *cri de coeur* came from the management of the San Carlo. Some wealthy Neapolitans had subscribed £20,000 to send a company to Covent Garden for a short season under the direction of Cleofante Campanini. Arimondi, Sammarco, Amato and Rina Giachetti would be worthy representatives, but Higgins and his colleagues had hinted that only a name like Caruso's could ensure success. He accepted the invitation, but he had not forgiven the San Carlo for his previous humiliation, and was only tempted by the thought of sweet revenge for those hisses back in 1902. He was possibly influenced by Rina, who needed reassurance for her début before a London audience. Condemned to stay behind, Ada may or may not have been too happy about this development. There is no evidence either way, but it could well have laid one of many smouldering fuses.

PART THREE

'La Donna è Mobile'

Chapter Eleven

Caruso had no time to ponder sisterly jealousies, if any. Early in October 1904 he sang at Berlin's Theater des Westens; ten nights later, when the San Carlo Company opened at Covent Garden with *Manon Lescaut*, he showed the effects of a cold but London was too delighted at having him back so soon to be overcritical. There was no question of Rina Giachetti's triumph in the title role. She sang and acted with such verve that the management, slightly nudged by Caruso, engaged her with the San Carlo Company for the following year. He recovered quickly enough to offer charming performances in both *La Bohème* and *Carmen*, but his Canio proved the company's true insurance against failure. *I Pagliacci* was now almost universally accepted as a 'Caruso opera', with the certainty that 'Vesti la giubba' would spark off as many encores as his tonsils could withstand.

In his second Metropolitan season he gave thirty performances at the increased fee of $1152 apiece, apart from making two dozen appearances in Philadelphia, Boston, Pittsburgh and other cities. It was a strenuous schedule, and without Scotti's company for relaxation and Barthélemy to nurse him through several jittery hours before appearances, he could not have stood up to the pressures. In this vintage period his phrasing was immaculate and the high notes so clearly sustained that only his intimates knew the agonies he suffered before putting on make-up and costume. Only then would he start to unwind. Few of the other artists suspected these torments as they saw him standing unconcernedly in the wings, often doodling on his sketch-pad. Once a performance was going smoothly he often felt relaxed enough in the lighter operas to seize a cape and hat and, unrecognised by the audience, skip on stage again with the chorus. But parts like Cavaradossi and

Canio, demanding 'a passionate something in the heart', always sapped him physically and emotionally. He sweated heavily in dramatic roles and lost as much as three pounds in weight during a performance. After singing 'Vesti la giubba' with rarely fewer than three encores, he would stagger off with the tears streaming down his cheeks and grab a cigarette between trembling fingers. 'Whenever I sing,' he once confessed to Scotti, 'I feel that others are waiting to destroy me. I must fight to hold my own.'

That season would have been easier with Ada to comfort him and discipline his leisure. As their previous apartment had already been let, he had moved into the Hotel York on Seventh Avenue. Now there was no escape from the crush of admirers, operatic aspirants eager for jobs or advice, reporters on the scent of colourful copy and a practically nonstop relay of sociable compatriots. When Marziale Sisca, the genial editor of *La Follia*, a magazine widely read by New York's Italian colony, offered to pay handsomely for any caricatures he might care to contribute, Caruso at once handed him a batch and promised to do more each week without fee. 'I am paid for singing. Drawing is for my pleasure and to please my friends,' he said firmly. After a while he started sending Sisca his drawings from many different parts of the world.

He supplemented his stage appearances with concerts in several private houses. Although fatigued by a long season, he could not resist Simonelli's plea to star in a benefit performance of *I Pagliacci* in aid of New York's Italian Hospital. He gladly gave up his own fee and cajoled Scotti and the others to follow suit. Simonelli showed his appreciation by lobbying for his appointment as a Cavaliere of the Order of San Giovanni, the first decoration of his career and one which he wore with much pride.

Calvin Child considerately spared him too many recording sessions, but he now faced severe competition from the rival Columbia Company, licensees of the Edison phonograph cylinder patents. They had attempted to counter the Caruso vogue by starting their own Grand Opera series, using Metropolitan artists like Scotti and Marcella Sembrich for ten-inch discs selling at $2. High fees were paid, including $1000 to Edouard de Reszke for recording only three songs.

The Victor Company soon hit back with its magnificent Red Seal series, which most connoisseurs regard as the high-water mark of Caruso's recording career. Richard Tauber used to recall: 'I would listen to those records for hours and hours—the finest lessons any young singer could have.' But much technical research had still to be done before Caruso's voice would reach its full bloom with an orchestra. In February 1905 he made five recordings at the Carnegie Hall studio with piano accompaniment. They sold so many thousands of copies at $3, particularly the lyrical 'Cielo e mar' from *La Gioconda*, that Child began hopefully to schedule for duets with Scotti and even Melba.

Caruso rejoiced that his stepmother collected all his discs and played them day and night on the machine he had sent her from Milan. He liked recording—except in the mornings, when his throat was often clogged—but his head buzzed with more exciting plans as that Metropolitan season drew to an end. Puccini and Tito Ricordi had now formally invited him to sing Pinkerton in the London première of *Madama Butterfly*. As Melba was wrong for Cio-Cio-San, the role would be taken by Emmy Destinn, with whom he had already teamed successfully at Covent Garden. She looked like a cook and Caruso also thought her rather too tall for Butterfly, but he had no doubt of Scotti's complete suitability as the American consul, Sharpless. Together they went over the score again and again, assisted by Barthélemy.

One morning Caruso flourished a letter from Puccini, who congratulated him on his performances of *Tosca* and *Bohème* at the Metropolitan and looked forward to his 'refulgent voice and art' as Pinkerton ('I can hear you, I can see you in the part'). It was quickly followed by a rather nervous message from Tito Ricordi, who had agreed to the Pinkerton costumes being made in New York but feared the tenor's taste and implored him to order 'simple uniforms of a lieutenant in the navy'.

With an eight-week engagement at Covent Garden ahead, Caruso would have welcomed a longer breathing-space at the villa, but he could not resist the chance of a few days in London with Puccini, who would shortly be sailing for South America. Meantime he had to stop off in Paris following an SOS from Sonzogno. His old employer had arranged for a season at the Théâtre Sarah Bernhardt with the veteran Angelo Masini, Lina Cavalieri and Titta Ruffo, but the Parisians were apathetic until Caruso's name adorned the posters for *Fedora*. There was barely time for a single rehearsal of an opera which he had not sung for over two years. Furthermore, he would have to open his Covent Garden season in *La Bohème* immediately after this Paris engagement and without the usual week for rehearsal. Higgins had fortunately wired his consent.

Tickets for *Fedora* changed hands at profiteering rates. The first night's scenes, when the audience lost all control and wildly cheered Caruso's 'T'amo', were repeated throughout that week. The hysteria mounted to such a pitch and there were so many demands for encores that Campanini had to plead with the audience to allow his wilting orchestra a few minutes of extra rest between acts.

Caruso crossed the Channel on 21 May 1905, checked in at the Savoy Hotel and opened at Covent Garden the following night in *La Bohème* with Melba and Scotti. He sang throughout that season with such rhythmic power and all-round mastery that the writer Thomas Burke later recalled his enchantment in a panegyric almost unequalled in operatic literature: 'Gold swathed in velvet is his voice. . . . He is not a singer. He is a miracle. There will not be another Caruso for two or three hundred years; perhaps not then. . . . Jean de Reszke would heave and strain, until his audience suffered with him, in order to produce an effect which this new singer of the south achieved with his hands in his pockets as he strolled round the stage. . . . The house thrills. A short passage, throbbing with tears and laughter, has rushed, like a stream of molten gold, to the utmost reaches of the auditorium and not an ear that has not jumped for joy of it. . . . He carried a terrific crescendo as lightly as a schoolgirl singing a lullaby and ended on a tremendous note which he sustained for sixty seconds. . . . It is we who were exhausted. Caruso trotted on, bright, alert, smiling, and not the slightest trace of fatigue did he show.'

Burke was a diarist of London life and had no pretensions to musical expertise, but his rapture seemed to be shared by many professional singers, among them Caruso's staunch friend of the future, John McCormack. That spring the young Irish tenor had come to London to record ten ballads for a modest fee of £50. Caruso's high C in 'Che gelida manina' made him bounce up and down in his seat. He left the theatre almost drugged by melody and hero-worship. Next day he brought a photograph of his idol in *Manon Lescaut* and forged himself a dedication, 'Sincerely yours, Enrico Caruso,' He then spent several precious sovereigns on Red Seal records which soon forced him to interrupt his concert career for further study in Milan. 'That voice still rings in my ears after thirty-three years,' he once declared. 'It was like no other in the world.'

What Caruso jocularly called his 'musical box' now seemed to evoke divine echoes in all his partners, who in turn raised his own performances to supreme vocal glory. This mutual pollination flowered throughout that London season. He again partnered Selma Kurz, the slender and beautiful Viennese coloratura soprano, who possessed a magnificent trill, but was too inclined to hold it as she waltzed round the stage. In her Covent Garden début the previous year, while playing opposite Caruso in *Rigoletto*, she had to be sharply checked by the conductor, who drove his orchestra ahead and left her marooned on a high note. This time her Gilda, inspired and disciplined, brilliantly complemented his Duke of Mantua.

Melba had never been in better voice as Mimi, but Destinn's rapt and soaring urgency in the Nile scene from *Aïda* won almost as much applause. In *Madama Butterfly* her love duets with Caruso helped the hypnotised first-night audience to forget her sturdiness as a fifteen-year-old geisha and the undeniable fact that Pinkerton's overtight uniform and short legs made him a somewhat implausible naval officer. The curtain had to be raised again and again, but, to Caruso's regret, Puccini was not present to join his celebration supper at the Savoy. He had already sailed for Buenos Aires, where several of his operas were being staged; he had been paid 50,000 francs (£2000), plus free passage for his wife and himself, to launch the season. Before departing, however, he joined Caruso, Scotti and Tosti for a noisy stag party at Pagani's and also accompanied them to a reception at the home of the wealthy banker David Seligman. The latter's attractive if over-intense wife was herself a promising soprano and a former pupil of Tosti's. She complimented Caruso in fluent Italian, but was obviously fascinated by Puccini from the moment his lips brushed her hand. They soon became the most intimate of friends and would exchange visits and confidential letters for many years to come.

Caruso always sang willingly for her guests, asking 'only a plate of sphagetti' in return, but with twenty-four performances booked for Covent Garden he accepted few other private invitations. He had almost decided to turn down an engagement to sing at a party in Wimbledon with Emma Calvé, but could not disappoint her. As things turned out, he had no regrets about accepting. They had arrived rather early at the mansion, where the hostess mentioned that her music-loving son, an invalid, was too ill to leave his room in a small pavilion on the estate. Caruso at once suggested that he and Calvé should go over and entertain the boy while his mother waited for her guests.

Although he had already sung three times that week and had another performance scheduled for the following night, he gave the young invalid a 'recital' of operatic arias and some of his favourite Neapolitan canzonettas. Calvé offered her gayest French and Spanish ballads, ending with her Carmen dance, while Caruso snapped his fingers, stamped his feet in a burlesque flamenco and twanged an imaginary guitar. The boy howled with laughter and begged for an encore; they could not refuse him. They were in the middle of a duet when the hostess entered breathlessly and entreated them to return to the house; her guests had been fidgeting for an hour or more. Caruso was unrepentant. 'Look at your son's face,' he said gently. 'Isn't it better to sing for him alone than all the others put together?'

The highlight of that London season was an unexpected 'command' to sing with Melba, Destinn and Scotti at Buckingham Palace in honour of the young King of Spain. Among the guests was King Edward VII's niece, Princess Victoria Eugénie (Ena), who would soon marry Alfonso and survive an anarchist's bomb hurled at their coach on her wedding day in Madrid.

No hint of coming tragedy had clouded that state concert. It was far less of an ordeal for Caruso than his earlier appearance before the Romanovs. King Edward and Queen Alexandra loved Puccini's operas and were devoted to Melba, who had often sung at the Palace and Windsor Castle. She quickly put her fellow artists at ease. Caruso, as usual, had been very nervous, but Scotti joked with him as they drove together to Buckingham Palace, the tenor resplendent in his new well-cut Savile Row evening clothes and proudly wearing his Cavaliere insignia. It was the only extra touch which Scotti would permit, and that with some hesitation. He reminded his friend that the King was easy-going but could be a stickler for dress etiquette. Everyone at Covent Garden knew about the unfortunate woodwind player who had been whipped out of the orchestra by a royal equerry for daring to wear a black tie in the monarch's presence.

The extracts from *La Bohème* and a lesser-known opera were applauded, and the artists sat down afterwards to a delightful supper. A fortnight later Caruso received a charming letter from the Lord Chamberlain, together with a diamond and ruby tie-pin bearing King Edward's monogram.

Lord Farquar explained that it was in appreciation of his 'beautiful singing' which had given their majesties great pleasure.

A fellow guest at the Savoy Hotel was George A. Kessler, the ebullient Wall Street financier. Kessler had an international reputation for staging lavish and often eccentric dinner-parties, serving his guests vast quantities of Moët and Chandon, in which he had a major marketing interest. To celebrate his birthday he decided to dine and wine some two dozen friends, including Réjane and Edna May, the enchanting 'Belle of New York'. An incurable hunter of novelty, he had hit on the idea of a gondola dinner with Venice as the motif. The Savoy had *carte blanche* and an almost unlimited budget to provide 'the most novel little party I have yet given'.

The hotel forecourt was flooded and transformed into a miniature Grand Canal with miniature reproductions of St Mark's and other landmarks. The guests would float by in a vast gondola canopied in silk gauze and decorated with thousands of fresh roses and carnations, while an imported troupe tinkled appropriate melodies on mandolins. Waiters were dressed as gondoliers to serve a banquet of the rarest delicacies on a table adorned by the three great Lions of Venice sculpted in ice.

As a finale a baby elephant would plod over a gangplank and onto the gondola, bearing a five-foot-high birthday cake cut by the host and distributed by a bevy of Gaiety Girls with the inevitable magnums of Moët and Chandon. Mr Kessler seemed delighted with the preparations, but thought a little truly Italian entertainment might still be needed as the crowning touch. He approached Caruso, who was tempted but hesitated; the party had been arranged for 26 July, the night after a farewell performance in *La Bohème* to be attended by Queen Alexandra, and only a week before he would be appearing in Ostend to inaugurate the new Theatre Royal. But Kessler would not be denied. Asked to name his own fee, Caruso mentioned £450, almost double what he was then being paid for a performance at Covent Garden.* Kessler quickly signed a cheque and would no doubt have gone even higher (his staff tips alone for that gondola dinner were a trifling £1000!). Caruso delivered a luscious selection of arias and ballads under a melonlike moon, provided by the Savoy management.

He was very tired on arriving next day at the Continental Hotel in Ostend, but the sun shone invitingly and the sparkling water reminded him of the Bay of Naples. Instead of resting he was soon splashing about in the sea, watched by a crowd of holiday-makers who rushed headlong to the beach when his presence was reported. He delighted the children by puffing out his cheeks, spouting mouthfuls of water and generally behaving like a performing seal. Quickly circled by laughing swimmers and canoeists, he scampered off to his cabin, where he had to be rescued by the hotel porters, but not before he had sung 'Funiculí funiculà', signed dozens of autographs and kissed a procession of pretty girls.

Rigoletto was a success, although purists must have found it odd that Gilda and the others sang in French while Caruso had stipulated that he would only interpret the Duke in his native tongue. But the critics were too occupied with coining superlatives ('he sounds like a clarinet played by an archangel') to find fault. The King and Queen of Belgium sat in the royal box, where Caruso was afterwards received and complimented on his performance. After giving some concerts in aid of Belgian charities he added the Chevalier's Cross of the Order of Leopold to his Italian decoration.

Caruso had by now acquired both a valet and a far more imposing country seat than the Villa alle Panche. His income from the Metropolitan and appearances in various other cities was approaching $100,000 per annum, treble the proceeds from his first American season. He was also benefiting from recording fees and his $2000-a-year retainer from the Victor Company.

* In the first decade of the century a middle-class London family could be housed, fed and served by two resident maids on £400 a year.

He could amply afford a more luxurious way of life, but his engagement of Martino as valet and general factotum and the purchase of the Villa Bellosguardo were not symptomatic of *folie de grandeur*. Both turned out to be excellent investments in terms of the comfort and relaxation which had become almost indispensable to a career under growing pressure. After Lorello had finally left, with a lavish bonus, Caruso managed almost incredibly without a full-time secretary until late in 1917. His own scrupulous book-keeping enabled him to keep his accounts up to date, and he also wrote personally to friends all over the world, always in the language of the recipient, however quaintly phonetical. If he was submerged by urgent business correspondence or his mass of fan mail in London, Milan and New York, he conscripted willing countrymen and rewarded them with tickets for the opera and 'presents' in cash or kind. His contract with the Metropolitan allowed him fifty free seats a performance, but he insisted on paying the full box-office price, and he gave away so many more that his bill sometimes reached $10,000 in a season. This largesse had its practical side, too, for he would carefully place his friends in different parts of the house to form a strategic private claque.

An improvised secretariat could not of course handle the constant queue of callers, many of whom would arrive unannounced while Caruso was resting or at work with his accompanist. Tact was often needed to turn them away. He also required a valet to keep his clothes and theatrical costumes in faultless condition, quite apart from supervising his numerous trunks and making his complicated travel arrangements. Martino, calm and dignified in dark suit and polka-dot bow tie, seemed almost predestined for his difficult role.

Not only was Caruso excitable before any performance, but his neuralgic headaches made him intolerant of the smallest break in routine. He had a wardrobe of at least eighty pairs of shoes, fifty suits and more than a dozen assorted hats, and he insisted on apple-pie order and impeccable valet service at all times. His chronic dread of infection also imposed heavy demands on Martino. Shirts might be discarded two or three times within a few hours, and he would change from head to foot after only a short walk. He took two long baths every day and had his rooms sprayed constantly from a mammoth atomizer of Caron perfume. Only Martino was entrusted with the armoury of syringes, gargles and sedatives which had to be labelled and packed in a special trunk before any journey.

Martino's snub nose and toothbrush moustache would appear peripherally in scores of Caruso photographs. He soon became more companion than manservant. While he dabbed his master's temples with witchhazel and gently massaged tired neck muscles, he also listened with sympathy to a catalogue of irritations from 'the Signor Cavaliere'. He was confidant and friend almost from the first and remained so until the tenor's last breath.

The Villa Bellosguardo, which Martino later ruled as majordomo, was a four-hundred-year-old mansion at Lastra a Signa, forty miles from Florence, commanding a view of violet-tinged mountains and the famed Chianti-bearing slopes. Built on the summit of a hill and surrounded by a high wall, its towering gates opened on a long avenue of cypress trees. It overlooked an estate of forty-seven farms cultivating olives, wines and vegetables. On his first visit to Baron Pucci, the owner, Caruso was charmed by the sound of bells from a monastery five miles away. This seemed such a good omen that he bought the property without further delay. The price was easily within his means, although building renovations would be costly, quite apart from the necessary expenditure on new furnishings. He quickly won the farm-workers' goodwill by pledging himself to improve their holdings and replace run-down machinery. He also volunteered to forgo all rents in exchange for fifty per cent of the produce, a generous arrangement which had given excellent results in other parts of Tuscany.

Caruso liked trotting through the baronial rooms and noting possible alterations. He was enchanted by the seventeenth-century chapel and an adjoining *presepio* with a fifteen-foot stage. He and Ada spent several days inspecting the

133

gardens, accompanied by landscape artists from Florence who proposed elaborate plans for beautifying them. He was determined to spend far more time here than had been possible at the Villa alle Panche, which he had been unable to visit for more than a few weeks in all during the past three years, but Ada remained sceptical. He had been equally well intentioned about their other villa. She was at first reluctant to become chatelaine of this vast house and estate, which meant longer exile from her friends and city delights like the Galleria and La Scala, but there would be consolations. Caruso had engaged an English nurse-governess, Louise Saer, to take Mimmi off her hands and also provided an automobile for her journeys between Milan and Signa. She soon bought house dogs and other pets which Caruso had always refused to keep in the city, but no caged birds were allowed in the villa or anywhere else on the estate.

She was apparently reconciled to abandoning her operatic career. She had two sons, money in plenty, elegant clothes, a jewel box worthy of any contessa and was respected as the wife in all but name of the most celebrated tenor in the world. In every way she was more fortunate than the Signora Puccini, whose marriage had failed to bring her either happiness or real security. The composer, although diabetic, seemed to grow more handsome and dashing in middle-age, while Elvira had become a discontented and insanely jealous woman; once she lashed out with an umbrella at a pretty young singer. It was openly rumoured that she filled Puccini's trouser pockets with camphor balls and even mixed an anaphrodisiac in his coffee and wine when he was engaged in one of his many love affairs.

Caruso used to chortle over these stories and congratulate himself on his own excellent relationship with Ada, who was still attractive and desirable but had never inspired the smallest whisper of scandal. She might sulk over his long engagements in England and America, but their reunions held all the fascination of short honeymoons. Lovely Bellosguardo could only add to their bliss.

His one disappointment, which Ada did not wholly share, was the point-blank refusal of his father and stepmother to retire to the peaceful luxury of the villa. Marcellino had finally quit his part-time work at the factory and after some argument with Caruso consented to rent a more comfortable apartment, but nothing could persuade him to leave Naples. He and his invalid daughter would have profited from the mountain air, but he preferred to play expansive host to local hangers-on and boast endlessly of his 'Rico', whose records were being played everywhere. The Neapolitan newspapers often carried photographs of Caruso in New York and reported fully on his clothes, his diet, his friends and even an attack of mumps. There was endless comment on his phenomenal earnings. Marcellino still found it impossible to believe that the Metropolitan Opera House could be paying his son $1300 a performance, or that he had been driven by limousine all the way to Washington and back merely to sing a few ballads at some party for a fee of $2500.

The 1905–06 season had opened with *La Gioconda*. Tickets were sold weeks ahead and with only a handful on sale by the scalpers. A Caruso Night was now a social event whether or not he sang familiar roles or made débuts in *La Favorita*, *Martha* or *Carmen*. W. J. Henderson of the *Sun*, so often critical of the tenor's costumes and outlandish headgear, was finally captivated by his performance in *La Gioconda*. 'One cared not a whit what he wore,' he enthused. 'It was one of the supreme pieces of singing of our time. . . . The fact now to be recorded is that the public has gone to the opera almost solely for the purpose of hearing Enrico Caruso. . . . The invariable request at the box-office has been, "Can you let me have seats for Caruso's next appearance?" '

That season he sang sixty-four times in New York and other cities, not missing a single performance. It pleased his public, but above all it pleased Conried, whose penny-pinching had started a crisis at the Metropolitan early in January 1906. The $15-a-week chorus, with whom Caruso openly sympathised, decided to go on strike just before the curtain went up for

Faust. Caruso, Emma Eames and the other principals had to carry on without their help while Conried improvised effects with an offstage orchestra and organ. Between acts he went before the curtain and stolidly lectured the restive audience with his views on the artistic advantages of an open shop in opera!

Conried's anxiety to lift the Metropolitan's accounts out of the red caused him to over-use Caruso, whose name alone seemed to guarantee a full house. This led a writer to protest in *Forum*: 'What are the principal operas performed at the Met? Caruso's. Who sings the chief roles? Caruso. Why is German opera given so little? Caruso. Finally, what is Italian Opera? *Caruso.*'

The public could not have enough of him either in or out of the theatre. He had moved into an apartment on West Fifty-seventh Street which was large enough to accommodate Barthélemy and Martino, but offered even less privacy than the Hotel York. He had become such a cult with New Yorkers that passers-by would often stop to point out the house. During a performance of *L'Elisir* he accidentally cut his head with a bottle but went on singing while the blood poured down his face. For days afterwards his apartment was jammed with anxious countrymen who brought flowers, wine and even cans of fortifying soups, while a temporary secretary had to be recruited to answer the hundreds of solicitous messages.

A small crowd regularly waited for him to emerge from the house. They gave him a friendly cheer whenever he bounced out in full evening-dress, wearing his decorations and often with a crimson-lined cape billowing behind him, to sing at Mrs Vanderbilt's palatial mansion on Fifth Avenue or for other social leaders like Alva Vanderbilt Belmont and Mrs Reginald de Koven. For these musicales the whole of Fifth Avenue became a slow-moving procession of stately limousines, but Caruso always felt guilty about the chauffeurs, who shivered in the cold wind while he was being paid two or three thousand dollars to warble a few arias and romanzas. He went out of his way, even in the middle of an exhausting season, to sing at benefit concerts, and usually sent back the fee after personally reimbursing the Metropolitan. He once accepted a last-minute invitation to appear at a Waldorf-Astoria concert in aid of a new tuberculosis hospital in the Adirondacks, although he had to leave immediately afterwards to sing in Philadelphia and Washington. The orchestra was under the direction of Victor Herbert, who would become a lifelong friend, though only a few days before this occasion he had declared sourly, 'Our Fifth Avenue hostesses expect the whole country to gape if they engage Caruso and two horn players for a single night.'

He liked pinning on his decorations and being introduced as 'Signor Cavaliere' to fashionable private audiences but was never obsequious to wealthy dowagers and refused to audition their daughters. Gracious little Belle Goulet, Mrs Cornelius Vanderbilt's sister, was among the very few hostesses to whom he gave a second thought once he had pocketed his cheque. Her husband owned the largest piece of Manhattan real estate after the Astors, but she also happened to be a truly *grande dame* with a genuine appreciation of opera. She occupied Box One among the red and gold lacquer caves of the Diamond Horseshoe and showed so much interest in what went on behind the scenes that Caruso took to calling on her and talking about his work and composers like Puccini, Boito and Giordano. Herself on Christian-name terms with most of the crowned heads of Europe, she could divert him for hours with her irreverent stories of court life. Whenever he made his first entrance he used to smile up at her box and ritually presented her with an autographed copy of every new opera.

One night she asked him to sup with her either in her house or at the Plaza, leaving the choice to him, but he had previously arranged to eat at Del Pezzo's little restaurant and could not disappoint the owner, an old friend. Mrs Goulet smilingly agreed to accompany him to West Thirty-fourth Street, where she created a minor sensation by arriving on his arm in

137

diamonds, sables and glittering tiara to eat a bowl of good spaghetti on Del Pezzo's checked tablecloth.

The Victor Company had begun to market a horn-enclosed phonograph, the Victrola, on which thousands could now hear Caruso's voice accompanied by an orchestra. It coincided with a new and very generous agreement which would earn him some $2 million in royalties during his lifetime. In February 1906 he recorded half a dozen arias at the studio in Carnegie Hall, including the now inevitable 'Che gelida manina', followed a month later by his first duet with Scotti, the 'Solenne in quest' ora' from Verdi's *La Forza del Destino*. It would sell in vast numbers for many years.

Only small orchestras could be used. A short square horn was linked to the recording machine and musicians would be seated at varying heights. The trombonist was perched on a high platform, the oboeist and cellist sat on tall stools, and the violins had horns attached for amplification. The recorder was stationed behind a long window through which he directed vocalists by prearranged signals either to expand or, more usually in Caruso's case, to keep the voice down. If he came too near the horn the resulting blast would ruin the record; if too far out of range there was a danger of fuzzing the *mezza voce* with needle scratch and other surface noises. Despite these difficulties, which were only overcome with endless patience and constant repetition, his timbre came through splendidly. Compton Mackenzie, a distinguished editor of *The Gramophone*, has recalled those pioneering days in an eloquent tribute: 'We today with our symphonies and quartets owe our good fortune to Caruso. When violin solos sounded like bluebottles, overtures like badly played mouth organs, chamber music like amorous cats, brass bands like runaway steamrollers and pianos like an old woman clicking her false teeth, Caruso's voice proclaimed a millenium and preserved our faith.'

It also stimulated Chaliapin and other leading artists to persevere with what a less far-sighted English writer than Mackenzie had dismissed as 'the monstrous trumpet'. Once Melba had overcome her first repugnance, she became a fervent convert to a medium that paid her as much as $50,000, plus royalties, for only a week's recording. She soon discovered that by listening to her own records she could detect technical faults and improve her performances not only in the studio but on the operatic stage. It was a lesson which Caruso had absorbed from that very first session with the Gaisbergs in the Grand Hotel, Milan.

Caruso had barely had time to record his duet with Scotti at the end of that Metropolitan season before they again appeared together at a benefit performance at the Waldorf-Astoria in aid of Miss Leary's Italian Settlement. They then hurried off to Grand Central to join the company that Conried was sending out to tour various cities from Baltimore to the West Coast. In Washington, where he sang in *Lucia di Lammermoor* and the sure-fire *I Pagliacci*, Caruso was delighted by the breezy warmth of President Teddy Roosevelt, who presented him with a framed autographed portrait which Martino packed with special care.

As the train carried them from Washington to Pittsburgh and on to Chicago, St Louis and Kansas City, Caruso was in an ebullient mood. He played cards with Scotti and the other men until late at night and continually made jokes which kept not only the company but all the Pullman car attendants laughing. Audiences had been so enormous and enthusiastic that the tour developed into a series of gala performances, each more triumphant than the last as the advance publicity gathered momentum. But he was becoming exhausted and yearned for a spell of Californian spring sunshine before starting his next season at Covent Garden. He planned to spend the rest of the summer at the Villa Bellosguardo with Ada and the children.

Apart from his headaches, which attacked without warning and vanished as suddenly after an hour or two in a darkened room, he had no anxieties. His income was already vast and increasing year by year, with larger fees from the Metropolitan and Covent Garden, reinforced by the new royalty arrangement with the Victor Company. Above all, the serious critics had at last given up measuring him disparagingly against their former idols. James Huneker spoke for most of his colleagues on both sides of the Atlantic when he declared: 'Some have outpointed him in finesse, like Bonci; Tamagno could have outroared him; Jean de Reszke had more personal charm and artistic ability; nevertheless, Caruso has a marvellous natural voice, paved with lyric magic. . . . Why, there are men in this land of ours who would rather be Caruso than the President of the United States of Europe.'

Few would have argued with that verdict on 13 April 1906 when the train pulled out of Kansas City and roared westward towards San Francisco.

Chapter Twelve

Caruso owed much of his stamina to the practice of regularly going to bed before midnight, except when he was enticed into a card game by Scotti and other cronies. His dislike of taking siestas probably helped to ensure a sound eight hours' sleep. But in San Francisco on the night of 17 April 1906, nobody slumbered through until daybreak, and many thousands would never awake.

That sultry evening Caruso had sung a graceful Don José and returned jovially to the Palace Hotel, assured of an excellent short season ahead. At 5.13 a.m. the hotel rocked and beams began to crack like damp cardboard, the splutter of hot cinders providing a macabre firecracker display. His bed wobbled, then tilted over, and finally dumped him on a carpet of ceiling plaster. Terrified shrieks could be heard above the grinding and creaking of nearby buildings.

He must have been in a state of traumatic shock. He dressed mechanically and at the last minute wrapped a towel round his neck, no doubt in reflex defence against the night air. Scotti was astonished to see him fully dressed and hugging his silver-framed photograph of President Roosevelt when he walked glassy-eyed into the lobby. Most of the other singers were still in dressing-gowns and slippers. Pol Plancon's beard looked grotesquely greenish-grey without its usual morning dye.

Masked by handkerchiefs to protect their eyes and repel the appalling stench of charred flesh, they picked their way through razor-edged rubble towards the St Francis Hotel, where several of the others had quarters. Caruso was anxious to make a detour for the Opera House and salvage his costumes, but someone reminded him that it was already ringed by smouldering fires. He looked blankly at the speaker and muttered, 'Vesuvius.' His face was pallid and glistening with sweat. Before either Scotti or Martino could stop him he broke away, mumbling that he had to get back to the Palace and pack his trunks.

As the St Francis was unsafe, Scotti had decided to make for a friend's house in the suburbs. He found a wagon-driver who demanded $300 in advance to take his horses through the broken glass and clouds of acrid smoke. Scotti paid him at once and climbed in with Eames, Sembrich, Plancon and the others. They managed to locate and pick up Caruso, who had somehow got his valises down into the hotel lobby but still seemed to be in shock. He rambled on about fighting some Chinaman who had tried to rob him on his way back to the Palace. Although calmer by the time they reached Arthur Bachman's house some miles out of town, nothing would persuade him to sleep indoors. 'It's Vesuvius,' he kept repeating. He lay all night under a tree in the back yard with his towel muffling throat and mouth.*

Next morning they piled into the wagon and headed for the bay, where other members of the company greeted them with relief. They reported that several looters had been shot and hundreds of people were camping in the Golden Gate Park. Flames still crackled all over the city, and practically every water and gas main had been wrecked. While Scotti, by far the calmest amongst them, was making arrangements to hire a launch and cross to Oakland, Martino announced agitatedly that his master had again disappeared. He hurried off to search for him, praying that he was not buried under masonry or pinned down by some beam.

Time was now running out. Almost everyone else was on board and impatient to start, but Scotti refused to leave without his friend. He finally discerned Caruso's stocky figure and green scarf at the dock gates, where he was gesticulating violently to officials who blocked his path. Martino could not force his way through the milling crowd of refugees, but the singer was at last allowed to pass. Nobody had recognised him or could make much sense of his hysterical American-Italian gibberish

* Scotti's own account of this episode is quoted verbatim in Pierre Key's biography.

142

until he thrust the silver-framed photograph under the nose of a dock policeman. The officer glanced at the inscription, 'To Enrico Caruso, from Theodore Roosevelt,' and hastily issued him a boarding ticket.

He would never again sing in San Francisco, which was added to Barcelona and Palermo in his list of cities with 'the evil eye'. From this time onwards he had a premonition of violent death. He was also terrified of falling out of bed, and would not travel without his own down pillows, linen sheets and a special double mattress to be wedged firmly under the usual one.

He did not stay long in New York and arranged to sail almost at once for Europe, feeling even more need to rest before the opening of the Covent Garden season on 15 May. It was dispiriting to watch Conried wringing his hands over the San Francisco disaster. The Californian tour was of course abandoned, as all the scenery, props, costumes and musical instruments had been destroyed when the Opera House burned down. Many thousands of dollars had to be refunded for the cancelled bookings.

Kahn and his fellow directors were already worried by the rival Manhattan Opera House, which Oscar Hammerstein was building five blocks away at West Thirty-fourth Street and Eighth Avenue. The loss of a sell-out Californian tour had been yet another strain on their finances. They were therefore looking forward with even more anticipation than usual to a big Caruso season in the autumn. He would be joined by the beautiful American soprano Geraldine Farrar, who was to make her New York début after several successful years in Europe. It was hoped that she and Caruso might even rival his box-office triumphs at Covent Garden with Melba.

Caruso was too preoccupied with his own plans to share Conried's anxiety over the future. Oddly enough, he had become one of the few Metropolitan singers to feel much warmth for the gruff-spoken managing director. He sympathised with his crippling attacks of sciatic neuritis and sometimes visited him in his apartment to eat a bowl of goulash, which Conried cooked superbly. He no longer took offence at his stinginess and dismissed it as a joke when Conried wrote to him that summer at the Villa Bellosguardo, authorising him to choose his own steamer for his return to America but reminding him characteristically, 'I know you too well to be sure that you will not spend more money than is absolutely necessary.'

He had never shown extravagance at the Metropolitan's expense but lavished enormous sums on the villa. It was being furnished in luxurious style, based mainly on the florid nineteenth-century Neapolitan taste for shallow, high-backed sofas, red plush curtains and ornate tapestries with African jungle motifs. He was canvassed incessantly by dealers in objets d'art, sumptuous velvets and brocades, and also signed cheques freely for landscape gardeners, who produced more and more blueprints. He pottered about, discussing seeds and plants with an enthusiastic ignorance, invariably ending up by giving them a free hand, subject only to Ada's approval. He had a blind faith in her taste, which was, however, rather better on house decoration and bric-à-brac than on horticulture.

Sitting on the wide verandahs overlooking his estate, his sense of opulence and well-being had been fortified by the lucky escape in San Francisco. He had stocked his cellar with admirable wines to supplement those grown in his own vineyards, and the villa buzzed day and night with the chatter of house-guests, reporters, conductor friends like Mugnone (who helped to prepare him for Covent Garden), music publishers and composers imploring him to record their songs. His brother, Giovanni, and his wife stayed throughout the summer and others from Milan and Naples brought entire families for vacations at Bellosguardo, where food and drink was abundant and a huge staff of servants in attendance.

Many of the visitors were shallow Galleria acquaintances eager for favours and offering nothing but flattery and false bonhomie in return. Caruso was far more comfortable with old friends like Eduardo Missiano, whom he could at last repay for his first free lessons in Naples. As Missiano's family had lost their wealth and he could no longer depend on them for a precarious singing career, Caruso arranged to have him booked at the Metropolitan for several small but fairly lucrative parts. (Unfortunately, Missiano soon collapsed and died while rehearsing *La Gioconda*, leaving his wife and three children almost destitute. Caruso had the body sent home for burial and at once cabled $2000, his own fee for the performance, to the widow. He also urged her to turn to him in any future emergency.)

With so many house-guests and visitors, his three-week stay in Signa was anything but restful, but the smiling faces had a tonic effect. Ada seemed as loving as ever, although she was still prone to jealous sulks. She was no doubt nettled by a New York newspaper story of an incident during *Tosca* when Caruso had apparently kissed the American soprano, Emma Eames, with a realism beyond the call of duty. He had successfully laughed this off, but she was less easily soothed over her sister's rapid success compared with her own enforced retirement from the operatic stage. Rina had scored heavily at Covent Garden in the previous autumn with the San Carlo Company and was rated by some English critics as second only to Destinn herself in *Madama Butterfly*. She was now being coached for *Tosca* by Caruso and Scotti and would shortly be leaving with them for England.

Caruso's London engagement was even more triumphant than the last. The public sympathised with him over his San Francisco ordeal and he was flattered at being invited to dine at Lady de Grey's to recount his experiences of the 'airthquake' to her guests, including King Edward and Queen Alexandra. He sang thirty times at the Opera House that season and seemed to be vocally impeccable. His ten performances of *La Bohème* with Melba touched every heart, but all the other operas were sung with equal mastery. His Canio had not yet become over melodramatic; Radamès seemed more imposing with each performance; while his fine legato singing as Pinkerton had made *Madama Butterfly* almost as positive a draw as the well-tried favourites. The critics now raved over the unerring pitch

145

of every aria he delivered, from his nonchalant 'Questa o quella' and the gay magic of 'La donna è mobile' to the crackling electricity of 'E lucevan le stelle'. After the acclaim for his Cavaradossi, in which he was strongly supported by Rina Giachetti and Scotti, he could not resist rushing out to a leading London gunsmiths and buying an expensive sporting rifle for Puccini.

The Covent Garden management now proposed raising his fee to £400 a performance, equalling Melba's, but she at once objected to a parity which might reflect on her supreme status. Caruso shrugged and agreed to keep the peace by accepting £399, knowing perfectly well that his generous 'expense allowance' would amply compensate for the lost sovereign. He was far more put out by her brutal treatment of Frances Alda, who had been engaged to sing eight performances of *Rigoletto* with him. Melba had allowed her to sing only once before having her paid off. Caruso was relieved when the disappointed soprano dried her tears and soon made a hit at La Scala.

It was already clear to him that the singers with whom he performed at both opera houses were always more relaxed in New York without Melba's jealousy and front-office intrigues. Although his own position in London was invulnerable, he too felt more at home at the Metropolitan, but for other and mainly personal reasons. To him London had become synonymous with cheerful Pagani suppers, the luxury of the Savoy Hotel, and the Tostis' warm affection. He also relished the atmosphere of Covent Garden, both for the exuberant Italian gallery and for the sophisticated elegance of the stalls and tiered boxes. The Diamond Horseshoe's dowagers could not compete with the royal hallmark of an opera house which was the very hub of a London Season, with its presentations at court, Goodwood, Ascot, Henley, the Eton and Harrow cricket match and other annual splendours unknown to Manhattan.

He liked the glitter of gala nights when the programmes were printed on silk and a potentate like the Maharajah of Nepal wore 'a head-dress made entirely of diamonds and emeralds', according to *The Times*, but nothing could replace the camaraderie at the Metropolitan. London's eight-week season was too short for Caruso to familiarise himself with the rank-and-file backstage. Performing for four months a year in America, he knew the Christian names and often the family histories of almost every musician, carpenter and electrician who worked with him. They were also more easy-going and informal and made allowances for his quaint English. In polyglot New York, with its large Italian colony, he could wander through the streets and greet almost as many casual acquaintances as in his native Naples. Moreover, he had so far never sung outside London, whereas his tours with the Metropolitan company had led to valued friendships in a dozen American cities.

When the Covent Garden season ended on 26 July with the usual acclaim for *La Bohème*, he felt almost homesick for New York and in his mind was already savouring Del Pezzo's clams, spaghetti and zabaglione. He was imperceptibly moving into a régime in which New York would become home and the Villa Bellosguardo a holiday retreat where he could relax for a few weeks with his mistress, his children and congenial friends while simultaneously playing Santa Claus and patriarchal lord of the manor to his farm-workers. Perhaps unconsciously he had slipped into the role of a very wealthy bachelor whose work and tastes offered mobility, luxury and immunity from boredom.

Ada was still physically exciting to him and there was nobody so comforting or understanding in his darker moments, but he had grown rather more free and easy towards the women who wrote him passionate notes of adoration. He indulged in nothing more serious than mild philandering and often play-acted ludicrously to keep a flirtation alive, but it was difficult not to be influenced by his almost inseparable companion, Scotti, who had made womanising a second career and vigorously echoed Puccini's philosophy, 'On the day I am no longer in love, you can hold my funeral.' With Caruso this found expression in public kissing, sending huge bouquets and taking women on

147

calm him, but great drops of sweat ran down his face while Kane gave his evidence. The policeman stated that he had become suspicious when Caruso showed no interest in the monkeys but started following a girl of about twelve. Apparently he had also sidled up to three women, one of them a buxom Negress, and ogled them offensively. He was alleged to have moved in on the complainant and squeezed her behind. She struck him in the chest and screamed, 'You loafer! You beast!' Kane had then taken him into custody. His testimony was supported by a man of dubious reputation who told his story glibly enough and could not be shaken by the defending attorney.

Caruso denied pinching the woman or even touching her. He asserted that she had smiled at him and he had smiled back politely. Surprisingly, she was not called as a witness. The judge clucked sympathetically when the prosecuting attorney explained that she was terrified of Caruso's Italian friends who had threatened to beat her up if she took the stand.

Worse followed. On the second day of the hearing an attractive woman, dramatically veiled in white, came forward to testify that in February of that year she was leaving the Metropolitan when Caruso, in the audience that night, brushed against her and began to fondle her. Caruso vehemently denied this fresh and completely uncorroborated accusation. It was dismissed, but the public seats hummed with indignation. Nobody seemed impressed by Mrs Graham's absence or by the remarkable coincidence that Officer Kane happened to have been best man at her wedding to a janitor acquaintance of his.

Deputy Police Commissioner Mathot was practically in a lynching mood as he stood up to defend American womanhood against this vile foreign seducer. His voice grew hoarse when he denounced Caruso as a moral pervert who ought to be kept out of decent society. To strengthen his case but without producing any evidence to support it, he informed the court that a year earlier, after a Fifth Avenue reception, a woman guest had given Caruso a lift in her car, which he repaid by molesting her. According to Mathot, a mounted policeman had offered to arrest the singer, but the woman refused to prefer charges.

The bench found the case proved and fined Caruso $10. The conviction was upheld on appeal, Recorder Goff taking an even sterner view than his colleague in the lower court. He ruled astonishingly that it had not been essential for Mrs Graham to appear in court as 'the offence was not so much against the individual as against public order and decency.'

The 'Monkey House Scandal' spawned almost as many columns as the San Francisco earthquake. American public opinion was split down the middle. Most people readily accepted Caruso's guilt but seemed amused rather than shocked by this latest exuberance from a volatile tenor who had so often kissed pretty girls at the stage-door. Others, however, seethed with moral indignation and demanded that he be deported.

He would always protest his innocence and could hardly do otherwise. The whole truth remains in doubt. Mrs Graham would have not been the first American woman to smile at him in public, and he was not one to avoid returning the compliment, usually with a vigorous hug or some absurd piece of gallantry for a laugh or a newspaper photograph. Fondling or tweaking a lady's behind was—and remains—so prevalent a male pastime in Italy and Latin America that he might well have acted instinctively and without considering it more personal than a playful kiss.

In view of the flimsy and unsatisfactory evidence, it is equally possible that the whole affair was, as Puccini suggested, 'put up by some hostile impresario'. In this context one cannot entirely rule out the possible complicity of Oscar Hammerstein or his very resourceful press agent, William J. Guard, who afterwards manufactured a whole series of lurid stories to discredit the rival opera house. The Metropolitan season was scheduled to start on 26 November. With the Manhattan due to open only a week later, the downfall of the Metropolitan's outstanding attraction could obviously prove a most damaging opening shot in the so-called Battle of the Opera Houses.

Otto Kahn and Conried did not minimise the threat. Caruso had been their gilt-edged investment year after year. Nobody could safely predict how audiences would react to the fallen idol. The Diamond Horseshoe dowagers could turn fickle and even this solid bloc of admirers in the cheaper parts might hesitate to accept a convicted bottom-pincher as sentimental Rodolfo, the noble Radamès or Lieutenant Pinkerton.

Young Geraldine Farrar was scheduled to partner Caruso for the American première of *Madama Butterfly* in the presence of Puccini. This was to have been the highlight of the coming season. The directors had confidently expected not only to spike the guns of the Manhattan Opera House but to recoup some of the heavy losses that had been suffered in San Francisco and were only partially covered by insurance. All was now in jeopardy. Caruso had convinced himself that the stage-hands and even his fellow singers were sniggering behind his back. He looked jittery at rehearsals and, on returning from the theatre, refused to go out for meals or to see any visitors except Scotti. He was receiving a daily batch of abusive and often obscene letters, which disturbed him far more than the crackpot anonymous threats to castrate him. A vein had started to swell automatically in his temple, followed by blinding headaches and a racing pulse. Martino used to place ice on his wrists and constantly dabbed his forehead with a soothing lotion. The doctors diagnosed a nasal infection, but Caruso guessed more accurately that only a favourable verdict from the public would cure him.

Geraldine Farrar, a refreshing change from the familiar run of veteran prima donnas, made her American début in *Roméo et Juliette* on 26 November. It would be the only opening night not graced by Caruso in his seventeen years at the Metropolitan. Conried told the press he had reserved this date to launch his new star, but few doubted that such an obvious break with tradition was connected with Caruso's recent troubles. The tenor himself did not seem to take offence and was probably relieved at being spared a first-night performance. He sat beside Kahn in the Director's Box and joined in applauding the

American girl, whose verve and sparkle captivated her audience. Their cheers were echoed next day in every newspaper. The critic of the *Evening Sun* declared that 'such lovemaking has not yet been seen since Aunty Calvé, such joyous grace since Grandmother Sarah [Bernhardt].'

Caruso's own ordeal followed two nights later in *La Bohème*. He prayed with more than his usual fervour before going on stage and amazed Marcella Sembrich, his Mimi, by hurrying to her dressing-room to assure her of his complete innocence in the Central Park affair. He was in a cold sweat for his first entrance, glancing up instinctively at Mrs Goelet who blew a kiss from Box One. Scotti (Marcello) gave him a wink straight from Naples and warmly reassuring, but he trembled when a slight hissing came from one part of the house. This was instantly counterblasted by cheers from Italians in the gallery, soon taken up all over the auditorium. His first aria ended to frantic applause, as did each of his duets with Sembrich, whose performance, perhaps generated by the emotional atmosphere, matched his own that night. They took a dozen calls together before he returned to his dressing-room and embraced Conried and Martino, both almost as relieved as himself. 'New York still loves me,' he kept sobbing.

This would soon be put to a more practical test. On 3 December he won an ovation for *Martha*, but the special excitement of a 'Caruso night' was oddly absent. The lobbies seemed almost subdued between acts, and only a handful of spectators had gathered outside to gawk at the celebrities. Hundreds more were jamming West Thirty-fourth Street to admire the brightly lit new Manhattan Opera House, on which all the sleekest carriages and automobiles in New York City seemed to be converging.

It was the curtain-raiser for an operatic battle relentlessly fought out over the next four years. Oscar Hammerstein was not only determined to end the Metropolitan's monopoly but had a private score to settle with Conried. In addition to money, flair and showmanship, Hammerstein had far more taste than his opposite number. All he lacked to put Conried out of business was either Caruso himself or some equally potent attraction.

He opened his campaign by boasting characteristically that he had persuaded Jean de Reszke to come out of retirement. This was fictitious, like much of the other publicity with which he and 'Billy' Guard bamboozled the public, but there was still enough genuine gold dust in their pans to reduce the proud Metropolitan to near bankruptcy. Caruso's own box-office supremacy was not seriously challenged by the engagement of his old rival, Bonci, as the Manhattan's leading tenor, but far stronger competition would come from such glamorous international stars as Melba, Mary Garden and, even more unexpectedly, Tetrazzini.

Chapter Thirteeen

There was some irony in the Manhattan's bid for operatic control of New York. Two decades after the Vanderbilts had struck back at the Astors, the arrogant Diamond Horseshoe itself was now threatened by Mrs Clarence Mackay and her friends, who saw no reason why a new opera house should not put on better productions and still show a profit. Oscar Hammerstein, with his nose for scenting public taste, seemed ideally equipped to take charge of the campaign.

He had arrived from Germany during the American Civil War and first set up as a cigar-maker. It was not long before he had built ten theatres, including the Victoria at the junction of Seventh Avenue and Forty-second Street, where some of the best vaudeville acts were presented. He was himself musically gifted and had once won a $100 wager by writing a producible comic opera, both libretto and score, in forty-eight hours. Conried had worked for him as an actor in his early managerial days when both were still struggling for a foothold in New York. After they parted in bitterness, Conried's successful running of the Irving Place Theatre, followed by his emergence as the tsar of the Metropolitan, caused him to look down on Hammerstein, who reciprocated with almost pathological envy and contempt.

The Manhattan Opera House opened at the precise moment when the Metropolitan was still reeling from the San Francisco disaster and heading for its worst deficit in years. Under-rehearsed and often shabby productions could not be salvaged even by star names like Caruso, Eames and Calvé, while Conried's dislike of spending money on any but Italian works had led to a stale repertory. This estranged serious critics already incensed by his business tactics. In a rare effort to vary the operatic diet, he had not scrupled to pirate *Parsifal* despite Cosima Wagner's strong objections to having it performed outside Bayreuth. In the absence of copyright protection in the United States he was backed by the courts and made use of his 'good fortune' by putting up the price of stalls to $10.

Not only had morale slumped at the Metropolitan, among leading artists as well as the rank and file, but Conried was in poor physical shape to fight off the Manhattan's challenge. He hobbled about on crutches during his bad spells of sciatica while Hammerstein enjoyed an oxlike constitution and could go without sleep for a week. With stage-managers and others nearing collapse, he would sit on a plain kitchen chair in the wings and cast a martinet's eye on the minutiae of delivery, acting and make-up. He was quite as ruthless as Conried, but he had far more style and rarely became flustered. When a soprano threatened to shoot herself unless he granted an audition, he agreed reluctantly to give her ten minutes in his office. After hearing a few opening bars he lit one of the two dozen cigars he smoked every day, reached into his desk drawer and silently handed her a revolver.

Short, stout and bewhiskered, he favoured a very tall conical silk hat which he wore in his office and even inside the theatre. It became as much his trade mark as the gold-knobbed cane and Prince Albert coat. He never carried a dollar in his pocket and once left his fur-collared topcoat as security for a bowl of oyster stew in a restaurant where he was unknown.

His idiosyncrasies endeared him to journalists, who disliked Conried's habit of bursting into the press room at the Met and helping them with their notices. They also distrusted his hand-outs, even with the fifty-cent cigars, whereas Billy Guard, Hammerstein's publicity agent, had worked on newspapers and was always good for anything from a spicy paragraph to a full-column feature. He was tall and thin as a celery stick, with a head which rose to a high dome and a sleek helmet of hair parted dead-centre. He continued to smile and dispense blarney throughout the Manhattan's precarious early weeks.

The new opera house had 700 fewer seats than the Metropolitan's 3800, but still found it difficult to fill them once the novelty had worn off. Patrons appreciated the excellent lighting and acoustics, but the Manhattan could not compete with a star attraction like Caruso or the exciting new soprano, Geraldine Farrar, already capturing a younger generation of opera-goers.

Hammerstein had displayed a shrewd touch of showmanship in approaching Melba, who had never been happy at the Metropolitan since the end of her glamorous reign with de Reszke. Accustomed to being coddled at Covent Garden, she resented Conried's impudence in bracketing her with Eames and other singers. Hammerstein offered the *prima donna assoluta* treatment together with an appetising bait of $3000 a performance.

She had been engaged for ten performances but sang fifteen. From her début in *La Traviata* early in January 1907 to the farewell appearance two months later, every house was completely sold out. Although she was now forty-six and no match in looks for slender Geraldine Farrar, the majesty and range of her voice thrilled audiences already tingling from Billy Guard's high-powered publicity. She reacted to the adulation with a graciousness that astonished Guard after the many alarming stories that preceded her. She autographed dozens of photographs for very high prices but delighted the public by handing over all the proceeds to a home for blind children on Long Island. Before sailing back to England she was invited by Calvin Child to record the 'O soave fanciulla' duet from *La Bohème* with Caruso. The disc, most professionally made and for once without the slightest sign of 'temperament' on her part, sold enormously for many years.

Her season at the Manhattan salvaged Hammerstein, who desperately needed to offset the réclame for Puccini's six-week visit to New York. Conried had given him an $8000 fee to supervise the premières of *Manon Lescaut* and *Madama Butterfly*. Billy Guard had already spread the usual false reports that Caruso had lost his voice, but even he was powerless to discredit Puccini, who made front-page news from the moment he landed. His boat had been delayed by fog and docked only two hours before the opening of *Manon* on the night of 18 January

157

1907. He went straight to the theatre from the pier and seemed quite overwhelmed by the fanfare and a standing ovation from the packed house as he entered the Director's Box. He reported to Sybil Seligman that Caruso was 'amazing' and had sung 'like a god'.

At the Astor he often entertained Caruso, who reciprocated by introducing him to Del Pezzo's and other favourite restaurants and often took him for drives around New York, carefully avoiding the Central Park Zoo, which Puccini had solemnly wished to include in his itinerary! They were mobbed wherever they appeared together in public. One rich autograph hunter accosted the composer and begged him to write out and sign the opening bars of his Musetta Waltz. Puccini agreed to do so for a fee of $500 and immediately used it as a down payment on a new motor-boat, which he shipped out to Leghorn and thence to Torre del Lago.

He began a series of flirtations which inspired one of Caruso's crudest and most ill-advised pranks. A young American matron used to attend all the Met rehearsals during Puccini's visit and was soon involved in a passionate affair with him. It had to be conducted in pidgin French as she spoke no Italian and his English was confined to very few words. Caruso, moved either by envy or by some imp of mischief, casually drew Elvira Puccini's attention to one of her husband's diamond rings, which the woman was flaunting on her engagement finger.

She was watching a rehearsal of *Butterfly* from a box when Elvira stalked into the theatre with Puccini. After a vicious exchange of insults she made him go straight over and ask for the ring to be returned. That night she went carefully through her husband's clothes while he was asleep. In the lining of his silk hat she discovered a note from her rival arranging a rendezvous for the following day. A violent scene followed which may have added to Puccini's touchiness over the first performance of *Madama Butterfly*. He thought the production under rehearsed, dismissed Vigna's conducting as 'asinine, listless time-beating', and was less than complimentary about Geraldine Farrar, who had assumed the title role when Destinn declined to leave Europe. The only word of praise was reserved for Scotti, whose Sharpless seemed to him far more successful than Caruso's Pinkerton. 'C. won't learn anything,' he wrote waspishly to Mrs Seligman. '*Your god* is lazy and too pleased with himself—all the same his voice is magnificent.'

Caruso had much to answer for, but not this charge of laziness. He gave sixty-two performances in five months, including a most exhausting tour of ten cities. Strain and occasional hoarseness caused him to miss half a dozen appearances, although he often went on rather than give the Manhattan any scope for rumour-mongering. Billy Guard had kept up the myth of Jean de Reszke's 'imminent' return while simultaneously announcing the engagement of Bonci ('the new and better Caruso') with Maurice Renaud, the French baritone, and Campanini as conductor at $1000 a week. Hammerstein also signed agreements with Arimondi, the basso, and a graceful young tenor, Giovanni Zenatello, whose fine upper register had triumphed at La Scala. As Pinkerton many Italian critics considered him superior to Caruso. He was short, blond and stocky, but had such a fine stage presence that Melba, who had often sung with him at Covent Garden, recommended him to Hammerstein. The latter quickly decided to challenge Caruso's popularity on records by signing contracts for Bonci and Zenatello with the Columbia Company. Their discs were issued at $1.75 but made little impact on Caruso's Red Seal labels, which continued to sell in tens of thousands at $3.

With Melba's departure the Manhattan was again in critical need of a soprano to offset Geraldine Farrar's sensational impact in her very first season. Her glorious singing made box-office music, although Conried had to pay very dearly. He was no match for her mother, who argued over the fine print of every contract, regularly demanding higher fees, and soon forced him to provide Geraldine with her own dressing-room for a vast wardrobe of low-cut Paris gowns, fans and dozens of pairs of exquisite slippers.

Like everyone else in those early years, Caruso admired Farrar's acting ability, which had impressed David Belasco

159

enough for him to invite her to give up opera for the legitimate theatre. Her fresh, lyrical soprano lacked, perhaps, the magic of Destinn, Melba or Tetrazzini, but her sparkling personality gave a new dimension to every performance, notably in *La Bohème* and *Madama Butterfly*. Scotti lost his always susceptible heart to her, while Caruso designed a professional emblem to please her. It was a robin perched over a buckled wreath enclosing her initials and surmounted by the prophetic motto 'Farrar farà' (Farrar will make it). All the others were a little scared of her mother, who made them keep their distance on the Metropolitan's special train to Philadelphia every other Tuesday. She and Geraldine would sit apart, sipping their coffee and munching free chicken sandwiches while they hatched schemes to squeeze more cash out of Conried. Only Caruso managed to charm Mrs Farrar, whom he soon addressed affectionately as 'Mammina'.

He ended that American season with a powerful performance of *I Pagliacci* in Milwaukee and sailed for Europe over $100,000 the richer for his Metropolitan contract and another series of recordings for the Victor Company. He had time for only a few days at the Villa Bellosguardo, its gardens gay with spring flowers, before departing for London. The various pieces of furniture he had shipped over from New York were tastefully arranged by Ada, but she sullenly brushed off his compliments and seemed so prickly that he dared not reproach her for drawing mammoth cheques during the past few months. The domestic staff had almost doubled and the house was bursting with guests, many of whom he scarcely knew. They appeared to be theatrical bohemians from Milan and Florence with quite a sprinkling of French acquaintances picked up during her frequent trips to Nice.

He checked in at the Savoy Hotel in London and immediately began rehearsing *La Bohème* with Melba. On the opening night she took her high Cs with miraculous ease and seemed to have fully recovered from an attack of bronchial pneumonia after the Manhattan engagement. His own legato was so faultless that the *Times* critic eulogised, 'Caruso was at his finest, singing the phrases with a beauty of tone and an *entrain* that have made him famous all the world over.'

Between appearances he made a rushed visit to Paris to perform at the Trocadéro in aid of Belgian charities and felt amply rewarded by the gift of a gold cigarette case from the Duc and Duchesse de Vendôme, who had organised the concert. He was also invited to record his voice for posterity. This disc and others waxed by Kreisler and Kubelik were sealed in urns and deposited in the Opéra vaults with the strict proviso that they would not be opened for at least a hundred years.

One of several highlights in that glittering London season was a concert, directed by Tosti, at Buckingham Palace on 8 June 1907. Caruso partnered Melba after a state banquet given for the King and Queen of Denmark, who three nights later also attended a gala performance at Covent Garden. The Royal Box, occupied by King Edward and Queen Alexandra, had been linked with five others, all decorated with Danish and English flags and many hundreds of red and white roses representing the national colours of Denmark. Campanini conducted a programme which closed with Melba and Caruso singing their duet from the first act of *La Bohème*.

A month later he was made a member of the Royal Victorian Order, an honour inspired by the good offices of Paolo Tosti, who would himself be knighted within a year. Caruso prized this decoration above all others except those from his own sovereign, but Puccini did not share his delight. Fifteen years later he was still writing petulantly to Sybil Seligman, 'I think I might have received some form of recognition from your great country. . . . The father, no less than the son, the present King, loved and love my music.'*

The season ended, as it had begun, with *La Bohème*. As

* His disappointment was understandable, if based on self-deception. King Edward VII enjoyed Puccini's music, but his son, George V, did not inherit the taste. He once gruffly assured Sir Thomas Beecham that *La Bohème* was his favourite opera only because it happened to be the shortest!

Caruso was leaving the stage door a swarthy youth rushed out of the crowd and offered him a small package, which he refused to accept. Even in London he was still receiving threatening reminders of the Monkey House episode and feared that the parcel might contain a bomb. He recoiled when the young man tossed it into the cab. It turned out to be a gold-mounted fountain pen engraved with his name, the accompanying note explaining that it was from his admirers in the gallery in appreciation of so many memorable nights. Caruso quickly summoned a press conference at the Savoy to apologise for his discourtesy.

It was to be his last appearance at Covent Garden for five years. The syndicate was reluctant to meet Conried's inflated terms and felt confident of continuing to draw patrons with Melba, McCormack and other favourites. Caruso was not altogether sorry. His American commitments had become more strenuous now that he had to supplement appearances at the Metropolitan with the regular tours which Conried was frantically organising to help balance his books.

Well-paid concerts in England and on the Continent would more than compensate Caruso for his Covent Garden seasons. Although he missed the help of a prompter, he had already found it far less demanding to sing his favourite arias and a few ballads with the words and music in front of him than to memorise and perform the whole of a difficult opera. Moreover, by spacing out his concert appearances it would also become possible to enjoy longer vacations at the Villa Bellosguardo.

He was still very much in love with Ada, as Mrs Seligman and her son discovered when they travelled back to Italy with him that summer. Before the train drew in at the station in Milan he jumped onto the platform and threw himself passionately into her arms. Their joyful reunion soon ended in recrimination, though. From time to time he had heard disquieting reports of her familiarity with a handsome young chauffeur who was driving her to and from the French Riviera in a huge forty-horsepower limousine, one of the many extravagances to which he had turned a blind eye. He had dismissed the stories as tittle-tattle and thought she would be delighted to join him in America for part of the season. To his surprise she had seemed apathetic and obviously anxious only to resume her own operatic career. On impulse he taxed her with the stories that had reached him in London, confident that she would deny them indignantly. He was horrified when she broke down and hysterically asked for his forgiveness for having been indiscreet. She assured him, however, there had been no misconduct with the chauffeur, Cesare Romati, who had apparently confided that a secret society had hired him to murder Caruso. Afraid to dismiss him, she had parted with large sums of money to save her beloved.

It was a fantastic story but skilfully aimed at the tenor's paranoia, which had become more acute after his arrest in Central Park. They argued violently—according to Ada, he also struck her several blows—but the scene dissolved into tears and hot kisses. She promised to send Romati away, and Caruso departed to fulfil several important engagements before the opening of the next Metropolitan season.

He seemed to have shelved his domestic anxieties when singing for the first time in Budapest, but the recent quarrel may have had a delayed action. His performance in *Aïda* was so dispirited that the gala audience sat on its hands and failed to call for a single encore. Two nights later, however, he sang Radamès with such power and authority in Vienna's State Theatre that they stood up to cheer each act.

His tour of sixteen performances at $2000 a night became a triumphant procession through Leipzig, Hamburg, Berlin and, finally, Frankfurt. This time he did not spend the customary few days with Ada before leaving for the United States. Instead he sailed almost immediately from Bremen, where reporters were surprised to see him clean-shaven. One can only surmise that he had removed his moustache to look more youthful, possibly a reaction to Romati's good looks.

While he was waiting for the ship to cast off, Martino thrust a German newspaper into his hands. It displayed a photograph of Luisa Tetrazzini being mobbed outside Covent Garden after her sensational début in *La Traviata*.

This had come about most unexpectedly. Melba had left for Australia to rest for several months before returning to London. As Covent Garden needed a stop-gap for the sluggish autumn weeks, Campanini had suggested his sister-in-law. Harry Higgins was apathetic but agreed to engage her at only £120 for each of ten appearances, a fraction of the fees she commanded in South America. He then became so nervous of introducing this fat unknown in Melba roles, even in the off-season, that he asked her to cancel the contract and offered £300 as compensation. She refused, and made operatic history.

There was little or no advance publicity and so few bookings that the more expensive parts of the house had to be 'papered'. That opening night in early November 1907 also coincided with a pea-soup fog, which did not, however, stop London's Italian colony from arriving in force to hear Tetrazzini's Violetta. Even they could not have anticipated her triumph. Their delirious joy echoed through every section of the theatre. The ovation was comparable only with the season's first and closing nights for Caruso and Melba. The top notes were magically true, but her fiery bravura, coupled with a sparkle which the majestic Melba had never attained, electrified the audience. She took twenty curtain calls that night, blowing kisses to the gallery and giving saucy winks to the box-holders, who laughed and clapped like hysterical school-children at a Christmas circus.

Next morning the London critics hailed 'the new Patti', 'the Voice of the Century', 'a peerless soprano,' and one of them dubbed her 'the Florentine Nightingale'. The queues stretched into the Strand for the whole of that month, tickets changing hands at a premium. Patti travelled up specially from her Welsh mountain home and wept unashamedly throughout the last act of *La Traviata*. Afterwards she congratulated Tetrazzini and invited her to lunch at the Carlton Hotel.

The new star repeated her triumph in *Lucia* and *Rigoletto*, in which she was teamed most effectively with John McCormack, then on the threshold of a brilliant career. They became so friendly, Tetrazzini generously insisting on sharing all curtain calls, that he was soon persuaded to join her for a season which Campanini was to conduct at the Manhattan Opera House. She left London to a rapturous farewell from hundreds of admirers, and with a contract to sing at Covent Garden the following summer, in which she would alternate with Melba in *La Traviata* and *Rigoletto*, apart from making exclusive appearances in *Il Barbiere di Siviglia* and *Lucia*.

Conried tried in vain to secure an injunction against the Manhattan, pleading Tetrazzini's unfulfilled prior contract with the Metropolitan. This, it will be recalled, she had refused to sign when he hedged over an advance. He was also regretting his failure to spot the potential of Mary Garden, who would now provide serious opposition to Geraldine Farrar during the next three seasons. Like Farrar she had both 'star quality' and a chic dress-sense rarely associated with sopranos. But Tetrazzini would be Hammerstein's real trump card in that 1908 season.

She was a press-agent's dream. Billy Guard kept the front pages crackling with her lovers, her diamonds, her furs and her temperamental tizzies. She was mobbed in the streets. Her sizzling performances seemed to charm critics as much as the public. Caruso rejoiced in her success and often invited her to lunch with him at the Plaza, where he had booked a four-room suite for the season. He had also bought himself a new green Lancia, in which he took her for drives into the country. When they were not singing there would be gay dinners at Del Pezzo's or at a little restaurant on West Forty-seventh Street owned by a countryman, Pane, whose niece cooked superb boiled chicken and specialised in Neapolitan dishes. Caruso subsidised the running costs of this establishment for years and reserved a regular table once a week for himself and several friends, always paying for the meal when he could not keep the date. He would often drop in to play *bazzica* after hours with Pane, who suffered dismally from homesickness in the sunless winter months.

Guard tried to exploit Tetrazzini's friendship with Caruso by hinting that they would soon be singing together for Oscar Hammerstein. At the same time he stoked up reports of an imaginary feud between Bonci and Caruso. According to him, they hated each other so bitterly that it could only end in a duel 'to the death'. It made good copy, but even Guard was powerless to nullify John McCormack's public confession that he had learned more from hearing Caruso sing than from any of his teachers. He always sent him a New Year's Day card addressed simply to 'The King of Tenors'.

This lifelong friendship stemmed from their devotion to Tetrazzini, whom McCormack called his 'fairy godmother' after she had sung a high A for him at Covent Garden while he was struggling with a bad cold. Nothing upset their cheerful bonhomie both on and off stage. Before one Manhattan performance of *La Traviata* she had left off her usual very tight corsets. McCormack embraced her in the dying scene and found himself clutching what he later described as 'a pair of Michelin tires'. He looked so startled that she could not help giggling even during Violetta's last moments.

In the winter of 1907–08 Caruso sang his fullest season at the Metropolitan, including a robust début in *Il Trovatore*, followed by two musicales at the Waldorf-Astoria, concert appearances in Canada and a barnstorming tour of several American cities. Judging from the crowded houses everywhere, few agreed with Henry E. Krehbiel, who declared sourly in the New York *Tribune*, 'It is beginning to be difficult to keep the Caruso cult on its old hysterical plane, which is no wonder with his two or three performances a week and the fifth year of his presence at the opera house.'

His earnings, including the proceeds from his autumn tour of Austria and Germany, amounted to close on $200,000, not counting his recording fees and royalties. He re-recorded many of his standard arias and also made several discs with Scotti and Farrar. One novelty was 'Adorables tourments', a slow waltz theme composed in collaboration with Richard Barthélemy, but he did not care for stunt records. He once tried to learn the flute, which encouraged a compatriot, sensing a quick profit, to cajole him into making a recording. Caruso good-naturedly gave in but, on hearing the replay, broke the disc over his knee and protested 'No, no! I'll sell you the flute instead!'

He could easily have coined a small fortune in royalties after an extraordinary unrehearsed episode during the last act of *La Bohème*. On the Metropolitan's 'special' to Philadelphia the basso Andrés de Segurola, an imposing figure with his monocle and cavalry moustache, complained of laryngitis and feared he would be unable to sing Colline. This would have meant cancelling the whole performance as there was no understudy for the role. He was particularly nervous of not doing himself justice in the Overcoat Song even if his voice lasted that long. Caruso sprayed his tonsils and advised him to sing in half voice for the first three acts, promising if necessary to take over the aria in Act Four.

De Segurola struggled through until the last act, when he signalled anxiously to Caruso, who promptly pulled a brown felt hat over his face and sang 'Vecchia zimarra' in a deep voice while his colleague mouthed the words. Suspecting nothing, the audience applauded generously. When Calvin Child heard of the incident he was eager to record the aria but agreed with Caruso to limit the edition to half a dozen private copies. 'I am not a basso,' Caruso had explained with a grin. 'Why I should then put my good friend, Chaliapin, out of business?'*

During the 1908 season he was delighted at being reunited with the Russian giant, who made his Metropolitan début the previous November in *Mefistofele*. The critics received it badly; they paid tribute to his voice but considered his interpretation 'too earthy' and were even less complimentary about his over broad Basilio in *Il Barbiere di Siviglia*. Caruso tried to comfort him, but Chaliapin sailed off to Europe in a fury. It would be

* De Segurola later sang with Grace Moore in *One Night of Love* and became a most successful singing coach in Hollywood. Deanna Durbin was among several of his well-known pupils.

many years before he reappeared at the Metropolitan, although he gave many concerts in America, thrilling his audiences but too often behaving like an irate grizzly bear. At rehearsals he tried to conduct the orchestras from the footlights and would tell the chorus exactly where he wished them to stand. In Chicago he once stopped a performance and yelled derisively, 'Pigs, imbeciles, artists—yah!' The infuriated conductor jumped on the stage and punched his nose. Chaliapin was too surprised to hit back.

The Russian's box-office failure, after so much réclame, proved to be the beginning of the end for Conried, whose accounts showed a loss of nearly $100,000 for that season, while the Manhattan had made a profit of a quarter of a million. It was an astonishing recovery by Hammerstein, who in the first precarious months had to empty the tills of the Victoria and other vaudeville theatres to pay his opera singers on Friday nights. One evening he had turned to Mary Garden and remarked mournfully, 'There isn't enough money in the house to pay the light bill.' Melba, Tetrazzini, Mary Garden, McCormack and other stars, magnificently directed by Campanini (so much superior to his rival, Vigna), changed the whole picture. The Manhattan could now afford to lose Bonci, who defected after Conried had offered him an extra $500 a performance, but Hammerstein still needed Caruso to bring the Metropolitan to its knees. He sent scouts to the Plaza with hints of doubling any fee Conried might propose, but Caruso assured the general manager, already under heavy fire from his own directors, that he would never leave the Metropolitan. Moreover, he bustled one morning into Conried's office and announced himself more than satisfied with $2000 a performance for the coming season. This was pure adrenalin for Conried, semi-crippled and losing his nerve, but it had come too late to save him.

In February 1908 he was curtly informed by Otto Kahn, now chairman, that his régime had ended. Only Caruso shed tears for the stricken dictator, but he could not help seeing the logic of Kahn's newly announced policy. He had decided to engage Gatti-Casazza, who hesitated to leave La Scala and only consented to come if he could bring Toscanini over with him. While negotiations dragged on, Andréas Dippel, the Wagnerian singer who had often deputised managerially for Conried during his illness, was engaged to run the administration. It was implied that he would act as co-manager with Gatti-Casazza when the latter arrived later in the year.

Caruso was elated at renewing his association with the gifted couple who had made La Scala the world's leading opera house and would surely inject new life into the Metropolitan. His own morale, reinforced by a comforting bank balance, had never been higher. His records were enjoying enormous sales and now had 'Commendatore Caruso' printed on them to publicise his recent elevation by the King of Italy. He had persuaded Tulluo Voghera, the distinguished conductor, to act as his accompanist in Europe and replace Barthélemy, who had other commitments. Voghera with another close friend, Father Tonello, and of course Martino sailed with him to Europe on 21 May 1908. The sun shone, the sea was placid, and everyone on board the *Kaiserin Augusta Victoria* was so cheerfully festive that Caruso quickly relaxed and began to air his 'musical box' for the very congenial itinerary ahead. Instead of facing a heavy Covent Garden season he would first appear at an Albert Hall benefit performance, soon to be followed by another concert in Paris in aid of the Académie Nationale de Musique. He then planned to visit his sick father in Naples before spending the rest of the summer—his first full vacation in several years—with Ada at the Villa Bellosguardo. After a short autumn tour of German cities he would sail for his sixth season at the Metropolitan, this time under exciting new management.

It was a pleasant enough prospect, as cloudless as the skies that smiled on them all the way across the Atlantic.

Chapter Fourteen

On Sunday, 24 May 1908, Father Tonello was dining with Caruso and Tullio Voghera in the ship's Ritz Restaurant when a steward handed him a radio message: 'Please inform Caruso that his father is dead.' Not until midnight could he nerve himself to break the news to Caruso, who began to sob like an abandoned child. His hysteria was all the more remarkable as he had never been close to his father, who, in any event, had been in poor health for some years. With Martino by his bedside he slept fitfully, rose at 5 a.m., and then sent off a wire of condolence to his stepmother. Others followed to Tosti and his Paris manager requesting them to cancel all his concert bookings. He spent the rest of the voyage in his cabin; meals were sent in to him and left practically untasted. He smoked incessantly between long periods of prayer with Father Tonello.

He looked pallid and red-eyed when the ship docked at Plymouth, where Tosti waited to embrace him. Among the sheaf of mail was a letter addressed in Ada's handwriting and postmarked 'Signa'. It informed him with brutal finality that she no longer loved him and had decided to leave for South America 'with another'. He burst into tears, quite unable to believe that, after sharing eleven years of success and hardship, she had now deserted him and their two sons for a worthless adventurer. Tosti was perhaps less surprised by her defection. He could understand how a woman of her age and temperament might prefer Romati, the lean and fascinatingly dangerous hawk, to a complacent pigeon. Although Caruso was over ten years her junior, she had worn better, and evidently imagined herself still attractive enough to captivate a man younger and far handsomer than her plump thinly thatched tenor. It was also an open secret among Caruso's intimates that she had grown jealous of both his limelight and her sister's success. Moreover, she was herself far too forceful and ambitious to play mistress indefinitely between his operatic engagements, despite the furs, the jewels and her retainers at the Villa Bellosguardo. The newspaper reports of his peccadilloes, culminating in the Monkey House scandal, had possibly helped to estrange them, but her decision to resume her operatic career immediately was clear evidence of the deeper dissatisfaction.

Tosti could not reason with the tenor in his mood of hysterical self-pity but gently reminded him of his obligations to his concert managers, fellow singers and, above all, the public to whom he owed everything. On 30 May, two days hence, he had promised to sing at an Albert Hall concert in aid of the League of Mercy. The King and Queen of England would attend and every seat had been sold for several weeks past. But Caruso was persuaded only when Father Tonello mentioned that his beloved 'Ciccio' (Tosti) had personally arranged the whole programme and would act as his accompanist. Even so, he was nervous of singing 'Vesti la giubba'. It had always been a strain and in his present frame of mind might cause him to break down. However, it was now too late to delete the aria, which had been announced as the highlight of the programme.

On that Saturday afternoon nobody outside Caruso's immediate circle knew that he had prayed for hours with Father Tonello before driving to the Albert Hall. The auditorium, packed to the roof, was festive with hangings of pale green and crushed strawberry, and dozens of flowers had been worked into crowns decorating the Royal Box. The King sported a pink carnation in his buttonhole, and Queen Alexandra wore a white boa and a pale mauve dress with matching toque. Caruso was doubly unfortunate in having to open the concert. Tosti advanced to the piano and discovered that it was pitched too high. This meant holding up the programme for a quarter of an hour, an additional torment for the tenor already sweating nervously under his clown's make-up.

The welcoming roar of applause only increased his agitation. Tears ran down his face as he sang Canio's Lament with a passion and poignancy that came from the heart. Once or twice he faltered, but this only heightened the effect. Many sobbed

with him and called again and again for encores. By the time
he reappeared for the Quartet from *Rigoletto* he had regained
control of himself. Afterwards he quietly informed Tosti that
he would leave for Paris and sing, as promised, on behalf of the
Disabled Artists Home with Melba and Maurice Renaud.

He gave a superlative Duke of Mantua for his début at
the Opéra. The audience, including the President of France and
most of the diplomatic corps, was enthusiastic but unaware that
after sending his fee of 12,500 francs ($2500) to the Metropol-
itan, Caruso had then reimbursed the sponsors with a cheque
for the full amount from his own pocket.

He departed for the Villa Bellosguardo, where he collapsed.
He kept calling Ada's name and wandered dazedly through the
huge echoing rooms, refusing to see anyone except Rina
Giachetti, who was looking after his elder son, Fofò, at her
home. He thanked her warmly but she was alarmed by his
deathly pale face and glazed eyes. His weeping fits alternated
with bouts of violence when he ripped the sheets from Ada's
bed and savagely tore up every scrap of clothing in her wardrobe. He became so distraught that Martino, fearing he might
kill himself, rarely left his side and slept outside the bedroom
door.*

He received many comforting letters from friends. Coquelin
commiserated with him in the loss of his 'charming gaiety' and
implored him not to be discouraged ('You have no right to be
that; nothing in this world equals the miracle of your voice...').
Others also wrote: Giordano, Scotti, Tetrazzini and Puccini—
soon himself to suffer an even more painful domestic tragedy—
but he still refused to see visitors. He paced his bedroom and
once turned fiercely on poor Martino, who had gently urged
him to resume his breathing exercises and start preparing himself for his autumn tour of Germany. He kept muttering that
Ada and her lover had emptied his cellar, leaving him 'without
enough to fill a glass'. It is more likely, however, that in one of

---

* 'Enrico went mad. He sent telegrams to every city where he thought
she [Ada] might be, but she never answered. His heart broke.'—*Enrico
Caruso*, by Dorothy Caruso (1946).

172

his rages he had gone down and smashed every bottle in sight. He found a cache of jewellery which Ada always claimed were gifts from him and her own property. According to her lover, Caruso had left her 'with nothing to wear but one slip', but she looked more elegant than ever when she began touring in South America. She could not have been entirely penniless. Caruso would later testify to the 'enormous sums' he had sent her in the weeks before she abandoned him, and few believed her claim to have spent 'at least £1000' in three months to pay the staff.

He departed for Wiesbaden that September after his German manager, Emil Ledner, had warned him of the serious consequences of breaking his contract, mentioning in sly parenthesis that Kaiser Wilhelm had arranged to give a dinner in his honour. Caruso informed him curtly that he had given up all social occasions and would make no exceptions, even for the Emperor. He relented after successful appearances in Wiesbaden, Frankfurt, Bremen, Hamburg and Leipzig, which helped to restore his self-confidence. On arriving in Berlin in mid-October he told Ledner that he would only dine privately with the Kaiser and on condition that Martino was in attendance. Ledner must have worked very tactfully behind the scenes to avoid offending Wilhelm II, who showed most unusual consideration when informed of the tenor's recent troubles. They duly dined at Potsdam with Martino behind his master's chair to serve him personally. Afterwards the host is said to have raised his glass and remarked with a whimsical smile, 'If I were not Emperor of Germany, I should have liked to be Martino.'

Caruso sailed for New York on 27 October with Bonci and Tetrazzini as fellow passengers. She was in a gay mood after her concert tour of England and Scotland, but for once failed to rally Caruso. He continued to feel bitter towards Ada and often skulked while he chewed cigarettes instead of tasting the spaghetti specially prepared by the ship's chefs. His clothes sat on him baggily and he was taking massive sleeping draughts.

Almost as soon as he arrived in America he began searching

for new quarters, an obvious attempt to forget his happier years with Ada. He settled into an eight-room apartment at the Hotel Knickerbocker and was pathetically grateful to Scotti, who volunteered to take a smaller suite on the floor below. They played cards for hours and usually dined quietly at Pane's or Del Pezzo's, discovering that their usual corner table in the Knickerbocker restaurant attracted far too many of Caruso's admirers and others begging for free seats or 'loans'.

The box-office was stormed for the opening performance of *Aïda* on 16 November 1908. Caruso's name on the billboards was enough to attract the crowds, but this time he would have Destinn, making her American début as his partner, and Toscanini in the orchestra pit. The Maestro had sailed triumphantly into New York with Gatti-Casazza and Frances Alda, who had become romantically attached to each other in Milan.

The whole company tingled in anticipation of a glorious new régime which would surely restore the Metropolitan's prestige and check Hammerstein's run of success. 'Mr Gatti', however, soon aroused hostility by his attitude towards Andréas Dippel, who had expected to continue as co-manager but was now brusquely informed that he would either have to resume singing or quit when his year's contract ran out. It was quickly made clear to him that his function would be that of an interim caretaker and very much under the thumb of the new impresario.

This displeased several of the leading singers, who thought Dippel was being shabbily treated. Scotti, who had himself secretly nourished quite ludicrous hopes of succeeding Conried, soon organised a backstage revolution on Dippel's behalf and roped in Caruso. This was surprising, as he had the warmest regard for both Toscanini and 'Don Giulio', dating back to his own early days at La Scala. He had everything to gain from their advent and scarcely knew Dippel, who had long disapproved of Italian bias at the Metropolitan and now denigrated the new 'Padrone' with Wagnerian fury. But Caruso's heart was always too big for his head; when Scotti, Eames, Sembrich and Farrar all signed a round-robin letter to the board demanding 'justice' for Dippel, he placed his own signature at the top. Gatti-Casazza snapped his fingers at the signatories and sharply reminded them that they were engaged to sing and not concern themselves with administration. Despite strong support from J. P. Morgan and other friends, Dippel was firmly squeezed out.

Backed by Kahn, the 'Padrone' soon declared his policy. He had no patience with the old star system, which, in his view, had led to leading singers being overpaid at the expense of the orchestra and chorus. He demanded large sums to redecorate the ceiling of the opera house and had the seats upholstered in an attractive red, adding several more. He also built a roof stage for rehearsals, which would henceforth be directed with all of Toscanini's perfectionism. Recalling his own first experience at La Scala, Caruso went out of his way to please the peppery Maestro by singing full voice at every rehearsal, but this did not spare him from being as sharply admonished as any scene-shifter. The orchestra suffered even more. During one rehearsal Toscanini snapped at a musician, 'Only you are standing between me and the composer's intention.' A few days later, unable to endure his lashing tongue, the whole orchestra walked out, but they quickly returned in the hope of a little more tolerance from Toscanini. He drove them even harder until one of the instrumentalists shouted, 'Oh, nuts to you!' It was lost on the Maestro, whose English was still imperfect. 'It's no use apologising,' he yelled back.

Caruso and the others all sang better under his baton, plainly benefiting from the team-work he inspired in musicians and choruses once they became reconciled to his bullying. He also distilled unexpected magic from Mary Garden, who had quarrelled with Hammerstein and signed on for the Metropolitan. Her voice lacked vocal allure and she was a frigid Carmen compared with Geraldine Farrar, but her stage presence was supreme. Audiences doted on her beauty, her jewels and a décolletage which once made Chauncey Depew, the elegant president of the New York Central Railroad, drawl at a party, 'I wonder what keeps that gown up.' 'Two things,' she replied

175

instantly. 'Your age and my discretion.' But her sharp tongue, coupled with a haughty distaste for all her colleagues, made her less than popular, particularly with Geraldine Farrar, who wrote acidly in her memoirs: 'I am sure it will make no difference to Mary Garden when I say I do not care for her Carmen, but she had her own ways and a devoted public.' Before Farrar won her own huge and ecstatic following of 'Jerry-flappers', Mary Garden was already commanding such hysteria that, after hearing her sing Marguérite in Philadelphia, one of her young admirers shot herself dead when denied admission to the dressing-room.

Caruso paired successfully with her but disliked her arrogance towards the rank and file. Although he tried every new perfume on the market, he stubbornly refused to buy a bottle of 'Gardenia', which an enterprising perfumer had named in her honour. He avoided receptions at her mansion on Madison Avenue but, with his incurable hypochondria, took a professional interest in her fad for iodine, which she used to mix into a glass of hot milk before retiring. He soon gave up the practice.

He rarely took sides in the prima donna vendettas, but adored partridge-plump Destinn, who was so often the butt of Farrar's sarcasm that 'Mr Gatti' would have to be called in to keep the peace. They never performed together. Another of Farrar's victims was Frances Alda, who received only a very offhand 'Good morning' even after she had married Gatti-Casazza. Their marriage also exasperated Toscanini, who thought his friend was making a fool of himself and accurately prophesied disaster for two people so different in age and background. He showed his displeasure by declining to act as a witness at the ceremony, and went out of his way to humiliate the unfortunate soprano. During a dress rehearsal of *Otello* in which she played Desdemona he interrupted Act Four to warn her: 'There will not be one smile, not one bow. You will not lift your eyes. You will just get into bed like a good pure virgin.'

Caruso felt sorry for Alda, who had a very rough passage

indeed in that first season. Her Gilda inspired a critic to write that 'the young singer comes from the land of sheep and she bleated like one of them'. She became knock-kneed with terror and tearfully offered to withdraw from *Faust*. Caruso went to her dressing-room, took her hand in his and assured her gently, 'I've never sung a single performance in my life without being nervous, miserable and afraid.' He partly overcame her panic by giving her a broad wink during the village scene in Act One but, unfortunately, some unknown member of the company had taken a dislike to her. He (or, more likely, she) had nailed the spinning wheel in the next act so that Alda was quite unable to turn it during her aria. The Jewel Song was warmly applauded until she tried to make her exit through the cottage door. Someone had nailed it so fast that the opera stopped while a stage-hand attempted to release it from the inside. Caruso comforted her with a merry supper at Del Pezzo's.

Throughout that season he gallantly gave her precedence at every curtain call. Although forced to endure his prankishness in the years ahead, she would never forget his kindness when everyone else, led by Toscanini, seemed determined to make her pay dearly for Gatti-Casazza's favour. Of Caruso she later wrote: 'I never knew him to be other than generous and encouraging, as interested in another's success as his own. He would often suggest and then show me how a phrase should be sung, or a bit of business played.' When a bouquet was offered to him after a performance with Alda, he made the audience roar by handing it over with a look of mock disappointment. She extracted one of the roses and presented it to him with a charming curtsey.

To help repair the damage of her first shaky season he had the kindly thought of introducing her to his own record-buying public. Calvin Child was easily persuaded to let them record the sombre Miserere from *Il Trovatore*. On a sleety December day, feeling the need of fresh air, Caruso suggested walking to Carnegie Hall but quickly called a cab and directed the driver to take them to the nearest shoe-store. 'You must wear overshoes in this weather,' he said firmly. He took the rubbers from a salesman and insisted on personally helping Alda to try them on. While he fitted her with one rubber he beat time with the other as he sang one of Rodolfo's arias from *Bohème*. Soon he had all the customers and shop assistants joining in.

But these bursts of exuberance were infrequent in the months after Ada deserted him. He mooned aimlessly about the vast hotel suite and only roused himself to practise scales and do his breathing exercises. He now gave even more time to studying his parts and worked extra hard to satisfy Toscanini. In early December 1908 he sang seven times in a single week, apart from giving a performance of *Aïda* at Philadelphia's Academy of Music. Kahn and his co-directors presented Caruso with a diamond-studded cigarette case to show their appreciation. Audiences were as enthusiastic as ever, and only Toscanini's sharp ear noted that the voice had 'darkened' and lost something of its lyrical freshness and clarity. He also covered up at times with an over-emphasis new to him. At one rehearsal, when he lingered theatrically over a high C, a mannerism first developed to please German and Latin American audiences, Toscanini called out sharply in Italian, 'Tell me, Caruso, when you have *quite* finished.'

He had become noticeably unhappy when singing three of his favourite operas. *La Bohème* inevitably reminded him of his first appearances with Ada in Livorno; *Tosca* recalled their triumphs together during the Treviso engagement; and, above all, it was no longer possible to sing Canio's Lament without shedding real tears. Only will-power and his anxiety to launch the new management enabled him to give forty-four performances that season. But early in 1909 he missed several appearances through indisposition, seven in a single month. He became desperate enough, after failing to sing throughout March, to write sadly to his brother, 'I do not know if I will be able to perform for the rest of the season or quit and rest one entire year at home. Pray for me.'

He was suffering from voice strain, aggravated by excessive smoking and an inability to relax, but his psychological condition was a major factor. He grew even more gloomy and tense after Ada arrived without warning in New York and demanded a meeting to discuss 'several outstanding business matters'. He refused to receive her at the Knickerbocker, where reporters might easily pounce on a scandal story. With some reluctance he arranged to call at the York Hotel with his attorney, who stood helplessly while they screamed in bitter recrimination.

Ada at once demanded her jewellery, which he flatly refused to return, suspecting with good cause that it would end up in her lover's pocket. She asserted, none too convincingly, that Romati now meant nothing to her and claimed to be almost destitute and in need of support while attempting to resume her operatic career. Caruso finally handed over a substantial sum and agreed to send her a monthly cheque for 500 lire ($100) if she would sign a letter renouncing all claim to the jewels. She also undertook to stay away from America, where her presence, particularly if she tried to secure singing engagements, could be exploited to his disadvantage. It was easy to predict how Billy Guard and others might handle the abandoned 'wife' who had sacrificed her own career for an ungrateful and ruthlessly ambitious tenor. She signed the document some weeks later. Caruso imagined that the whole sad business was over, although until that meeting he had still hoped they might be miraculously reconciled.

That April he sailed for home in the *Mauretania* with the intention of having his throat examined, followed by a long rest. He had planned to travel with Tetrazzini, but she was suffering from gastritis and left some days later. She would have been a comfort. On board ship he tormented himself—and Martino—with morbid fears of losing his voice permanently. Reporters were told that he was suffering from 'slight atony of the vocal chords', but a surgeon in Milan, who had treated him years before for similar trouble, removed a small node in the throat. The surgeon was indiscreet enough to announce details to the press, who played it up and soon hinted that Caruso might never sing again. This so incensed him that he refused to pay the surgeon's exorbitant fee of 60,000 lire and had it halved after bitter litigation.

He recovered quickly at the villa and was overjoyed to discover that his singing voice had been fully restored to him. While convalescing he started an affair with Ada's sister, who pitied him and would always be grateful for his kindness during her first season at Covent Garden. But it was joyless escapism for a man still mourning a lost love and subconsciously seeking both vengeance and a healing balm for his pride. Rina Giachetti soon tired of this liaison, although they stayed on good terms and she continued to devote herself to his sickly elder son, Fofò. It seems that he was not only an unsatisfactory lover but far too jealous and overpossessive for a high-spirited young woman.

Over the next few years Caruso would become steadily more uninhibited in his sexual relationships, although he wisely concentrated on Europe after his Central Park misadventure. Like most other famous singers he had long been exposed to adoring women, but had indulged in only harmless flirtations during his time with Ada. Now his wounded ego stimulated him to flaunt his conquests and exhibit symptoms of acute satyriasis. When he was not bedding his young ladies—they were all far more youthful than Ada, no doubt to proclaim his virility—he would conduct romantic sieges with bouquets, wildly extravagant gifts and tender messages worthy of some lovesick hero in a minor comic opera.

His chronically 'broken heart' gave Ledner and his other managers many difficult moments with husbands and fathers during the Continental tours. His reputation for womanising resulted in an amusing misunderstanding with Lotte Lehmann, whose superb lyrical voice in Strauss and Wagnerian roles had soon made her a star of the Vienna Opera. In October 1909 she shared a double bill with him at the Stadt Theatre in Hamburg, where her performance in Gluck's *Orfeo* preceded *I Pagliacci*. Already dressed to sing Canio, he stood in the wings for her finale as Eurydice. When the curtain fell to a storm of applause he grasped her hands impulsively and exclaimed, '*Ah, brava, brava! Che bene magnifica voce. Una voce italiana!*' He then asked her to dine with him and other members of the company after the show. In her memoirs she has recalled the overwhelming effect of his Canio: 'I choked for breath when he tore off the clown's cap with a wild gesture, wiped the paint from his face and sang, "Non sono piu Pagliaccio". Tears ran down his face, and at the end of the performance he was exhausted to the point of collapse.'

At dinner that night he insisted on her sitting next to him and paid her absurd compliments in pidgin French, as he could speak no German and her Italian was restricted to the operas she had learned by heart. He invited her to play Micaëla in *Carmen,* but she had never attempted it and had to refuse. After his own excellent performance as Don José he invited her to join him for supper in his suite the following evening. She had visions of seduction and hastily wrote him a note pleading sudden indisposition. She was on her way to deliver it at his hotel when a chance meeting with a fellow singer confirmed that Caruso was not planning to sup privately with her but had asked at least two dozen other guests to celebrate the end of his Hamburg season. She at once tore up the letter and hurried off to her hairdresser.

At supper he was flanked by two bosomy local beauties and gave Lehmann only a formal smile across the table. However, she screwed up the courage to send over one of his picture postcards and begged him to autograph it. Instead he did a self-caricature on the back of a menu and handed it to her with a deep bow. Next morning she was delighted to receive by special messenger one of his best studio portraits inscribed, 'A Mademoiselle Lotte Lehmann, la charmante et jolie Eurydice, très sincèrement—Enrico Caruso.'

She was far less experienced than the future Mrs Flo Ziegfeld, Billie Burke, one of the many women with whom Caruso professed to be madly in love at this time. He had often ogled her across the dining-room of the Hotel Knickerbocker, where she used to stay during her musical comedy runs in New York, but they did not meet until early in 1910. He was then singing *Aïda* and *Bohème* at the new Boston Opera House while she happened to be starring in a French farce at a neighbouring theatre.

On his non singing nights he would take a box to gaze longingly on the gay and lovely redhead to whom he sent enormous bouquets of American Beauty roses with notes announcing his helpless adoration. After persuading a mutual friend to arrange a luncheon with her, he called again and again at the Hotel Touraine and soon proposed marriage. He would drop on one knee to vow undying passion, usually ending up with a tender aria. It always brought a round of applause from the hotel residents crowding the corridor outside, but only a light peck from the very practical Miss Burke, who declined to take him seriously. They went for walks or drives together and often enjoyed after-theatre suppers, at which he customarily played host to a crowd of friends and fellow members of the Metropolitan Company. Their presence did not inhibit him from declaring his love between mammoth helpings of spaghetti.

This romance collapsed as soon as engagements separated them. Back in New York he recovered almost overnight from his failure to capture Miss Burke and joined in a round of welcoming parties for Engelbert Humperdinck, who had arrived for the première of his musical fairy-tale, *Königskinder*. He had been mobbed at the pier by a scrum of journalists and photographers. They seemed friendly enough, except for one reporter whose face was buried by a vast hat under which a black beard wagged fiercely. Notebook in hand, he shot a gibberish of angry-sounding questions. The composer took him for some crazy anti-German anarchist and edged away nervously until 'the reporter' pulled off his hat and false beard and kissed him on both cheeks.

Soon afterwards Caruso received a letter at the Knickerbocker, allegedly from the notorious Black Hand Gang of Sicilian thugs based in New York. They threatened him with death unless he delivered $15,000 in bank-notes to an address in Brooklyn. He thought it a hoax until he recalled how Ada had once babbled hysterically about a secret society plot to murder him. At the time he had pooh-poohed the story as an attempt to justify her liaison with Romati, but now he decided to call in the police. They at once gave him an armed body-guard and also had men watching from the wings at the Metropolitan while he was on stage. A trap was quickly set. Martino was sent off with a dummy package, which he left as instructed on the steps outside a house. Detectives waited until three men approached for the pick-up. One of them made off, but his companions, both Italians, were arrested and sentenced to long terms in Sing Sing and deportation. For some reason a campaign started to have them pardoned and Caruso, even more inexplicably, headed the list of signatories.

Admiring biographers have often cited this as evidence of his magnanimity, but it may equally be argued that he was anxious to placate his enemies and forestall other attacks from the same quarter. He lived for a while in terror of reprisals. Some months later, while singing Rodolfo in Munich, he was accidentally knocked out by a dislodged piece of scenery. He convinced himself that a Black Hand agent was responsible and for the rest of that season refused to go on in *Tosca* until every rifle in the firing squad scene had been carefully examined for live bullets.

PART FOUR

'Vesti la Giubba'

Chapter Fifteen

Caruso's relationships with women, notably in the years following Ada's departure, were either grossly undignified or revealed a callousness alien to his nature. By contrast, his business ethics remained irreproachable. The Metropolitan management would always be indebted to him for his loyalty when its finances were stretched and the rivalry with Hammerstein had reached a climax of bitterness.

They had weathered a $200,000 deficit in Gatti-Casazza's first season when his redecoration schemes and other innovations bit deeply into the bank account. Chaliapin's disastrous début and such prestige 'novelties' as importing Gustav Mahler as guest conductor had been costly, but far less crippling to the box-office than Caruso's throat troubles. He made only twenty-eight appearances during the 1909 season.

The Manhattan was in even worse shape. Mary Garden and Bonci had gone over to the enemy, and Melba could not be tempted back. Another blow was the resignation of their star conductor, Campanini, who had long complained of too little time to rehearse his musicians while trying to compete with Toscanini's two full orchestras. He abandoned his $1000 a week and departed in disgust for his native land.

Hammerstein still had Tetrazzini, Renaud and McCormack under contract but without such emphatic attractions as Geraldine Farrar and Caruso. The Opera War had become suicidal for both sides. New York audiences were enthusiastic but not numerous enough to support two major opera houses. Time was running out, particularly for Hammerstein, who needed some master stroke to stave off bankruptcy.

He had already made tentative but unfruitful approaches to Farrar, who had shrewdly weighed the odds and decided in favour of the Metropolitan, no doubt aware that her corps of 'Jerry-flappers' might not transfer their affections to the

Manhattan without Caruso as her partner and Toscanini in the pit. Hammerstein now took the desperate gamble of trying to seduce Caruso with a sky-high offer. He had visions of pairing him triumphantly with Tetrazzini and perhaps cracking the Diamond Horseshoe's allegiance, on which the Metropolitan relied so heavily for both prestige and profit.

William J. Guard suddenly stopped implying that Caruso had lost his voice. Instead he spread stories of internal rivalries at the Metropolitan, hinting brazenly that Caruso had quarrelled with Gatti-Casazza and Toscanini and was ready to sign with Oscar Hammerstein for a figure far beyond that ever paid by any opera house. After Caruso had politely rejected several overtures, including one or two half-hearted pleas from Tetrazzini, Hammerstein deputed his son, Arthur, to win him over at all costs. He made many attempts to corner him at the Knickerbocker, but Caruso took evasive action. Young Hammerstein finally shadowed him to the Café Martin, where he happened for once to be dining by himself. He sat down at Caruso's table and flourished an offer of $5000 a performance for a season of twenty weeks, intimating that he might sing as often as three times a week if he wished. The Manhattan would willingly deposit a large sum in escrow. Caruso shook his head and explained blandly that he had a superstition about losing his voice if ever he deserted the Metropolitan. This did not inhibit Guard from informing reporters that contracts were already drafted and about to be exchanged.

As the Metropolitan was still paying Caruso only $2000 a performance, Gatti-Casazza became understandably alarmed. He consulted with Otto Kahn, who authorised him to draw up a new contract with the figure of $4000 pencilled in. 'Don Giulio' then summoned Caruso to his office and announced that the Metropolitan might even be driven to matching Hammerstein's offer. He warned him mournfully, however, that this would mean using second-class singers in the minor parts and inferior or smaller choruses. Underpaid mediocre conductors might also have to be engaged when Toscanini was not available.

Caruso chuckled and lit a fresh cigarette. 'Two thousand dollars is enough for any singer,' he said quietly. 'But you will make me very happy by adding a cabin de luxe for my voyages between Italy and America instead of the single first-class cabin.' Gatti-Casazza embraced him with tears streaming down his cheeks. He then confided his plan to restore the Metropolitan's fortunes by sending a company, headed by Caruso, to sing in Europe for the first time.

Caruso was equally ungrasping in his dealings with Calvin G. Child. Some months after setting the Metropolitan's mind at rest, he had been approached by a rival gramophone company that offered him an immense sum, plus a higher royalty than Victor was paying him, to record exclusively for them. According to Pierre Key, he handed Child this draft agreement and authorised him to turn it down on his behalf. As his own contract with Victor would shortly be coming up for renewal, he now instructed him to draw up a new one but on the current royalty terms. 'Make it out for the rest of my life,' he added with a laugh. Child stammered his thanks and pointed out that, legally, it would have to be for a fixed term. 'Okay,' chuckled the singer, 'then I shall bind myself to you for twenty-five years, although you will have to pay me a very big advance, naturally.' Child opened his cheque-book and looked enquiringly across the desk.

'Twenty-five thousand dollars,' Caruso declared solemnly. He then reached out to grasp Child's wrist. 'No, my friend, let us forget the advance. It was my little joke.'

He never abused his status as the Victor Talking Machine Company's leading star and took infinite pains to perfect his records, rejecting wax after wax before deciding on 'the master'. While a recording was being played back to him he would listen tensely for a sour note and frequently demand a remake, although only one musicianly ear in ten thousand could have detected any fault. He was fascinated by technical developments and often accompanied Child to the New Jersey factory to follow every stage in the processing. Any new experiment found him eager to collaborate. He developed an early enthusiasm for wireless telegraphy and was exhilarated by his friend Marconi's Nobel Prize for physics. Soon afterwards, on the night of 3 January 1910, he made his own niche in radio history when part of *I Pagliacci* was transmitted by Lee de Forest from the Metropolitan stage to Victor's headquarters in Camden, New Jersey, with a private link to Gatti-Casazza's office, where several friends and employees had gathered. The songs were also picked up by hams in Connecticut and even in the wireless cabin of the steamer *Avon* at sea.

His driving urge for perfection demanded much patience from musicians, who willingly gave up weekends or worked at short notice to fit into his crowded schedules. He usually sang in an open shirt but did not go to extremes like Battistini, who progressively shed jacket, waistcoat, collar, and even his shirt, before finally stepping up to the funnel. Caruso showed consideration for the musicians and engineers and used to hand out appreciative little souvenirs like gold medallions or autographed caricatures. He rarely failed to notice when some regular member of the orchestra was away sick. He would send flowers or fruit to his home or the hospital, often enclosing a helpful cheque if the man had to be off work for any length of time. According to Pierre Key, he once plucked a gold and enamel pin from his cravat and presented it to the player of a difficult trumpet obligato. 'You deserve a little something,' he said gratefully. 'I thought you would surely crack before the end.'

Caruso's generosity became almost legendary, but he banked his recording fees carefully and, unlike Chaliapin, never regarded the Victrola as a horn of plenty endlessly dispensing gold coins. To celebrate his first HMV cheque for £1000, the basso gave a party at the Savoy Hotel in London. It cost him £950, and he distributed the odd fifty in tips among the waiters.

Hammerstein's failure to secure Caruso almost signalled the end for the Manhattan. He might have carried on for a time, but by now the Metropolitan could not afford to continue the battle for patrons. Early in 1910, Otto Kahn agreed to buy him out for $1.2 million, taking over his scores, costumes, scenery and the American rights in a number of operas. Hammerstein also gave up the Philadelphia Opera House and undertook not to produce opera in New York for at least ten years. The Metropolitan simultaneously acquired the services of Billy Guard, who would serve them with brilliant flair for many a year. Another valuable bonus was the unexpired contracts of John McCormack and Tetrazzini.

The genial Irishman's smooth and exquisitely pure voice immediately enchanted Metropolitan audiences, but he was altogether happier on the concert platform and in recording studios, where he had no need to act or concern himself with costumes and make-up. He used to suffer painfully from stage-fright and often recalled Caruso's kindness to him before his début as a Metropolitan guest artist in *Butterfly*. He had been gloomily making up in his dressing-room when Caruso, wearing full evening dress with decorations, poked his head round the door. He had stopped by on his way to some banquet.

'Rico,' exclaimed McCormack in surprise. 'What on earth are you doing here on your night off?'

'D'you think I could let you go on without wishing you well?'

The Irish tenor's gaiety, above all his passionate love of wine and spaghetti, made him a favourite with Scotti and the others whom he invariably saw under the table. Although some of his recorded ballads outsold even Caruso's arias, no hint of jealousy ever disturbed their friendship. One of Caruso's favourite anecdotes concerned an incident in Chicago. He was taking a short walk near his hotel when a complete stranger stopped him to confide gloomily, 'I've paid twenty bucks for your concert tonight and you can only make it worthwhile by singing one of my favourites as an encore.'

'Which one?'

'Mother Machree.'

For a special treat McCormack would take his high-spirited

children to hear Caruso sing at matinées. They sat in the front row of the stalls, where he could pull funny faces and wink at them even in the most serious parts of an opera. Caruso always tried to arrange to sail across the Atlantic with the McCormacks and loved playing deck games with the youngsters. On one voyage he persuaded Kreisler and, more incredibly, Toscanini to do conjuring tricks with coins while he tried some ventriloquism and drew caricatures for their albums. Their mother had briefed them to show proper respect for a man of world fame, but young Cyril accosted him one day on the promenade deck and piped up: 'Are you really the greatest Italian singer in the world?'

'That's right, I think,' he answered gravely.

'Well, my daddy's the greatest Irish singer.'

Not long afterwards the singers happened to bump into each other in the lobby of the Copley Plaza in Boston.

'And how is the greatest tenor in the world this morning?' boomed McCormack in his cheerful brogue.

'And since when, Mac, did you become a baritone?' quipped his friend as they walked off arm in arm for a reunion glass of champagne.

They were also linked by warm affection for Tetrazzini, who always treated Caruso's suite at the Knickerbocker as her second home in New York. She would startle visitors by suddenly rolling back and forth on the floor of his drawing-room to do her reducing exercises. Just before a performance of *La Traviata* she rushed into the apartment and sobbed hysterically that her voice had gone. Caruso steered her into the bathroom, where she flung off her chinchilla coat and sat obediently on the edge of the bath while he sprayed her tonsils with his own compound of salt water, glycerine and Dobell solution. It worked the usual magic.

Metropolitan audiences delighted in her trills and bubbling personality. For her farewell appearance as Gilda in 1912, with Caruso singing the Duke, hundreds stormed the doors after the 'house full' notices went up. Mounted police had to be called in to stop a riot. Soon afterwards he persuaded her to record with him in the *Lucia* Sextet and the Quartet from *Rigoletto* before leaving on her concert tour. She departed from Grand Central like an ermine-trimmed pigeon, pecking the cheeks of a dozen admirers but with a tearful hug and kiss for Caruso, who admonished her sternly to behave and look after her money.

It was wasted advice and he knew it. Her manager had tried for years to stop her from handing out cash and presents to plausible spongers. She once patted him on the cheek and gurgled, 'But don't you see that it makes me *happy*!' She also had a weakness for giving indiscreet interviews and mortally offended her brother-in-law, Campanini, now generalissimo at the Chicago Opera House, by telling journalists that he was 'merely a conductor'. He revenged himself soon afterwards when she sang Gilda for him and broke on a high note in the cadenza, 'Caro nome'. Campanini promptly signalled for a crashing chord from the orchestra. She never spoke to him or her sister again and refused to sing in Chicago during his régime.

Caruso tried to defend Tetrazzini from scandalous press gossip about her young gigolos, but would lecture her severely on the sanctity of contracts. One impresario whose season she wrecked by departing suddenly with some new lover had a squad of process-servers waiting for her at the gangplank of the *Mauretania*, in which she had booked passage for Europe. Tetrazzini dressed her maid up in chinchilla, sent her ahead by hired limousine, and sneaked unnoticed into steerage, wearing a shabby black coat and head-scarf. Caruso was in on the plot but disapproved. They next met some months later at the Savoy in London, where she invited him to share the cake she had baked specially for a tax-collector. The official departed, slightly dazed, with a kiss, a magnum of Bollinger and a bundle of one-pound notes, neatly tied with red ribbon, 'on account'.

Caruso could sympathise with her over British taxation. For convenience during his London engagements he had sometimes used a *pied-à-terre* at Clarendon Court in Maida Vale, where his son, Mimmi, stayed with his governess, Louise Saer. The tax inspectors thought this constituted British domicile and assessed him accordingly. In a fury of protest he stripped the house of all its furnishings and shipped them at considerable expense to the Villa Bellosguardo. He then transferred his son and Miss Saer to a house in Cricklewood owned by her family. Thereafter he always stayed at the Savoy.

His anger was prompted by 'principle' rather than tax evasion. He never had a dispute with the American tax authorities and was equally scrupulous in promptly settling his accounts with tradesmen and hoteliers, who sometimes took advantage of him. Immediately on placing a large order with a New York department store he sent off his cheque and was thoroughly put out when the goods fell below specification. 'Who pays before is always badly served,' he lamented afterwards.

Impudent attempts were constantly made to extract cash from Caruso, but he lost no sleep over a writ served on him in 1909 during his British concert tour. The plaintiff was a Mr J. W. Thorn of Argyle Street, Glasgow, described as 'a poetic author and medicated lozenge manufacturer', who claimed to have submitted four of his songs, which the tenor had failed to acknowledge or return. The case was thrown out.

A rich world celebrity like Caruso was an inviting target for begging letters ingeniously pitched to touch his heart. After parting with a large sum to some worthless stranger, he pleaded later in self-defence, 'How can I know which deserve and which not?' He found it almost impossible to refuse any appeal from a compatriot. While changing into his day clothes at the Metropolitan he nonchalantly scooped up a thick roll of bank-notes from his dressing-table. He noticed that his wigmaker was watching him. He peeled off a $500 bill. 'You like?' he asked with a laugh. 'How would you spend him?' 'I would send my wife back to Italy to see her mother, who is dying,' muttered the old man. Caruso at once flipped him the note. 'Take it for your wife.'

He was out driving one day in Washington when his car stopped at a crossing. He was recognised by an elderly Italian street-cleaner, who tossed away his brush and jumped on to the running-board. 'Caro Caruso!' he yelled exultantly. The tenor cracked some joke in Neapolitan slang and deftly slipped a wad of notes into the man's overalls as they embraced.

He was impulsive but would never lose his early habit of noting every item of expenditure, however small. He used to record waiters' tips and even minor card losses to Scotti or the restaurateur, Pane, with whom he often settled down after hours to play impassioned *bazzica* for fifty-cent stakes. Gambling had no appeal for him. He avoided the stock market and invested only in government bonds or blue-chip securities. Even when a racehorse was named in his honour he could not be tempted to back him for more than $10. It was just as well. This Caruso became a bookmaker's dream until even the tenor's army of admirers tired of losing their money on his lethargic namesake. A happier venture was Spaghetti Caruso, garnished with chicken livers, which an enterprising countryman marketed with considerable success, although—unlike Jean de Reszke—the singer declined to accept lucrative offers to sponsor brands of cigarettes.

He hoarded vouchers for share deals and bond certificates and noted precise details on all cheque stubs. He also kept tabs on box-office receipts to reassure himself of his continuing drawing power. This became highly personal during the Metropolitan Company's first foreign visit to Paris, in May 1910. Otto Kahn had agreed to underwrite the French impresario for fifty per cent of his outlay, but advance bookings at the Châtelet Theatre indicated clearly that only Caruso performances had any solid support. Patrons soon had to buy an additional ticket for some non-Caruso opera to ensure hearing him. This box-office blackmail angered the public but, fortunately for the company, Caruso had a delirious reception for his Canio, Radamès and des Grieux. After *Manon Lescaut* Réjane wrote to him: 'It is a real joy, and although I know you slightly, I would like to grasp your hand and thank you for that unforgettable evening.'

But even with Destinn, Alda, Scotti and Amato in the troupe, and Toscanini conducting, receipts slumped by half without Caruso on the stage. Schedules had to be frantically adjusted until he was singing half a dozen times in eight days. After an extra charity performance at the Trocadéro, for which he generously donated his 10,000-franc fee, he took the whole company out to supper in the Bois de Boulogne. He squatted in a side seat of the hired limousine which was so jammed that a door burst open and shot him into the road. He crawled back on all fours and chortled, 'See how Caruso bites the dust!'

That five-week engagement had been a strain and he was hoping to take his ease at Signa before a two-month tour of Germany in the autumn. This was to be followed almost immediately by his next Metropolitan season, during which he would sing in a new Puccini opera based on David Belasco's Broadway hit *The Girl of the Golden West*. The world première was scheduled for New York, but Tosti, always the courtier, had persuaded the composer to dedicate his work to Queen Alexandra as a conciliatory gesture to British admirers.

Caruso liked the score and for a while strutted about his music-room at the Villa Bellosguardo revelling in the un-accustomed role of Dick Johnson, the dashing bandit. How-ever, he soon began complaining of a sore throat and shut him-self away from his house-guests, emerging only for meals. He rarely walked in the gardens, which reminded him too pain-fully of serene hours with his Ada. Martino and a new assistant valet, Mario, were kept busy preparing a variety of inhalations and gargles. Mario, a good-looking young man with a mop of dark hair, was solemn in manner but a patient and sympathetic listener. He never became ruffled when Caruso's neuralgic headaches led to ill-tempered outbursts. In an astonishingly short time he had learned the elements of massage from Martino, whose fingers had stiffened with advancing years. He was also finding it difficult to support the singer's weight when his back or shoulder needed manipulation. There was surprisingly little friction between the valets, thanks to Mario's quiet modesty and devotion. He had been a porter at Milan's main railway station, where Caruso first noticed his courtesy and a most efficient way of stacking and carrying bags. He engaged him on the spot, an impulse he had no cause to regret for the rest of his life, particularly when Martino grew too old for his duties and took over as major-domo at Signa.

During those hot fretful weeks they needed considerable patience. Caruso had become more restless and seemed unusually nervous about his coming German tour. He dashed back and forth between Signa and Milan, seeing doctors or playing lavish host in the Galleria restaurants, which swarmed with admirers and autograph-hunters. He visited antique shops in search of rare pieces for his villa and also spent freely on new suits, hats, shirts and boots, although his wardrobes at Signa and the Hotel Knickerbocker were already bulging with unworn clothes.

In a department store he was attracted to a young, soft-skinned salesgirl, Elisa Ganelli, whose classic oval face and full red lips recalled Ada. He soon invited her to spend a few days at the Villa Bellosguardo and suggested that she might take a position as housekeeper or help look after his son, Fofò, while Rina Giachetti was away on her singing engagements. She thanked him demurely but refused, and this naturally fanned his desire. From Germany he wrote her several ardent letters professing his love. To his surprise and delight, she suddenly sent off a cable: 'I am ready to follow you. Come and fetch me.' He promptly mailed a large sum and implored her to join him in Berlin. She arrived there with her father in October 1910.

He booked them into a suite near his own at the Hotel Bristol. Signor Ganelli looked ill at ease in his rusty Sunday best but doggedly played chaperone while Caruso courted his daughter. She was soon introduced as his fiancée to his manager and friends. Within a very short time the tinselly idyll had dissolved into sawdust. Elisa was charming, if a little dazed by the hotel's rococo splendours and the confusing backstage chatter at the opera, but Caruso had taken a dislike to his prospective father-in-law, who badgered him to name the wedding date and kept dropping very broad hints about his dire poverty.

Caruso was not sorry to put them on a train for Milan. Before sailing back to America for his eighth season, he sent Signorina Ganelli a cable to announce that their 'private engagement' was at an end ('I cannot be married with anybody') and asked for his letters to be returned. For several months she continued to write passionately, but he did not reply and soon put her out of his mind.

New Yorkers welcomed him like an old friend and slapped his back enthusiastically whenever he appeared in the streets. At his usual corner table in the Knickerbocker dining-room he presided boisterously over his entourage of fellow singers, often joined by the Gatti-Casazzas, Toscanini, Rachmaninov and Fritz Kreisler. The violinist had to submit to much good-natured badinage over his remarkable resemblance to Puccini and sometimes amused himself by playfully signing autographs in his name. But Puccini looked a very different man when he arrived in late November with his son and Tito Ricordi for rehearsals of *La Fanciulla del West*. His tanned cheeks had hollowed and now showed deep furrows. He appeared to have aged by years since Caruso's last meeting with him in London, when they had dined so merrily with Tosti at Pagani's. His old vigorous handshake was now surprisingly uncertain and flabby.

Caruso was shocked by the change in his appearance. Like everyone else he had been horrified by a domestic scandal which had rocked Italy, but from all accounts Puccini had regained his peace of mind while working on the new opera ('the best I have written', he assured Sybil Seligman). He was now said to be living in comparative harmony with his wife, although he had refused to let her accompany him to New York. 'You have deprived me of a great satisfaction, that of participating in your triumph,' she wrote bitterly from Italy. 'Now you are a great man, and compared to you I am nothing but a pygmy.' His coolness was excusable enough towards a woman whose jealousy had driven him to the very edge of suicide.

In the autumn of 1908 her suspicions had fastened on Doria,

a pretty young servant, whom she falsely accused of sleeping with her husband. After driving her out of the house at Torre del Lago, she continued to persecute her victim. The girl finally broke down and poisoned herself. Her parents had the body exhumed to prove her virginity and then prosecuted Elvira for defamation. Puccini had bought them off with a large sum of money to save his wife from going to prison. Every year on the anniversary of the girl's death he placed a wreath on her tomb and could never rid himself of a sense of guilt for having inadvertently brought about the tragedy by a light-hearted flirtation that had meant nothing to him.*

Puccini's spirits improved in New York, thanks largely to Caruso, who took him for drives and gave several convivial supper-parties in his honour. He mellowed perceptibly during rehearsals of *La Fanciulla*, which he supervised with Belasco, looking episcopal as usual with his snow-white forelock and high clerical collar. Both were confident of a box-office triumph. Prices had been doubled for the première, and the scalpers were reaping a record crop of up to thirty times the face value of tickets. Caruso, an improbable cowboy with his unathletic stomach bulging over his belt, lapsed into Italianisms like 'Eep, eep, urra', but he sang with verve, supported by his fellow Neapolitan, Amato, as Sheriff Rance. The company took fifty-two curtain calls, with Caruso and Toscanini singled out for the loudest applause.

'Mr Gatti' added a touch of ballyhoo by bringing the composer on stage and placing on his head a silver crown beribboned with the national colours of Italy and the United States. That night Puccini reported joyfully to Elvira: 'Caruso is magnificent in the part. Destinn not bad but she needs more energy.' The public failed, however, to take this opera to their hearts, although it always played to full houses whenever Caruso's name headed the playbills in occasional seasons.

Ten nights after the opening the company repeated *La Fanciulla* in Philadelphia, Caruso then returning to New York for

* Doria is generally considered to have been the model for the doomed slave-girl, Liù, in Puccini's moving last opera, *Turandot*.

his Christmas shopping. It was, as always, a mammoth spree with $100 bills scattered like confetti at Tiffany's and almost every store on Fifth Avenue. He bought cigarette-cases, cuff-links, vanity boxes and bottles of perfume by the dozen. For close personal friends like Scotti, 'Don Giulio' and Toscanini he went more quietly in search of tasteful bric-à-brac or rare prints, often commissioning antique dealers to hunt down some special piece which might look well in their rooms. On Christmas Day he ritually took the centre of the Metropolitan stage and handed out gold coins from a huge pouch to the stage-hands and chorus. Each presentation was made with some personal quip and a warm handshake. The ceremony would later be repeated at the Knickerbocker, where chefs, waiters, doormen and cleaners were all remembered.

Caruso had seemed gay enough throughout the holiday, although Scotti, more observant than the others, thought he looked unusually flushed. But he was in high spirits when the train pulled out of Grand Central for Chicago in mid-January 1911. The familiar crowd of admirers and reporters surrounded him, while Mario led a squad of porters carrying the trunks of clothes, sedatives, pillows and monogrammed linen sheets. For once Caruso declined the Maine lobster Newburg and water-melon relish at dinner and complained of feeling off colour.

However, he appeared to have recovered and gave rousing performances of *I Pagliacci* and *La Fanciulla* at the Chicago Auditorium before the company returned to New York with a stop-over in Cleveland. Foolishly, perhaps, as he was un-doubtedly suffering from a slight cold, he insisted on keeping his promise to sing for Mrs Cornelius Vanderbilt at a musicale, quickly followed by another at the Waldorf-Astoria. Mean-time he was rehearsing for Baron Franchetti's unmemorable *Germania*, which opened on 1 February and was repeated five nights later. The following morning Billy Guard announced that Caruso was confined to his bed from the after-effects of influenza. Nobody took this too seriously until he sailed for Europe without warning at the end of the month. He would not sing again before November.

Reporters on both sides of the Atlantic were soon announcing that grave throat trouble had caused him to break off so unexpectedly in mid-season. His visit to a London laryngologist raised another crop of speculation. By now it was being hinted openly that over singing had caused irreparable damage to his vocal chords. He issued angry denials, but the wires hummed with the news that a surgeon in Milan had removed a node and prescribed complete rest.

This became difficult. He would have liked to scotch reports of his imminent retirement by giving a concert or two in England with perhaps a short tour of Germany, but his doctors advised strongly against taking the risk. His stepmother and his ailing sister, Assunta, came to join him at the Villa Bellosguardo, where he spent a few restless weeks before leaving suddenly for London to seek the congenial society of Tosti, Chaliapin and other soul-mates.

During that exceptionally hot summer, London's hostesses staged an almost unbroken series of lavish balls and receptions. Caruso had difficulty in securing his old river suite at the Savoy, already jammed with princes and American millionaires arriving in the capital for the Coronation of King George V. He was asked to numerous dinner-parties, but refused them all, nervous perhaps of being asked to sing afterwards. After much hesitation he attended a fancy-dress ball in the hotel as the guest of a titled box-holder at Covent Garden, one of his fervent admirers. He wore a heavy Moorish costume which made him so uncomfortable that he offered up a silent prayer of thanks to the management for thoughtfully spraying iced cylinders of ozone over the dancers.

He paid a sentimental visit to Covent Garden, which had opened its brilliant Coronation season with Nijinsky and Karsavina twinkling across the new £70,000 oak stage floor. He was touched by an invitation from the management to return whenever he desired. Soon he began to recover his old high spirits. One night diners at the Hotel Cecil were startled by a child's agonized cry of distress. It was Caruso practising a little ventriloquism.

While staying in Paris he received a most unpleasant visit from Elisa Ganelli and her mother, who demanded marriage or alternatively a sum to salvage the family honour. He practically showed them the door, but finally parted with a wad of notes on the understanding that his letters would be returned. Instead a lawyer quickly wrote from Milan claiming $50,000 as compensation.

He dismissed it as an impudent bluff until a writ was filed against him in July 1911. Some months later he had to appear in Milan and listen with burning cheeks while his high-flown letters were read out in open court. The case was clearly doomed under Italian law, which did not recognise breach of promise as a cause of action. The plaintiff obtained no damages, but the bench showed its sympathy by severely censuring the singer. 'There is no doubt whatsoever,' thundered the presiding judge, 'that Caruso promised Signorina Ganelli to make her his lawful wife and not merely to take her as governess or maid, as he would make believe, and there is no just motive for failing to fulfil his promise. It remains a morally deplorable act on Caruso's part that with the outlook of an imperishable love and a life abounding in splendour and ease he should have inveigled an inexperienced, ingenuous, upright girl, afterwards to abandon her without any reason to her fate. But whereas it is clear that, notwithstanding his blandishments and gushing letters, she succeeded in maintaining her unique source of wealth—the honour of a spotless life—intact, she cannot claim reparation for any damage.'

The proceedings started such an outburst of moral indignation against Caruso that Ada Giachetti was tempted to air her own grievances in an article published in the *Corriere della Sera*. She had lost her looks, her jewels and her lover, and was also finding it difficult to secure operatic engagements. Caruso was held responsible for all her misfortunes. Her complaint against 'the shameless tenor', as she described him, was threefold; firstly, she reaffirmed her own innocence and claimed to have been victimised by his insane jealousy; secondly, she charged him with the theft of jewellery worth £12,000; and, finally, he was accused of bribing a landlady in Milan to intercept a letter offering her an engagement to sing in New York. This she had never received, implying that Caruso had vindictively arranged for it to be destroyed.

The article excited popular sympathy in Ada's favour. Scenting cash, Romati and others then added their own quota of slander until Caruso was forced to bring an action against Ada and her former lover to clear himself. 'I am only here to defend myself, not to accuse anybody,' he told the court, which came down overwhelmingly in his favour, mainly because he had insisted on going into the witness-box and submitted to an hour's cross-examination while Ada avoided defending her accusations in person and prudently remained in Buenos Aires. She was found guilty *in absentia* and sentenced to a year's imprisonment and a fine of 1000 lire, the court refusing her the benefit of the law applicable to first offenders. Romati was condemned to a year and fifteen days' imprisonment for bribing a witness.

The volatile Italian public quickly took Caruso back to its heart. On a visit to Naples he was given almost a hero's welcome as he drove along the Toledo in an open *carrozza*, reaching out to shake dozens of hands among the cheering crowd. His carriage was soon joined by several others as he drove out to Posilipo for lunch. Characteristically he invited all his admirers to eat and drink with him, afterwards entertaining them and the entire restaurant staff to a ballad recital for which any Diamond Horseshoe matron would gladly have hocked her tiara.

The slander action had finally silenced Ada, without, however, giving Caruso much cause for self-congratulation. His 'confiscation' of her jewels could be excused by the bitterness of betrayal, but it had an unpleasant aroma of petty vengeance. He was less than convincing in his denials concerning Ada's draft agreement to sing in America. It had certainly been delivered at her *pensione* in Milan, and neither Caruso nor the landlady seemed altogether straightforward when cross-examined over its mysterious disappearance. His German manager, Emil Ledner, later disclosed that Caruso was always evasive over this matter and irritably discouraged further questions.

However, he acted with generosity in continuing his regular allowance to Ada, who might otherwise have starved between her modest engagements in South America. He would never mention her name, but tears filled his eyes whenever he handed his secretary the usual monthly cheque 'for the mother of my sons'.

Chapter Sixteen

Caruso was already past his vocal best by the time he reached the apogee of his fame and popularity. Two major factors account for this paradox. Firstly, the enormous sale of his records, backed by a dynamic personal appeal, made him such a cult figure that his name alone would automatically fill any opera house or concert hall and command dizzy fees. Secondly, although he would never recapture the lyrical purity of his first golden years at the Metropolitan and Covent Garden, he had gained in technical artistry. He would continue to sing with an incomparable intensity of feeling yet still leave an almost miraculous impression of having much more volume in reserve.

Nevertheless his nervous collapse after Ada's departure undoubtedly contributed to a change of timbre and early signs of 'darkening'. He would always retain his beauty of tone and warmth in the favourite arias, but over-use of his voice had combined with the onset of throat trouble to destroy an unflawed high pianissimo. In the immediate prewar years it was already being noted that his singing was most persuasive when he used less force to produce notes which had once cascaded so effortlessly.

During the last decade of his career it was apparent to all but idolaters that fairly average performances of even *I Pagliacci* and *La Bohème* were redeemed only by his spontaneity and fervour in the solos. Certain faults had developed which became chronic. He would tend to strain for more passion and habitually overdid 'the Caruso sob', often resorting to exaggerated sighing and groaning to register pathos, particularly for the benefit of his concert audiences. Nor could he always resist making little asides to his friends in the front stalls or even winking up at the gallery when he was not singing. An outraged dowager in the Diamond Horseshore was once almost persuaded to swear that he had spat at a soprano for going off key. No doubt, however, her glasses must have focused on him while he was seeking a quick gargle. To clear his throat of mucus he would have two small phials of salt water inserted in the pockets of all his costumes before going on stage.

Despite signs of hardening, notably in the 'heroic' roles, audiences continued to welcome every performance with hysterical approval. In the remaining years of his career no rival tenor approached within earshot, Beniamino Gigli only emerging as a potential successor during Caruso's dying months. But even Gigli's devotees had to admit that he was a lyric rather than a dramatic tenor and could not emulate his predecessor's Italian bravura in airs like 'La donna è mobile'. Bonci's supple vocalism and panache won admirers, but his limitations were exposed by the heavier demands of Alfredo or Cavaradossi. McCormack was a bewitching *tenore leggiero* and supremely alluring in creamy ballads, but he would never seriously dispute his friend's superiority as a dramatic interpreter.

Others were hopefully publicised as 'the second Caruso' during his long absence from Covent Garden. Giovanni Zenatello had made his début as Canio at San Carlo, followed by four impressive years at La Scala. His Radamès and Pinkerton (the latter in partnership with Rina Giachetti) had dominated several prewar London seasons. A more formidable Covent Garden recruit was the silver-voiced Giovanni Martinelli, twelve years younger than Caruso and in the same *bel canto* tradition. Puccini was among the first to notice his talent and had soon arranged for him to sing Dick Johnson in *La Fanciulla*. His vibrant trill and dramatic attack made him an ideal choice for most Puccini roles during his twenty-one seasons at the Metropolitan. He lacked Caruso's subtlety and acting ability, but the older man held him in esteem and always welcomed him to his corner-table at the Knickerbocker.

Caruso owed his mainly undisputed reign primarily to his voice. It remained 'an incomparable instrument for conveying either throbbing sensuousness or a phenomenal but controlled power'. The pitch might come under stress and occasional fault variations are apparent in some recordings (he sang an octave lower in the 'Ai Nostri Monti' duet from *Il Trovatore*, recorded before the war for Victor), but its unique quality was demonstrated for all time in an experiment by Dr Frank E. Millar, a specialist in reproducing voices on phonographic records. Caruso took and held the high C to such effect in 'Di quella pira' from *Trovatore* that the disc measured an astonishing fifty-eight feet.

His records had made him known to millions, including a significant majority of non opera-goers, but the Caruso cult owed as much to his almost magnetic rapport with the public, both on and off stage. After a year or two the Central Park episode would be recalled with only an amused shrug. If anything it rounded off the image of a volatile Latin who kissed pretty girls on the Grand Central platform and could be excused for bottom-pinching or indeed anything short of statutory rape. The beaming smile, lit by flashing white teeth, radiated an urchin exuberance and *joie de vivre*. Only Caruso would dare to go before the Metropolitan curtain, pat his stomach and implore the audience to go home 'because I'm so hungry and want my supper'.

On the sidewalks his fur-collared topcoat and twirling cane were as instantly recognisable as the inseparable black cigarette-holder, tilted upwards, and the gold cable-thick watch-chain stretched across a gaudy waistcoat. His variety of hats never failed to delight: derbies of every shade; boaters worn at the back of the head or over one eye; and of course the white curly fedoras favoured later by Al Capone. Sheet music of his most popular arias and ballads sold prodigiously on both sides of the Atlantic, particularly if his likeness adorned the covers. For years a British music-hall star, Wilkie Bard, brought the house down with his ditty, 'I Want to Sing like Caruso', audiences joining in the catchy chorus line, 'Signor Caruso told me I ought to do so'.

Billy Guard kept him and the Metropolitan in the news while his own publicist, Edward L. Bernays, coined the phrase,

'The man with the orchid-lined voice', and serviced a corps of gossip-writers and photographers. T. R. Ybarra says that newsboys could rely on a dollar at least from Caruso for every paper carrying his picture. Copies of *La Follia* quickly sold out whenever his caricatures appeared. They were just as eagerly snapped up by admirers who could not read a word of Italian.

He rarely turned down any request for a benefit performance even at the height of a busy season and would defy doctors rather than disappoint people who had paid high prices or been fleeced by ticket operators. For banquets he wore his breast-plate of decorations, but he disliked servility. Every morning he stopped for a shine from a gloomy old bootblack, whose troubles soon melted under the Neapolitan quips. He never missed calling at the Knickerbocker with a bunch of flowers on the tenor's birthday.

Recordings had won him the affection of millions, who sat by their phonographs and thrilled to the impassioned arias. His countrymen wept in exile over nostalgic folksongs wine-warm with sunlight. For a few precious minutes his voice would spread blue velvet skies over many cracked tenement walls. To New York's Little Italy he was far more than a voice; he had become a symbol of hope and laughter in adversity. They identified fiercely, patriotically, with the chubby little man who had escaped from a Neapolitan slum to win storybook success on alien soil but still spoke broken English and remained as Italian as macaroni.

Caruso's corps of pensioners was discreetly helped. After his death his personal papers would disclose a secret list of regular allowances to one hundred and twenty needy old friends in Naples and Milan alone. One of his dependants was Gravina, formerly a famed comic singer in Italy, who had fallen on hard times. Caruso enjoyed his clowning and took him along on several of his tours. Well-tailored and always with ready cash in his pocket, he passed easily for a private secretary. He was paid $100 a month merely to clip the tenor's photographs and reviews from newspapers. When he grew slipshod, Caruso

Dame Nellie Melba, whose long partnership with Caruso opened at Monte Carlo in Puccini's *La Bohème*, 1902.

Caruso poses for a bust in Genoa. He also had a weakness for casting bronzes of his own hand. Medallions of himself as Canio, Radames, etc., adorned his villa near Florence.

Above: Helen Keller, blind, deaf and dumb, 'hears' a passage from *Samson* by picking up vibrations from Caruso's throat.

Below: Pavlova and Chaliapin (whom he partnered in *Mefistofele*) were among Caruso's enormous circle of personal friends.

Caruso with his baby daughter, Gloria.

Caruso sails home from New York on 28 May 1921 with his wife, Dorothy.

Top: Tetrazzini makes a recording in New York, 1907. She and other leading artists followed Caruso, a pioneer in this medium. *Below left*: Puccini, whose operas provided Caruso with some of his most popular roles. *Right*: Caruso with baritone Antonio Scotti and Paolo Tosti.

As Eléazar in *La Juive*, one of his most triumphant but exacting dramatic roles. In this opera he made his last appearance at the Metropolitan, on Christmas Eve, 1920.

The last photograph of Caruso, on the terrace of the Hotel Vittorio, Sorrento,
6 July 1921. He died soon afterwards in Naples.

persuaded Jesse L. Lasky to employ him in some minor studio capacity.

He was over generous with needy compatriots but drew the line at operatic puppies eager to yap their 'Vesti la giubbas' at him almost as soon as they had trotted down the steerage gangway. One would-be basso burst into his hotel suite while Caruso, cocooned in a fleecy white dressing-gown and looking like an Eskimo over a water-hole, was busily inhaling before that evening's performance. He swore in choice waterfront Italian but had to submit to the Overcoat Song, which his unwelcome visitor had somehow memorised but nervously wished to transpose. 'A third lower,' suggested the weary accompanist. 'No, put it down an octave.' Caruso endured a few bars, then banged down the piano lid and advised the intruder to make his career in bricklaying or indeed anything but opera. Some years later, after giving a concert in Fort Worth, Texas, he was asked to supper by a local hostess, who soon presented a neighbourhood tenor and soprano. Their interminable repertoire kept him in anguish until 3 a.m. 'I were very rude,' he once told his wife. 'People have such nerve to come to me without voice and let me lose my time.'

He made a rare exception for the veteran contralto and teacher Ernestine Schumann-Heink, who pleaded with him to take over one of her pupils, a policeman from Paterson, New Jersey. Amused by the prospect of his 'singing cop' one day intimidating Toscanini at the Metropolitan, he agreed to give him a series of lessons. Ed McNamara was a hearty character with a bouncer's build and a voice to match. His musical knowledge was minute and his experience limited to sing-songs after political meetings, but the bulldozing tones would have crushed and buried Tamagno. Caruso good-naturedly risked the Knickerbocker chandeliers. One day he surprised his pupil by demanding still more volume, having suddenly remembered that Scotti was enjoying a romantic tête-à-tête in the suite below! McNamara did not pursue his singing career but had some success in the theatre, helped no doubt by the ambivalent accolade, 'Pupil of Caruso'.

Riccardo Martin, a handsome genial tenor from Kentucky, proved more rewarding. He started his career as a pianist and song composer but, unable to afford voice tuition, had almost decided to become a teacher when he chanced to hear Caruso sing at a benefit performance in Paris. He studied his technique and coincidentally received lessons from Lombardi, Caruso's own one-time teacher. By 1907 Martin had made his début at the Metropolitan and filled in with Canio and other roles when the star was on tour or needed to rest. He hero-worshipped Caruso, who coached him in phrasing and finally brought his talents to the attention of Covent Garden.

Caruso would occasionally be decried for refusing to audition or advise beginners, but this was less than fair. Apart from the strain of rehearsals, performances and recording, he spent several hours a day going over difficult passages or taking his breathing exercises. Each morning he would receive a procession of visitors: arrangers, recording technicians, agents, impresarios and recently arrived immigrants nibbling at 'a leetle chick' (cheque). As a national figure with the kind of adulation later accorded only to baseball kings, screen heroes and crooners, he had to autograph an average of two hundred photographs a week as well as writing thank-you letters for bouquets and gifts of Italian chocolate, cakes and wine. He was once sent a huge roast of beef from a fellow Neapolitan who had prospered as a butcher in Philadelphia.

He was far too impatient and also too much of a perfectionist to have enjoyed teaching others. Unlike Tetrazzini, he could read music but was unable to manage more than a few chords on his gilt and white Empire-style piano. Before attempting any new opera he needed much drilling from a *répétiteur*, supplemented by conferences on tempo with Toscanini and other conductors.

He was all the more surprised and flattered when, some years before the First World War, a London publisher invited him to write a book on the art and technique of singing. Alas, apart from one or two useful hints on correct breathing and some earnest advice to young singers not to take up smoking, his thoughts ran to very few pages. Among the clichés, however, was an interesting passage in which he scoffed at certain French singers who covered up their small voices with exaggerated diction and nasal intonation. 'Diction,' he affirmed severely, 'should act rather as a frame for the voice and never replace it.' The booklet, *How to Sing*, published at one shilling, sold many thousands of copies to amateur songsters eager for his secrets. They soon discovered that it was much easier to catch sunbeams with a butterfly net.

Desperate tenors were not Caruso's only afflictions. A rabble of dealers canvassed him when it became known that he had started collecting objets d'art. Often they swamped his suite with very dubious paintings and even stolen property. With the help of his countryman Amedeo Canessa, who owned a gallery on Fiftieth Street, he soon became canny enough to keep touts and confidence men at a distance.

His hobby took root inconspicuously in 1906 while he was in Paris for the benefit matinée arranged by Coquelin. He saw a Queen Arsinoë II gold piece in a numismatist's window, bought it and soon assembled many others until his hoard grew to over two thousand coins, some dating back to the fifth century B.C. He became an authority on early English and American gold coins and cherished a $5 specimen minted by the Mormons in Salt Lake City in 1849. Rare stamps also fascinated him, and he would enjoy long evenings inspecting perforations and watermarks through a magnifying glass.

He did not emerge as a serious collector until after the break-up with Ada. In his craving for solitude and anonymity he had begun haunting the Metropolitan Museum of Art, where he first gazed with longing on J. Pierpont Morgan's treasures. Later he bought several bronzes, enamels and three exquisite Riccio lamps when the collection came on the market. He liked to call unannounced on antique dealers but quickly gathering crowds made this both difficult and costly. He was so often overcharged that Canessa and a network of other middle-men had to be used more frequently in the years ahead.

At first he dabbled haphazardly in bronzes, enamels and cut-glass scent bottles, buying almost anything that took his fancy until the vitrines in his hotel suite overflowed with a higgledy-piggledy assortment. However, thanks to a serious study of catalogues and visits to museums in Europe, where he could move more freely than in New York, he started buying with discrimination and could describe the history and pedigree of every piece. He spent large sums on Louis XV snuffboxes and proudly displayed them in a separate showcase together with his jewelled watches from Alfred Rothschild's celebrated collection.

He purchased few pictures but envied John McCormack his first Corot, a magnificent Franz Hals and several Rembrandts. His own preference was for pottery and glass, which he used to fondle with almost sensual delight. He never tired of sorting and chinking his gold pieces. He also gathered much Greek and Roman glass from the pre-Christian era; rare faïence; Egyptian vases of the Ptolemaic period; mosaics from Imperial Rome, together with early Italian majolicas and terra-cottas. Although deploring some of his gold boxes and ornate kickshaws, connoisseurs gave him credit for some exceptionally fine Limoges enamels and Renaissance bronzes. His marble bas-reliefs included a favourite Quattrocento, which was placed on the chapel altar after his death.

To Signa he despatched appropriate sixteenth-century Italian furniture, velvets, tapestries and rare examples of early English embroidery, but his most satisfying find was a group of Nativity figurines, each exquisitely dressed in a costume made by the ladies-in-waiting to a former Queen of Naples. He had admired them at the Paris Exposition and outbid every dealer. This collection was set out on the stage of his *presepio* adjoining the chapel at Bellosguardo, to which he often retreated after long hours in the music-room. With the help of the custodian, a retired local artist, he used to carve wooden figures, never having forgotten the skills first learned from his sculptor friend in Buenos Aires.

Favoured experts would often be invited up to his Knickerbocker suite to dine and talk shop. They sipped his Signa wine from crystal goblets and dutifully admired the Florentine refectory table covered with an antique lace cloth. He rarely failed to exhibit a bronze plaquette which he had picked up in a junk shop near Covent Garden for only ten shillings. It was later authenticated by a New York antiquary as the work of the sixteenth-century Venetian, Tullio Lombardi, and valued at $500.

His library was remarkable only for the number of works on Napoleon and for the many bookplates designed by himself. The rest was an unread miscellany of first or early editions chosen for their bindings and possible scarcity value. It included an early *Decameron*, Balzac's *Contes Drolatiques* with the Doré illustrations, a 1776 *Don Quichotte* and a copy of *Madame Bovary* from a numbered edition. He also treasured coloured costume plates of stage and military subjects.

Collecting gave Caruso deep personal satisfaction. It was of course a rich man's pastime, but the beehive was bursting with honey. In the last decade of his career his income would rarely fall below a quarter of a million dollars a year, almost forty per cent from recording fees and royalties.

In his 1911–12 season Caruso sang to full houses in New York, Boston, Philadelphia and Atlanta, giving fifty performances at his regular $2000 fee and without missing one through indisposition. Audiences, sympathetic over his troubles with Ada and Signorina Ganelli, and delighted that he was again singing with the old mastery, gave him a frenzied reception everywhere. He wisely saved his voice by turning down all invitations for concerts and private parties but cut twenty-six records for Victor, two of them with Tetrazzini. One novelty was Sullivan's 'The Lost Chord', which he rendered in phonetically memorised English. He had chosen the ballad for a Metropolitan benefit performance after the *Titanic* disaster.

He was again breathing perfectly and showed no ill-effects from his long season when he arrived in Paris in May 1912 for half a dozen appearances at the Opéra. The supporting baritone,

Titta Ruffo, was a gay supper companion but cost him many hours of sleep. However, Caruso was able to spend a few restful weeks that summer at the Villa Bellosguardo before starting to prepare for his forthcoming German tour. His repertoire would be strenuous—*Tosca*, *Rigoletto*, *I Pagliacci* and *La Bohème*—and he was more than doubtful of his welcome by German audiences after an absence of two years.

The opera-goers of Munich and Stuttgart quickly reassured him. His hotel was thronged at all hours by people who camped in the lobby and clamoured for autographs. Street traffic would often be held up while admirers surged forward to congratulate him, many content only to touch his sleeve. But he was homesick for America and jumped up and down on the ship's deck as Manhattan's skyline rose through the morning mist. A laughing crowd of reporters awaited him at the pier. Now clean-shaven, he whisked out a false moustache and rolled his eyes for the photographers.

He opened at the Metropolitan that November in Puccini's *Manon Lescaut* with Scotti and a captivating new soprano, Lucrezia Bori. He varied the usual operatic fare with five performances of *Les Huguenots* and impressed the critics with his improved dramatic style, although one or two thought he was forcing his voice. But it withstood fifty appearances in New York and other cities. Although he had decided to turn down all outside bookings, he could not resist a plea from the governor of the Federal Penitentiary in Atlanta. Before leaving the city he treated the inmates and staff to a generous two-hour feast of song, although at the end of a heavy season during which he had made several recordings for Victor, including Kahn's 'Ave Maria' and Massenet's 'Elégie Melodie' with Mischa Elman. Between appearances he had also been busily preparing for his return to Covent Garden after five years. He would be paid £500 a performance, £100 more than his fee from the Metropolitan.

There was scarcely time to catch his breath in New York before sailing for France. He spent a fortnight almost incognito in Paris, going over his notebooks and visiting antique dealers while Martino kept out stray callers. They departed for London and checked in at the Savoy, where his suite was soon swamped with bouquets and so many complimentary letters that a temporary secretary had to be recruited by the hotel management. The whole Covent Garden staff greeted him like a beloved old friend. Even Melba, excited by her own return after missing the previous season, had embraced him with quite unusual fervour.

He opened in *I Pagliacci* on 20 May 1913 with Sammarco in support as Tonio, but it was indisputably a traditional Caruso night. Prices had soared to gala heights, but the box-office was sold out within half an hour. Queues had formed at six that morning for unreserved gallery seats, many of Caruso's countrymen joyfully singing Tosti choruses while they stood in the rain. Extra stall seats overspilled into the gangways and the King's box was solid with British and Swedish royalty. As always, 'Vesti la giubba' intoxicated the audience. Caruso took eight solo calls. If some of the critics seemed less ecstatic over the performance as a whole, they were too enchanted to have the *primo tenore* back at the Royal Opera House to be anything but cordial. One reviewer paid brief tribute to his 'intense emotion and absolute vocalisation' and gave up the rest of his notice to recording the public's hysterical approval.

Two nights later Melba celebrated her silver jubilee at Covent Garden with McCormack in *La Bohème*, but everyone was agog to hear Caruso's Rodolfo. They had to restrain their impatience while he sang in *Aïda* with Destinn and Scotti, followed by *Tosca*, exciting performances both but without Melba's alchemy. The box-office had long discontinued all bookings for their *Bohème*, which opened to an acclaim more explosive than anything Caruso had experienced even at La Scala premières under Toscanini's baton. Osbert Sitwell, wedged among the glittering audience, would later recall the splendour of that night in his memoirs. He wrote flippantly that Melba's soprano 'was not invariably true, having about it something of the disproportion of the Australian continent from which she had emerged', but having accustomed himself to the spectacle of Mimi and Rodolfo, 'fat as two elderly thrushes, trilling at each other over the hedges of tiaras', he succumbed like any Soho waiter to Caruso's magic. After thirty-five years he could still rhapsodise over a voice that carried 'the warm breath of southern evenings in an orange grove, and of roses caught in the hush of dusk at the water's edge'. The miracle was repeated on the night of 23 June in the presence of the King and Queen accompanied by the Prince of Wales, who, like his father, did not care for opera but had to endure this Covent Garden visit as part of his nineteenth-birthday celebrations.

For Caruso that short five-week season was an exhilaration. London had never seemed gayer or so carefree. The men, elegant in tail-coats and gardenias, escorted pink-cheeked young goddesses dressed by Paul Poiret. At the Savoy the chatter was all of Ascot, parties in Park Lane mansions and the enchantment of Diaghilev's Russian ballet. Caruso's one regret was Tosti's absence from the convivial suppers at Pagani's. Illness and advancing years had forced him to desert England for the warmth of Rome.

Caruso spent many enjoyable hours with Chaliapin, whose Galitzky in *Prince Igor*, under Beecham's baton, thrilled Covent Garden audiences. The basso chortled over Caruso's account of the Metropolitan première that March for *Boris Godunov*, which Toscanini had rehearsed for two months. As there were not enough Russian-speaking singers, it was given in Italian with a Pole in the Chaliapin role and such un-Mussorgsky artists as Louise Homer in support. The two friends often went out together on gay shopping expeditions. On one of these sorties to collect his patent-leather hand-made boots, the Russian giant stopped in St James's Street to buy himself a grey top-hat for Ascot. With Caruso trotting breathlessly alongside, he could not resist opening the hatbox to survey himself in several shop windows on their way back to the Savoy. He ate and drank prodigiously but showed no ill-effects, attributing his constitution to Turkish baths, which terrified Caruso almost as much as the slightest imaginary draught. He had even less use for Chaliapin's theory that skin demands air. The basso would lounge about his suite in a vast flowered silk kimono or sometimes stark naked while his pet monkey, Boris, contentedly munched chocolate by his side.

Chaliapin also tried without success to persuade Caruso to take more exercise and join him in his own dieting spells. It was sound advice. At forty the tenor looked quite ten years older with his thinning hair and thickening waist. He adored spaghetti *à la Napolitaine* which he often attempted to cook but rarely failed to burn the sauce. He had similar touching faith that his throat could withstand endless cigarettes if he wore amber beads or a fillet of anchovy round his neck.

He used to make a light breakfast of black coffee, a brioche and the first of several Egyptian cigarettes. Occasionally he ventured a few knee-bends and hopefully waved his dumb-bells. After luxuriating for half an hour in a hot scented bath he received his daily visit from the hotel barber and manicurist. He was always nervous on the day of a performance and played many games of solitaire, nibbling a sandwich and some fruit with his glass of Chianti, or often only a salad-bowlful of raw fennel, sometimes varied by spinach and hard-boiled eggs cooked for exactly half an hour. After the theatre, however, he attacked an enormous meal with *pasta* as the centrepiece. He drank far less champagne than McCormack and lacked Chaliapin's head for red wines. He contented himself with several bottles of mineral water at a meal, but his daily intake of calories would have filled any average sextet. Ice cream, tapioca, custard and semolina were lowered in bulk after his favourite double helping of boiled chicken.

Caruso had an odd taste for bread crusts, which he thought good for his teeth, but, one suspects, made an even better excuse to reminisce about his hungry early days in Naples. One evening he kissed his son, Mimmi, before leaving for Covent Garden. 'Where are you going, Papa?' the child asked. 'I am going to work so that you can have food to eat and clothes to wear,' laughed his father, but then rounded on him and growled, 'At your age I worked.'

Fortunately, the boy had a sense of humour. Caruso called

one afternoon at the house in Ealing to find him with several young friends crouched round a phonograph and chuckling over a Harry Lauder song.

'You like his records?' the tenor asked in surprise.

'Oh, yes, much better than yours,' replied the eight-year-old without hesitation. His father shared his taste for Lauder. He once entered the consulting room of his London throat specialist, Dr William Lloyd, and cheerfully burst into 'I Love a Lassie' with a strong Neapolitan accent.

Mimmi proudly wore evening dress for the first time to see an end-of-the-season performance of *La Bohème*. Sitting with Miss Saer in a stage-box, he was delighted when his father, taking a solo curtain call, bowed and blew them a kiss. After promising the Covent Garden management to return next season, Caruso went off to spend some weeks at the Villa Bellosguardo, soon joined there by his brother's family and his elder son, Fofò, who would shortly be leaving his academy near Florence but seemed indifferent to his future. Caruso gave him a new bicycle and other presents but could not penetrate a shell of surliness that so often recalled Ada. While in London Caruso had seriously thought of sending him to an English public school, Charterhouse, where Sybil Seligman's son was a boarder. It would have had the advantage of bringing the brothers together, after years of separation, but Rina Giachetti adored Fofò and argued passionately for keeping him close to her. Caruso put off the decision while running over his repertoire for appearances in Austria and Germany.

Vienna gobbled encores like pastries, but nothing approached the hysteria of Caruso's German audiences, fortunately unaware that they would never hear his voice again. After a final performance of *Rigoletto* in Stuttgart, crowds stood for hours outside the hotel and would not disperse until he had appeared on a balcony and waved to them like some beloved monarch. Only the chill night and Martino's warnings restrained him from giving them 'Vesti la giubba'.

Caruso was a very tired man when the ship docked in New York, but the city air invigorated him almost as much as the friendly sidewalk greetings whenever he took a short constitutional. Only Scotti was told in confidence of his crushing headaches in Germany and his anxiety about overstraining his voice during the whole of the London engagement. However, the New York doctors attributed his headaches to a minor sinus disorder and detected no signs of fresh nodes in the throat.

He was careful to avoid private concerts but could not turn down Calvin Child's plea for more labels. He made another seventeen recordings, including a duet from Verdi's *Otello* with Titta Ruffo. That season he appeared over fifty times at the Metropolitan and other opera houses, giving hard study and effort to *Julien*, Charpentier's hapless sequel to *Louise*. Even Caruso, with Geraldine Farrar in support, could not keep it alive after five performances, the only disappointment that season.

The Metropolitan had been a little nervous that Caruso might demand exorbitant terms when his contract came up for renewal in March 1914, but he seemed perfectly satisfied with a $500 raise, bringing his fee up to $2500 a performance. Never the most open-handed of managers, Gatti-Casazza had every cause to congratulate himself. After one superb performance he murmured to Toscanini, 'Any amount you pay Caruso, he is always the least expensive artist to the management'.

Covent Garden echoed that verdict. Advance bookings for the 1914 summer season climbed to peak figures when it was announced that Caruso would again be partnering Melba in company with Destinn and Scotti. He had complained of tiredness before sailing, but his 'ozone tonic' helped him to survive sixteen incisive performances at Covent Garden and a round of supper-parties. One unexpected diversion, however, would give him recurrent nightmares for years to come. On Sunday, 24 May, he had joined some friends for a holiday outing to the London Aerodrome at Hendon. Cheered by the crowd and over excited, he rashly accepted an invitation to fly in a Forman biplane piloted by Claude Grahame-White, the first Englishman to gain an aviator's certificate. Caruso amused spectators by scribbling various little notes and inserting them in his overall pockets. 'My last will and testament,' he explained, rolling his eyes. Only Scotti knew that he was almost paralysed with terror and would gladly have backed out. When the plane landed after several circuits at eight hundred feet, he pronounced his flight 'magnificent', but looked quite remarkably wan. Without pausing to sign any autographs, he hurried back to the Savoy's safe carpets.

He appeared in the last prewar royal gala performance in Verdi's *Un Ballo in Maschere* and was presented afterwards to Queen Alexandra and the Dowager Empress Marie of Russia. *La Bohème* had been scheduled to end the season, but there were so many pleas for one extra Caruso performance that the management decided to stage *Tosca* on 29 June. From early that morning hundreds had queued cheerfully for the gallery, kept in order by a squad of good-natured London bobbies. Italians picnicked on salami and cheese while the British munched veal and ham pies with fruit peddled by enterprising market porters. The sun shone and nobody seemed much concerned with that day's newspaper accounts of the assassination of an archduke in some impossibly remote town called Sarajevo.

Chapter Seventeen

Caruso's daunting seasons at the Metropolitan and Covent Garden ended in complete nervous exhaustion. A physician in Milan advised him against going to the Villa Bellosguardo, where he would have to play host to a houseful of rackety guests and might also start preparing too soon for his next series of appearances in America. After some argument he retired for a few weeks to the mountain spa in Montecatini above Lucca. There he loafed aimlessly, bored by an enforced diet and holiday-makers who rubbernecked whenever he took the waters. He kept more to his room, gloomily spraying his throat and making a half-hearted study of his notebooks. He had anticipated a few lively meetings with Puccini but found him distracted and irritable, having recently quarrelled with the Ricordi firm and involved himself in wrangles with Mascagni over the rights to an Ouida novel which both had decided to adapt for a light opera.

Locked away in the mountains, Caruso began to miss his collection and, even more, the Knickerbocker côterie. With only the taciturn Mario and a squad of obsequious waiters for company, he longed for Scotti, Gatti-Casazza and, perhaps most of all, Kreisler, whose talk of politics, religion and other non-musical topics always stimulated him. The newspapers haphazardly delivered at Montecatini afforded little comfort during that endless doom-laden summer. Until Austrian shells landed on Belgrade and Russia mobilised, followed at once by German intervention, Caruso had not taken the threat of a general war too seriously. For weeks he had been overwhelmed by depression and only glanced nervously at the headlines. Now he wrote asking Giovanni to meet him at the villa but urged him to clear it first of all visitors. With the outbreak of hostilities between England and Germany, he also arranged for Miss Saer to bring Mimmi to Livorno. They would stay with Rina until the boy could go to his brother's school near Florence.

He received frantic messages from Gatti-Casazza, who had spent most of the summer in Milan and was now trying to assemble his leading Metropolitan artists, either vacationing in Italy or on singing engagements elsewhere on the Continent. Like Caruso and everyone else, he was certain that Italy would stay neutral but thought it prudent to return to America while it was still possible to book passages.

Caruso reported at last and quickly agreed to sing at a concert to raise funds for Italian workers desperate to leave Germany. But first he had to go to Paris in response to an urgent wire from Raoul Gunsbourg. They dined at the Grand Hotel, the little Russian almost in tears over the war news but still resolved to go ahead with his plans. 'I'll open the season at Monte Carlo,' he declared, 'even if nobody comes.' Caruso grasped his hand and assured him firmly, 'I will come. You can announce that I shall open for you next March. On that you have my word.' They embraced emotionally as Caruso boarded the Rome express.

On the night of 19 October 1914, the Costanzi patrons cheered every excerpt but became feverish when Caruso sang 'Vesti la giubba'. Toscanini had angrily tapped his baton for a full fifteen minutes until the manager, terrified of a riot, implored him to allow encores from Caruso.

With the Maestro and the other singers he hurried from the theatre to catch the train for Naples, where he was seen off at the pier by his stepmother and Assunta, now very frail and scarcely able to stand on her rickety legs. Elisabeth Schumann, Lucrezia Bori and Geraldine Farrar were already aboard the *Canopic*. 'Mr Gatti' had presented each of them before sailing with a bouquet of tired-looking carnations bought cheaply from some waterfront stall. Caruso was impatient to sail but throughout the next fortnight could not be separated from his life-jacket, morbidly convinced that every flying fish would transform itself into an enemy periscope. Toscanini was calmer and soon had a piano installed in his cabin, where for several hours each day he drilled Caruso, Farrar and Pasquale Amato for *Carmen*.

It was performed in mid-November, with Caruso and the others in prime voice and Farrar acclaimed the best Carmen since Calvé. It prompted her manager, Morris Gest, a former ticket-scalper, to approach Jesse L. Lasky with the suggestion that she might one day repeat the role on film.

War seemed remote as one glittering production followed another at the Metropolitan. Caruso had fully recovered and was now singing twice a week without sign of strain. He had informed the directors of his pledge to sing in Monte Carlo, but this had evidently not been taken too seriously. In mid-season he walked into the head office, where Gatti-Casazza and Otto Kahn were conferring, and announced that he had booked passage for Europe to keep his promise to Raoul Gunsbourg. The chairman puffed hard on his cigar and made no comment, but Gatti-Casazza jumped to his feet, yelling, 'You're mad! This could cost you one hundred million francs in stage and recording fees alone. And I must warn you that we will sue for one hundred thousand dollars for breaking your agreement with us.' Caruso shrugged and expressed polite regret, while Kahn tried to pacify his general manager. The latter finally calmed down and tried another tactic. 'Let us pay Gunsbourg to tear up his contract,' he now proposed. Caruso shook his head. 'We have no contract,' he replied sharply, 'except my word, and I will not break that for any money.' While 'the Padrone' raged and Scotti anxiously warned his friend that nobody could afford to defy the mighty Metropolitan, Mario packed his master's bags and Caruso sailed for Naples, where the mayor and council stood on the quay to welcome him.

He sang for a month at Monte Carlo, enchanting the Casino patrons in *Aïda*, *I Pagliacci* and *Lucia*. His appearances undoubtedly saved Gunsbourg, who had recruited a company of useful singers although none of the Melba or Farrar vintage. But for his 'gentilhomme tenor', as he called him, the season could have been a total disaster.

Taking his ease at the Hôtel de Paris, where relays of impresarios called with offers, Caruso seemed composed and very confident. In fact he was worried about his future with the Metropolitan. Gatti-Casazza had apparently forgiven him, but disturbing reports of policy changes continued to reach him. The management had not only stopped all salary increases after Caruso's departure but were introducing several petty economies. No elaborate house bouquets would in future be presented on the stage and only one or two sent to the dressing rooms, thereby saving a few dollars but antagonising the stars.

Backed by his directors, Gatti-Casazza had taken full advantage of his near-monopoly of artists starved for work now that so many European opera houses were shuttered. Toscanini quickly took issue when faced with under-rehearsed productions, smaller orchestras and a ruthless pruning of choruses. He had complained to 'Don Giulio', who blandly shifted all responsibility to Kahn and his fellow financiers. The conductor had asked for a larger budget, failing which he threatened to resign, plainly expecting his old friend and La Scala partner to back him. He packed his bags in anger, giving up his salary of $42,000 a season when Gatti-Casazza continued to hedge. Kahn hastily intervened and agreed to meet all his demands, but by then it was too late. Toscanini returned to Milan and would not make his peace with the Metropolitan for seventeen embittered years.

New York seemed unimaginable to Caruso without Toscanini. He had almost decided to spend the rest of the summer at Sigma when his dilemma was temporarily resolved by Walter Mocchi, who booked artists for some of the leading theatres in South America. The impresario hurried to the Hôtel de Paris and offered him a contract on almost any terms. Half in jest Caruso suggested 35,000 francs ($7000) a performance. Astonishingly, this was agreed on the spot. They sailed within a week for Buenos Aires, where Caruso had last sung in July 1903.

There was no question of his welcome. Audiences rose to

him at every performance, hotly brushing aside the occasional pedant who dared to grumble at over-emphasis and a possible loss of lyrical gold. Latin America, like Germany, could not have too much passionate volume or theatricality so long as Caruso was generous with his encores and justified the high price of their tickets. No Toscanini graced the orchestra pit and, apart from Sammarco, the company lacked Metropolitan calibre, although Caruso was much impressed by a young coloratura, Amelita Galli-Curci, whose spectacular style and bravura as Lucia thrilled even Tetrazzini's supporters. She was still slender and without hint of the goitre that would force her retirement from the operatic stage. More than once she praised his recordings and would later partner him in sessions at the Victor studios. Warm-hearted by nature although acidulous at times about rivals ('To hear Melba sing "Lo, Hear the Gentle Lark", when she has finished you would think it was a turkey'), Galli-Curci comforted him when he received news of his sister's death. Bouquets and hundreds of sympathetic letters descended upon him. Before leaving Buenos Aires for a short season in Montevideo, he was presented with a gold cigarette case from Mocchi, who inscribed it gratefully, 'To Caruso, dearest of all friends, and the *least* dear of all artists'. His takings had more than justified that unprecedented $7000 fee for each of twenty appearances.

Caruso returned to Italy in September and prepared himself at the Villa Bellosguardo for his next Metropolitan season. He would open in Saint-Saëns' *Samson et Dalila*, a challenging and powerful role, but he was far more disturbed by an unexpected personal attack in *Le Matin* accusing him of pro-German sympathies. This was particularly hurtful as he had recently sung for the French Red Cross and other Allied benefits. In the past he had freely given his services to French causes and worn his Legion of Honour ribbon with so much pride that the accusation caused him considerable anguish. Soon after arriving in Buenos Aires, he had first heard and welcomed the news that his country was at war with Austria, but failed to appreciate the angry reaction to Italy's fence-sitting over the Germans. French journalists grew so incensed at the antiwar stand taken by the Vatican, royalists and leading industrialists that they now denounced any Italian celebrity suspected of pro-German sympathies.

Caruso's prewar popularity in Vienna and Berlin made him an easy target, but more probably he was singled out for attack because of his friendship with Puccini, whose provocative statements early in the war, while Italy was still neutral, had been much resented. He had unwisely proclaimed his warm feelings of gratitude to *any* country performing his music. As his operas had enjoyed far less favour in France than in either Germany or Austria, the implication was transparent. Toscanini threatened to slap his face publicly when they next met.

The Maestro was such an ardent francophile that he would never have agreed to conduct for Caruso if the slur in *Le Matin* had had the smallest justification. He did not hesitate to invite him to appear at a concert in Milan that September on behalf of needy singers and musicians. They embraced affectionately before Caruso began rehearsing for two performances of *I Pagliacci* at the Dal Verme Theatre. His Canio was received with the usual furore but, almost as important to him, stopped all rumours that his voice had faded since the former days of glory.

At the Villa Bellosguardo he had made use of the coaching talents of Richard Barthélemy as well as taking advice from Mugnone, Tullio Voghera and a number of other friendly conductors who volunteered or were cheerfully recruited. From 1916 onwards his full-time accompanist, advisers and *répétiteur* would be Salvatore Fucito, who was entrusted with the keys to the music trunk containing hundreds of scores and the precious notebooks. Arriving at the Knickerbocker sharp at 9 a.m., Fucito would sit himself at the piano in the studio and play softly while Caruso was shaved and manicured before issuing his orders of the day to Mario or one of his corps of temporary secretaries. Once his correspondence was completed and the most urgent callers disposed of, he would settle down with Fucito, who played through the whole score of any opera being performed that night. Caruso used to whistle or hum phrases before singing in half voice and finally, after much discussion, with the full volume. There would be pauses for throat spraying and vocal warm-ups to facilitate proper breath control, but the major part of the session, often lasting several hours, was devoted to the niceties of phrasing and diction.

He prepared more intensively for his first Samson than any other role in his entire career. He copied out page after page of the score, interpolating each passage in French, a difficult language for him, and laboriously memorised phrases by singing them phonetically. He also took unprecedented pains over make-up and the subtlest nuances of interpretation. His vocalism, particularly in the middle range, was now matched by an acting power that astounded audiences long accustomed to Canio and Cavaradossi.

This 'New Caruso' offered an unforgettable experience, almost a revelation, to his faithful public, but his determination to stretch himself in weightier parts imposed still more strain on a constitution already vulnerable to obesity and excessive cigarette-smoking. A testing role like Samson demanded far more punishing hours of rehearsal than the 'standard' operas. Instead of restricting his working schedule to allow for the new challenge, he simply added it to his repertoire.

He had argued himself into believing that, without Covent Garden and his Continental engagements, he could easily recuperate from a full six-month stretch in America by spending a few weeks at Signa, forgetting that the villa might not be quite so restful or congenial in wartime. Moreover, since the Monte Carlo dispute he had won complete freedom to organise his own future outside engagements without any control or financial participation by the Metropolitan. It was a lucrative concession but tempted him to accept an increasing number of private engagements, although he once turned down $6000 to sing at a party given by J. Pierpont Morgan because he had arranged to dine that very evening with Scotti and other friends.

In addition to his periodic Bagby Musicales at the Waldorf-Astoria and occasional Friday-morning concerts at the Biltmore Hotel, Caruso pocketed handsome fees for appearing at parties given by James Henry ('Silent') Smith in the former Whitney mansion at Fifth Avenue and Sixty-Seventh Street, where the guests sometimes dined on gold plate and the fountains gushed champagne. He was paid $10,000 (exactly double the fee for Paderewski) by Charles M. Schwab of Bethlehem Steel to give an after-dinner recital at his seventy-five-room palace on Riverside Drive. He rubbed his eyes at the three passenger lifts with their crimson-cushioned banquettes, but was even more impressed when his host sat down at his $50,000 miniature pipe organ and proved that he could not only read music better than Caruso but also had a pleasant singing voice.

In the 1915–16 season he missed only a single one of his full quota of fifty Metropolitan appearances. A severe sinus attack demanded minor surgery, but within a few days he felt well enough to attend a dinner given in his honour by the Lotos Club of New York and organised by Victor Herbert. Whenever Caruso was in Philadelphia he never failed to call on the twinkling white-haired composer at Willow Grove Park and always sent him affectionate greetings and a gift for his birthday. Herbert proposed his friend's health and ended with a loudly cheered eulogy: 'There is only one, our Caruso, standing today at the top of the ladder, in the glory of his God-given, golden voice, and in the warm glow of his democratic modesty and personal charm.'

Throughout that winter he was racked by severe headaches, but his début as Samson encouraged him to repeat it five times. His success tempted him into a characteristic piece of buffoonery. As the curtain fell, with a huge papier-mâché rock pinning him to the stage, he raised a guffaw from the gallery by doing an arms bend and upward stretch.

One of the highlights of that season was his Don José to

228

Farrar's Carmen, although the opening performance provided an unexpected sensation. 'Geraldina' had returned to New York after making a five-reel *Carmen* with Wallace Reid. In Hollywood she was pampered by Lasky, who supplied a house, servants, limousine and a private dressing-room with grand piano. Less fortunately she also acquired a husband, Lou Tellegen, the handsome Dutch actor. The marriage would soon end in divorce, but Farrar's pretty head was still in the clouds when she returned to a wild reception from her 'Jerry-flappers'.

Fresh from Cecil B. de Mille's full-blooded direction, she was soon tempted to indulge in capers more appropriate to celluloid than to the operatic stage. On 17 February 1916 she decided to inject some extra 'realism' into her interpretation of Carmen. In the cigarette factory scene she mauled one of the girls and almost shook the life out of her. The matinée audience applauded, but Caruso, watching from the wings, snorted: 'What does she think this is? A cinema?' During her stage fight with Don José she writhed so melodramatically that the audience almost ignored Caruso's singing. In the finale she struck him hard on the jaw with her fan. He seized her wrist and held it so firmly that she bit his hand and drew blood. He then clutched her, wriggling like a captive eel, and tossed her smack on her bottom across the stage while continuing with his aria. The curtain fell to a tremendous ovation, the public thoroughly relishing Farrar's fiery acting. There was loud laughter when Caruso came forward and ruefully rubbed his jaw. Behind the velvet curtain, however, they resumed their wrestling until the stage manager had to separate them. 'If Caruso does not approve my interpretation,' threatened Farrar, 'they can get another Carmen.' He replied icily, 'We can prevent a repetition of these scenes by getting another Don José instead.'

Billy Guard, always an opportunist, encouraged the newspapers to play up the incident. This upset Caruso rather more than the prima donna, who had accurately sensed its publicity value. For months afterwards, even without the fisticuffs, it became almost impossible to buy tickets for *Carmen*. Farrar had apologised charmingly and never had another cross word with Caruso either on or off the stage. His attachment to Mrs Farrar grew so strong that he once pleaded with her to adopt his son, Mimmi, who was being coddled by Miss Saer and needed a stronger hand.* 'Mammina' thanked him for the compliment but made it clear that Geraldine had first and exclusive call on her services.

Mimmi was not his only anxiety when he returned to Signa in the summer of 1916. He had delayed sailing until his astrologer, Evangeline Adams, assured him that he was safe from torpedoes. Nevertheless, he would not go aboard without a small armoury of good-luck and holy medals. He also had an 'unsinkable' suit specially made to keep him afloat in mid-Atlantic in case Mrs Adams had chanced to get her stars crossed.

The Villa Bellosguardo's sumptuous furnishings looked shabby to his critical eye. Martino explained sadly that many of the servants had gone off to the army. Those too old to serve had tried to cater to scores of Caruso's relatives and the horde of acquaintances whom he had carelessly invited to make themselves at home. As food and drink were still plentiful, thanks to produce from the estate, soldiers on leave or convalescent from the Isonzo front were now given hospitality, with Caruso's warm-hearted approval.

The news of heavy Italian casualties and an Austrian breakthrough in the Tyrol had spread alarm in Milan, where many feared invasion from the north. Caruso became aware of hard looks and occasional newspaper hints that he was earning 'millions of dollars' in comfortable New York, while many of his countrymen were being slaughtered or suffering want. He did not attempt to justify himself but felt acute resentment. His own position seemed unequivocal. Now approaching his mid-forties and unlikely to satisfy even the most casual army doctor, he was an obvious military reject. In Italy he might have given a few benefit concerts, but could raise far more cash

* *Caruso*, by T. R. Ybarra.

230

from personal appearances in the United States. He would never contemplate following John McCormack in adopting American nationality, but his allegiance was plain. Years before, at a gala performance in Berlin, the Kaiser had jocularly suggested that he might consider returning to Europe for good and perhaps even make his home in Germany. 'Your Majesty,' Caruso had replied very solemnly, 'my gratitude to America will be extinguished only with my death.' He had often confided to Scotti and other intimates that the United States would remain his true home until the end of his operatic career, when he planned to retire to the Villa Bellosguardo. He had also left detailed instructions for burial in Naples. Meantime, he felt deeply for the land of his birth and had made no effort to remove his elder son to the safety of America or any other neutral country. Fofò, now eighteen, would soon be called to the colours.

At the villa he practised long hours with Barthélemy and his old conductor friend, Mugnone, who coached him zealously for the coming Metropolitan season. It would open that November with a revival of Bizet's *Les Pêcheurs de Perles*, which, it was hoped, might repeat the success of *Carmen*. Caruso had not sung Nadir since his appearance in Genoa in 1898 and needed to refresh his memory. He had also agreed to give another half-dozen performances of Samson but would seek light relief by performing *L'Elisir d'Amore*, the opera which had once rescued La Scala from disaster.

During that gloomy summer at the Villa Bellosguardo he found it difficult to project himself into the comedy role of Nemorino. He had to strain even for the magic of 'Una furtiva lagrima', which had always tripped from his lips. Instead of strolling through the gardens after hours of practice with Mugnone, he played solitaire or did a little carving, but more often he sank into introspection. He had returned with red eyes from Rome after visiting the dying Tosti and avoided all his old friends, even Puccini, who was nursing his melancholia at Torre del Lago and, according to the Galleria gossips, dosing himself with 'rejuvenating' potions. Caruso also grieved for

Emmy Destinn, now a virtual prisoner in Prague, with only her cats and a collection of antique treasures for comfort. Her passport had been impounded by the Austrians when she publicly announced her intention to return to New York and take out first citizenship papers.

Nijinsky was more fortunate in being able to leave Vienna, where he had been under house arrest as an enemy alien. He was allowed to join Diaghilev's ballet company in New York, thanks to the intervention of Otto Kahn and the State Department. The Metropolitan badly needed this new attraction. For some time past it had been under attack for patchy or mediocre productions between the Caruso-Farrar peaks. However, the arrival of the Russian dancers gave Gatti-Casazza's enemies a welcome chance to snipe at him. They fêted Diaghilev and touted his name as the Metropolitan's next general manager.

Caruso took no part in these manœuvres but hospitably entertained the Russians, particularly the Nijinskys and their enchanting baby, Kyra, whom he helped to instal more comfortably at the Majestic. He took them on sight-seeing tours and played host at his favourite restaurants, as Nijinsky was partial to Italian food. The dancer never seemed to tire of riding up and down hotel elevators, which Caruso found less alarming than driving with him in his new Peerless. Nijinsky drove like a charging Cossack, using the wrong side of the road and often reversing unintentionally. But Caruso revelled in his company and loved to air his Russian vocabulary whenever they met. He introduced him to Long Island hostesses, who swooned when he dived gracefully into their swimming pools and performed superb acrobatics. He also took naturally to tennis and hit astounding volleys with his galvanised salmon leaps.

These social triumphs did not please Diaghilev, who was still boiling with spleen over his former bedmate's marriage to Romola. From the Ritz, where he was staying with Massine, he sneered at Nijinsky for being under the thumb of his 'unprincipled' wife. Nor did he spare Caruso, whose voice he had formerly proclaimed one of the world's true glories, ranking equally with the music of Tchaikovsky and Stravinsky. He now released twin barrels at both tenor and faun. According to him, Nijinsky had become fat, old-fashioned and 'the Caruso of the Dance'. Nobody took this very seriously, but Gatti-Casazza was not too sorry to see the troupe off on their national tour.

Caruso's opening night in *Les Pêcheurs de Perles* on 13 November 1916 was given almost a twenty-one-gun salute, with all tiaras and lorgnettes firing. One breathless columnist reported: 'The Diamond Horseshoe was ablaze with jewels which answered each other from box to box until their brilliancy dimmed even the auditorium's flashing lights. Paquin, Worth and Poiret were in their glory.' Caruso did lyrical justice to Bizet's music, but the opera, while sensitively directed by Toscanini's successor, Maestro Giorgio Polacco, had to be dropped after only three performances.

Caruso gave fifty appearances that season, plus concerts for Italian war funds and three for his own benefit with the Cincinnati Symphony Orchestra. These netted him $12,000. He was also honoured with a dinner by the Friars, America's top society of theatrical press agents, and blushed at the tributes paid to him by one speaker after another, led by Gatti-Casazza, Scotti and Victor Herbert (who addressed him in Italian). But he was unusually subdued that night and had only accepted the invitation to avoid offending Herbert.

Caruso continued to take his routine sidewalk promenades with the inevitable cordon of admirers and photographers, but had become noticeably less cordial towards uninvited callers at the Knickerbocker. He could not, however, refuse to see five Italian miners from New Mexico on their way home to join the army. They camped outside his suite until Mario had to admit them. Their leader dumped two hundred grubby dollar bills in Caruso's lap and begged him to sing a few Neapolitan songs before they left America. It seemed that they had failed to secure seats at the Metropolitan and found the scalpers' prices quite beyond their means. Caruso sympathetically handed back the cash and invited them to return next day with as many friends as they liked. Almost two dozen crowded into his suite the following evening. He gave them an hour's recital of 'Santa Lucia', Tosti's 'Ideale' and other ballads.

A ten-year-old American girl, Elizabeth Rodewald, also benefited unexpectedly from his good nature. She had long treasured a Red Seal recording of 'La Donna è mobile' but saw Caruso for the first time on the Back Bay Station platform in Chicago. Enveloped in a fur-collared coat and with the familiar velour twirled over one eye, he was blowing kisses from the train window. He then reached forward to catch some Parma violets which a woman had unpinned from her muff and tossed to him. As the train moved off he retired to his private drawing-room and bolted himself in. The school-girl, brought up in a strict Quaker household and ordered never to speak to strangers, least of all high-voltage Latins, yielded to temptation and tapped on his door. He opened it with reluctance but laughed when she timidly begged his autograph.

He had been playing patience and soon persuaded her to sit down and learn double demon. After a while she screwed up enough courage to ask him to sing something for her. He offered little snatches from his operas and one or two Neapoli-tan folksongs, pulling faces all the time until she was weeping with laughter. Although he had planned to settle down with his notebooks, the five hours' journey passed so pleasantly that they were chatting and laughing like old friends when the train puffed into Grand Central. He buttoned her coat snugly under her chin but clucked in disapproval when she put on her severe little brown hat. 'It makes you look like a mouse,' he declared. On the platform, ignoring the waiting throng of photographers and reporters, he took Elizabeth by the hand and delivered her to her very astonished father. 'We have spent our afternoon at the opera, Mr Quaker,' he explained with a chuckle. 'And, pliz, I beg of you, buy her another hat—*with flowers.*'

He was far less amiable with backstage visitors. In the past

234

his dressing-room had always been jammed with friends and a procession of autograph-hunters, who could be sure of a signed portrait and a cheerful joke. Reports of heavy Italian war casualties had saddened him. He would hurry from the theatre for a quiet dinner with Scotti either at some restaurant, where he would be unmolested, or more often in his suite. On most free evenings he was closeted with his coins and stamps. Occasionally he visited the circus in Madison Square Garden and amused the crowd by jumping over the rail to shake hands with the clowns, but he very rarely went to the theatre unless comrades like Victor Herbert and George M. Cohan had shows running or Ethel Barrymore specially invited him to see a performance.

He had become friendly with the actress after a concert at the Metropolitan in aid of the American Red Cross. She was scheduled to recite 'The Battle Hymn of the Republic' as the finale but seemed terrified of forgetting her lines. As a precaution she had begged her brother, Lionel, to go into the prompter's box. When the huge golden curtains parted and a vast sea of faces heaved before her, she became acutely nervous and stumbled over the last verse. Lionel's promptings came through the mist in such a dull roar that she froze altogether for a few seconds before recovering. The performance ended to tremendous applause. Caruso, standing in the wings with John McCormack, rushed forward to congratulate her on that dramatic and highly effective pause at the end, but she could never be sure whether there had been a genuine tear in his eye or, as she rather suspected, a mischievous wink.

The cinema attracted him even less than the theatre, which perhaps explains his somewhat offhand treatment of Chaplin. In 1916 the comedian had made a two-reel burlesque of De Mille's *Carmen* and was eager to see Geraldine Farrar and Caruso in the Metropolitan production. He arrived for a matinée performance but learned with disappointment that Farrar had a cold and *Rigoletto* would be put on instead. After the first act he asked Morris Gest if it might be possible to meet the tenor. Gest brashly assured him that nothing was easier and promptly buttonholed 'Mr Gatti', who seemed rather more doubtful but ordered the stage-manager to conduct Chaplin to the star's dressing-room. He was finally admitted after some parley with the dresser.

Chaplin recalls that the singer was clipping his moustache when the stage-manager announced nervously, 'It is my great pleasure to present to you the Caruso of the cinema, Mr Charlie Chaplin.' Caruso went on snipping and said over his shoulder, 'You have big success, eh? You make plenty of money?' Chaplin nodded. 'So,' commented the tenor, dismissing him with a cool handshake.

Others, however, were shown more consideration. Exhilarated by America's entry into the war on 6 April 1917, he at once agreed to give a benefit performance eleven days later with Sarah Bernhardt, Alda and a chorus of five hundred directed by Ivor Novello's mother. Rouged and raddled, with her red frizz straggling over kohl-rimmed eyes, Bernhardt hobbled about on her one good leg. But she was still a magnetic personality even in her seventies, and Caruso, not waiting for a formal introduction, hastened to pay his tribute. He presented himself humbly at her hotel and knelt to kiss her hand. He was even more impressed by Helen Keller, whose book, *Optimism*, he had long admired. When the deaf and dumb author expressed a wish to 'hear' him sing passages from *Samson*, he was much touched and consented without hesitation. She rested her fingers on his throat and picked up his vibrations to register what she later recalled as 'a magnificent experience. . . . Spellbound, I followed him in a perfect glory of tone. . . . His voice swelled and surged in harmonious billows.' His cheeks were moist with tears when she leaned forward to kiss him. 'I have sung the best in my life for you,' he assured her very gently.

At the end of the 1916–17 season he desperately needed to rest. In normal circumstances he would have returned for his usual few weeks at the villa, but with every available ship crammed with soldiers and equipment, even the world's top singer had a low-priority rating. Not that he was too anxious to defy the German U-boats. To avoid the heat and discomfort of an American summer, he therefore accepted a return engagement with Walter Mocchi, but refused to sail until his astrologer had consulted her charts and cleared the south Atlantic of enemy submarines. He embarked early that June in the S.S. *Saga* with his linen sheets, mattresses and trunkfuls of costumes, music, inhalants, sedatives and other essentials, including Swedish snuff. He also took the 'unsinkable' suit and half a dozen life preservers.

The South American tour lasted five months and presented him to fanatical audiences throughout the Argentine, Uruguay and Brazil. It would have been a most gruelling schedule even without several benefit performances in aid of the Red Cross, Italian and American, and other Allied causes. He did not forget London's Charing Cross Hospital, which he had often strolled past in happier days on his way back to the Savoy. When an English resident in Buenos Aires mentioned the hospital's need of funds, he at once volunteered to give a concert at the Teatro Colón.

One of the theatre's conductors, Vincenzo Bellezza, had become a close friend. He gladly agreed to sail back with Caruso to New York and help prepare him for his next Metropolitan season. As this would open a bare fortnight after his return, Caruso spent most of the voyage going over his repertoire with Bellezza. En route they learned with horror of the disastrous defeat at Caporetto, where the whole Italian front had collapsed with a massive toll of killed and wounded.

Immediately after landing in New York he wired $10,000 to Rome for the relief of war refugees and added another block of Italian bonds to those already standing in his name. He also announced himself available for benefit concerts and any fundraising rallies where his name or voice might help. But he deplored Gatti-Casazza's jingoistic flag-waving, which seemed to him hysterical and overdone. The Metropolitan had dropped Wagner and Mozart from its wartime repertoire and ostentatiously dismissed Frieda Hempel among other 'enemy aliens'.

This stimulated several concert impresarios, whatever their private misgivings, to follow suit.

Caruso felt sad when Kreisler became a marked man and was not only denied the opportunity to work but often humiliated in public. He had been called to the colours by the Austrian army in 1914 and, after being declared militarily unfit, quickly returned to the United States to perform unmolested until America entered the war. He could easily have won immunity from persecution by buying Liberty Bonds but, as a dedicated pacifist, refused to do so. Many of his former friends predictably went to ground or even denounced him as pro-German. Others showed more charity. Geraldine Farrar had her faults, but not disloyalty. She continued to ask Kreisler to her parties and regularly joined him at Caruso's corner table in the Knickerbocker dining-room, where he remained an honoured guest, as always.

Although the Diamond Horseshoe box-holders had transferred their jewels to safety vaults and the Metropolitan's wings grew chillier with the coal shortage, there were few other signs of national distress when Caruso opened the season in *Aïda*. The touts quickly sold out of stall tickets at $20, but nobody complained, least of all the frenzied gallery, when their idol gave yet another magnificent Radamès. To the usual repertoire he added several performances as Samson and also proved his newly found dramatic supremacy with a powerful characterisation of Johanns Van Leyden in Meyerbeer's *Le Prophète*, following such interpreters as Mario and de Reszke. Thanks to Caruso, it soon re-established itself as a Metropolitan favourite.

He continued to record for the Victor Company and paid several visits to their spacious studios at Camden, New Jersey. They were less adjacent than the old room in Carnegie Hall but far better equipped. Every fresh Caruso record was snapped up on the day of issue. Sales, together with royalties from the standard favourites and his $125,000 from the Metropolitan, had enriched him but also the Internal Revenue: they billed him that year for $59,832.15. He took his cheque to the collector's office on the same day as a patriotic gesture. At least three times a month during 1918 he sang at Liberty Bond rallies or for Allied benefits. His own outlay on bonds was matched by other heavy disbursements. At one war charity auction he cheerfully handed over $4000 for a box of oranges.

The heavier demands on both time and cheque-book forced him at last to engage his first full-time secretary, Bruno Zirato, a tall compatriot of stately presence but also an unruffled disciplinarian with a quite remarkable memory. He was paid a large salary, but worked all hours and had a genius for dealing tactfully with people. He quickly took over all the paperwork and routine book-keeping, which relieved the tenor of entering details of his earnings and outgoings in his ledger, as he had done for so many years. Mercifully, he had now placed his complicated and large-scale investments in the hands of a trust company, relying heavily on expert advice from his friend Constant J. Sperco.

The new secretary helped to catalogue the Caruso Collection, which had expanded considerably over the past few years. The bulk of it was now housed in the Canessa Galleries on Fiftieth Street near Fifth Avenue. More important, Zirato had the right kind of qualifications for his post and had previously taught music at New York University.* Another of his invaluable assets was a capacity to pacify 'the Commendatore' when he raged at an occasional bad press notice or had a tantrum if Mario misplaced a favourite necktie or ran out of the glycerine-free cold cream which his master always used for removing make-up. It was specially prepared by a New York Italian pharmacist and Caruso would use none other.

For several years Mario had been unofficially engaged to Brunetta, an attractive brown-eyed Milanese, but was threatened with instant dismissal if they dared to marry. 'No man can serve two masters,' he would be sharply reminded. Caruso had often told reporters that he himself would never marry.

* After Caruso's death he became for a time a talent scout for the Metropolitan and later joined the New York Philharmonic Symphony Orchestra, retiring as managing director in 1959.

'I am a great singer because I have always remained a bachelor,' he once declared flippantly. 'No man can sing unless he smiles and I should never smile if I were married.'

All this changed dramatically after a chance meeting in the autumn of 1917. Caruso had gone to a christening party for the son of Fernando Tanara, a well-known singing teacher to whom he often sent promising pupils. The baby was to be named 'Enrico' after his celebrated godfather. Caruso made a boisterous entrance in his fur-collared overcoat, under which he wore an overtight suit of electric blue.

Among the guests was Dorothy Benjamin, a tall wide-bosomed young American with smooth corn-coloured hair and a swimmer's breadth of shoulder. She seemed rather lost in that swarthy volatile crowd, with everyone gabbling Italian and exchanging private jokes that meant nothing to her. Caruso had detached himself from his friends and addressed her amiably in his very fractured English flavoured with American slang. At first she gaped like a cod when he congratulated her on her large wine-red hat, but she had pleased him by recalling that his Don José, five years earlier, had been her first experience of opera. They were soon joined by an Italian woman in her mid-thirties who introduced herself as Anna, Miss Benjamin's 'companion'. She had a coquettish manner and gushed over Caruso, mentioning archly that she was training for the operatic stage and knew Pasquale Amato, who had dined more than once with the Benjamins. Caruso paid her flowery compliments in Italian, while Dorothy shifted uneasily and went crimson when he winked at her behind Anna's back. She looked drabber and far less assured than the older woman, who brashly invited him to dine at the Benjamins'. He thought this came oddly from a companion instead of the daughter of the house, but accepted. He was rewarded with a shy smile of gratitude from the American girl, whose skin, he noticed approvingly, was as smooth as porcelain.

That year he had only dined out with Scotti and other intimates or accepted invitations to formal banquets in his honour.

His friends naturally assumed that he had been smitten with Anna. Otherwise his decision to dine with the dull and rather priggish Benjamins seemed quite inexplicable. Unfortunately for all concerned, Anna had formed the very same impression.

PART FIVE

'The Star-Spangled Banner'

Chapter Eighteen

Dorothy Benjamin's background was remote from any slum tenement in Naples. Almost from her cradle days she had known the crackle of old money and New England starch. Her grandfather, editor of *Avant Garde*, enjoyed close friendships with Poe, Longfellow and Oliver Wendell Holmes. His son, Park Benjamin, had served as an ensign under Admiral Farragut in the Civil War and edited *The Scientific American* before setting up in lucrative practice as a patent lawyer. The panelled walls of his library were adorned with autographed royal letters and others signed by Washington and Benjamin Franklin.

After the death of his first wife he married a younger woman who gave him a son, Romeyn and Dorothy. Their dinner-parties included members of the inner White House circle and celebrated inventors like Edison and Marconi. But Ida Benjamin's health had collapsed soon after the birth of her daughter. She became a helpless invalid and spent the rest of her days in a series of private nursing homes.

Dorothy had been tutored by governesses until she was packed off to the Sacred Heart Convent at Torresdale, although she was brought up as an Episcopalian. On school holidays she and her brother huddled against their father's icy reserve. He had hardened into a sour, gruff-tempered martinet without much affection for his younger children. Their half-sisters had thankfully escaped into marriage.

Dorothy's four years with the nuns had been reasonably happy, but often she was punished or gently ridiculed for being so clumsy and absent-minded. She was the tallest girl in the school and tripped over her large feet at games. Gentle by nature and introspective, she was quite exceptionally ill equipped to keep house for her father. He resigned himself to having a graceless spinster permanently on his hands and saw no point in making her a decent dress allowance or encouraging visits from young men, whom he soon scared off with his sarcasm.

His temper improved, but not towards his unfortunate daughter, after Anna came to live with them. His sister-in-law, Mrs Walter Benjamin, hailed originally from Florence and befriended the signorina, who had arrived in America to study for an operatic career. She became governess to Mrs Benjamin's three daughters before being taken on by Park Benjamin. In return for her singing-lesson fees she acted as his part-time housekeeper and soon found ways of pleasing him. He gladly pumped the pianola while she sang and was easily amused by her lively chatter. 'She invited people to dinner and father spoke to them amiably enough,' Dorothy would recall sadly. 'They ignored me, although I sat in Mother's place, and I felt unwanted, alone and very stupid.' She had even less defence after Romeyn went overseas with the Marines.

Anna had no difficulty in persuading Park Benjamin to welcome the famous tenor, whose performances they had often enjoyed together at the Metropolitan. She hoarded all his records and for several days before his first visit directed the cook to prepare spicy dishes, sauces and Neapolitan pastries. She also bought herself an elegant new toilette for the occasion. Dorothy's blue silk dress matched her eyes but otherwise seemed more suited to some demure lady's companion than to the nominal mistress of the house.

Caruso had raided his operatic wardrobe for the occasion, finally deciding on an outfit adapted from his costume in *Julien*. He wore a powder-blue tuxedo with blue velvet lapels, white silk socks and patent-leather slippers. A cape was flung over one shoulder, topped by a wide-brimmed felt. Park Benjamin, high-collared and stiff in conventional evening dress, concealed any sartorial shock with patrician fortitude as he gave an arm to his very nervous daughter, while Caruso led Anna to a table sparkling with damask, silver and crystal.

The tenor had discovered in advance that Mr Benjamin was an authority on Poe and thoughtfully read up a few biographi-

246

cal details, which he aired in his pidgin English. The host seemed more amused, however, by his backstage anecdotes and reminiscences of the Tsar, the German Emperor and Edward VII. He also talked with quiet authority about his own coins and bronzes, while tactfully admiring Mr Benjamin's treasures. To Anna he addressed amiable gallantries without once slipping into doubtful taste. Either by accident or design he was not over-attentive to Dorothy but considerately avoided talking too much music, which would have left her even more adrift. A few days later he sent over three front-row tickets for *Aïda*, and soon afterwards invited the young women to drive out to the country with him. Mr Benjamin did not object, imagining that his daughter would be playing chaperone, a delusion which Anna fostered coyly.

Caruso behaved with rare decorum during those winter months at the turn of the year. He amused them with droll stories of his boyhood, and Dorothy soon found herself warming to him. She began accompanying Anna to the Metropolitan although not really caring for opera ('It seemed to me noisy and unnatural,' she would later confess.) The celebrated voice attracted her far less than Caruso's kindness and jollity. She had also glimpsed a lonely man inside the opulent fur-collared coat.

One evening in late February 1918, just after celebrating his forty-fifth birthday, he at last found an excuse to be alone with her for the first time. While returning from one of their afternoon drives she had happened to mention casually that she would be dining that evening with family friends. He asked Mr Benjamin's permission to drive her there. In the car he took her hand and blurted out, 'Now, Doro, when can we be married?' To his delight she murmured gently, 'You must ask Father's consent.'*

He presented himself the following day while Dorothy eavesdropped at a ventilator connecting her room with the

* Mrs Caruso's own account of her courtship and marriage not only offers revealing sidelights on the tenor's psychological make-up but provides an unconsciously charming self-portrait.

247

library. Park Benjamin seemed too startled to raise much objection but, as a seasoned lawyer, insisted upon time to consider this quite unexpected proposal. He then gave his provisional approval, subject to a six-month's engagement. Anna offered tight-lipped congratulations but henceforth, and very naturally in the circumstances, declined to act as chaperone to the starry-eyed couple. Dorothy's half-sister, Mrs Torrance Goddard, came up from Alabama for some weeks.

Once Caruso's friends had recovered from the shock, they teased him unmercifully but wished him happiness, only a minority prophesying disaster. Their attitude was understandable, although with hindsight one can rationalise even such an apparently grotesque union between the middle-aged tenor and a top-drawer Cinderella, twenty years his junior. Any latter-day psychiatrist could have filled a convincing dossier without even advancing to the couch. After Ada's departure Caruso had inevitably turned to younger women and would probably have married Elisa Ganelli but for his snobbish aversion to her family. The Benjamin pedigree and superior caste must have added spice to this romance.

He was a tired man, physically and mentally, during the last phase of the war, and had become almost a solitary. He did not conceal his depression from Scotti and other close friends who saw through his exuberant salesmanship at bond rallies and knew how he worried that Fofò, now in the army, might be killed or taken prisoner. He also brooded over reports from Signa that his agents and farm stewards were fleecing him. He had wept on hearing that his exquisitely carved doors were worm-eaten and all the gate hinges rusted.

Psychologically he was ripe for a new adventure which might help to nourish his middle-aged ego. This well-built blond young woman radiated a calm serenity and must have twitched certain delicate nerves never far below the surface. Since his early youth he had developed an Oedipus complex as wide as a barn. His beloved mother had been replaced by an almost equally indulgent stepmother before Ada Giachetti took over. He had then turned for sympathy to various matrons:

'Mammina' Farrar, stately Belle Goelet and Chaliapin's aged mother whom he used to slobber over like a spaniel.

Dorothy's reaction to him was less complicated. She could not help being flattered by the attentions of the world's most acclaimed singer. After years of neglect she was like a bemused child at a Christmas tree when he began buying her expensive gifts as soon as they were betrothed. As a substitute 'father figure' he must have had overwhelming appeal, but a chord of mutual sympathy was also struck by his orphaned childhood. He soon discovered that she could be moved to tears like any emotional Latin.

Between their almost daily meetings and chaperoned suppers he had to deal with his business affairs and the ceaseless routine rehearsals or appearances. He now confided more in Dorothy and often turned to her for advice. They spent anxious hours discussing an offer from Jesse L. Lasky, who seemed confident that Caruso could repeat Geraldine Farrar's box-office success in *Carmen*. He and his wife, Blanche, would never forget that far-off November night in 1903 when they had failed to book seats at the Metropolitan for *Rigoletto* and stood cheering wildly at the back of the gallery with half of 'Little Italy'.

Caruso had inconsequentially given Joseph Schenck an option on his film services, but neither had shown much enthusiasm to pursue it. Lasky now decided to buy out Schenck's rights for $40,000 and offered the tenor a fee of $100,000 for each of two pictures to be shot at the Famous Players Studio on Fifty-sixth Street. He dithered. Although his Samson had grown in dramatic stature, he was very doubtful of taking non-singing roles. But the terms were tempting, and Calvin Child predicted that millions of cinema-goers would boost the sales of his records. Guessing Caruso's true inclination, Dorothy prompted him to accept but had her private doubts. She was far happier teaching him the lyrics of 'Over There' which his friend, George M. Cohan, had sent him. She read the words over to him several times until every vowel and consonant had been memorised. He delivered the

249

song with enormous gusto at an Ocean Grove concert on 27 July, his audience cheering and waving flags, many of them in tears despite the rolled Italian r's and words which emerged strangely as 'Hover Dere'. The record was issued soon afterwards. An autographed copy, auctioned at the Waldorf-Astoria in aid of the *Sun's* Tobacco Fund for Soldiers, realised $125,000.

More than once during that blistering summer he regretted yielding to Lasky. Shooting went on from 8 a.m. until late at night, often between benefit concerts and recording sessions. He became more and more depressed about the two pictures. The first, *My Cousin*, was tied up with the release of a catchy Gus Edwards song of the same title but had little else in its favour. The so-called script called for Caruso to play two parts, a clean-shaven barber and his moustachioed cousin, a famous tenor who arrives unexpectedly in New York. Trick photography proved equal to this challenge, but Caruso's best acting was done between takes, when he clowned behind the cameras or fooled about with the props. The second picture, *A Splendid Romance*, was even weaker, but Lasky continued to hope desperately that Schenck would soon be chewing his fingernails in envy.

During weekend breaks from the set Caruso hurried off to the Benjamins' summer house at Spring Lake, New Jersey. He always arrived with a carload of gifts: Havanas for his future father-in-law; perfume to placate the still sulking Anna; and jewellery for his fiancée, who was, however, far more excited by a police dog puppy, Spoletta. After the dusty drive Caruso would at once strip off and splash about in the sea. He also liked dressing up in khaki overalls to mow the lawn or clip hedges, often singing a gay *canzonetta* which the gardeners applauded rather more than his carefree handling of the shears.

His antics were possibly a little too vulgar for Park Benjamin's prissy taste. Anna may also have found the couple's hand-in-hand bliss intolerable. Whatever the reason, Mr Benjamin turned hostile and began denigrating Caruso's 'frivolous' profession. He reminded Dorothy that her brother had been severely wounded making the world safe for democracy and fat tenors too cowardly to fight. Caruso's sordid history was now recalled in detail: the bottom-pinching episode in Central Park; his two sons born out of wedlock; and finally a catalogued list of women with whom his name had been associated. In short, he had become a most undesirable son-in-law and Dorothy was forbidden to see him again. Shocked at first, she now guessed what must have been discussed in the library where her father and the housekeeper were closeted for hours when they returned from Spring Lake. Anna had no doubt made it clear that her good name would suffer if she remained in the house after Dorothy's departure.

Mr Benjamin soon discovered that his ugly duckling had not only grown prettier but seemed to have developed a backbone as stiff as his own. She refused to give up seeing Caruso even if he were barred from the house. Her father at once changed his tactics and now announced blandly that he would give them his blessing if the tenor proved his bona fides by settling half a million dollars on his bride. It was a most preposterous condition, but made from a lawyer's shrewd assessment. Through his Wall Street contacts he had learned that Caruso's assets, although considerable, were mainly tied up in bonds and other securities. His liquidity would not run to anything like half a million. Moreover, the quick-tempered Italian might well resent an implied charge of fortune-hunting and abandon the whole affair.

Dorothy went tearfully to the Knickerbocker and informed Caruso of this new ultimatum. For some minutes he was speechless and quite unable to adjust to a situation completely foreign to anything in his previous experience. In southern Italy a bride's parents ritually provided the dowry, however small. Only in the rarest cases where the girl came from an impoverished and destitute family, or was being 'sold' to some rich old man practically on his deathbed, would there be any departure from this centuries-old tradition.

Mr Benjamin's demand had shocked him almost as much as

251

being locked up in that cell in the Central Park police station. He began pacing the room furiously, puffing on one cigarette after another. Dorothy dabbed her eyes while he babbled about stocks and shares and told her angrily that he could not put his hand on a cool half million without realising securities on a war-depressed market. That would clearly be both foolish and unpatriotic. But how, he kept asking her and himself, could anyone seriously doubt his financial stability? His combined income from the Metropolitan and the Victor Company still averaged well over $250,000 a year; his bonds and blue chips were worth a couple of million dollars, while his other assets included the valuable collection in the Canessa Galleries, apart from his Villa Bellosguardo, on which he had already spent the better part of $175,000.

Once he had calmed down, he saw through the manœuvre. He grasped Dorothy's hands and told her very gently that he would never sell his Liberty Bonds or anything else as a prerequisite to marriage. Afterwards she could have anything he possessed. He begged her to think the matter over and decide between her father and himself. She telephoned him next morning and they were married later that day.

Dorothy arrived at the Hotel Knickerbocker wearing a dark blue satin gown, bought off the peg, and a simple toque trimmed with a white wing at the back. An old family friend Mrs Keith, had arranged for her to use her charge account. They departed in Caruso's car to City Hall for a special licence and went on to the Little Church Around the Corner, but the pastor became flustered and wanted proof that the tenor was not already married! They at once moved off to the Marble Collegiate Church at Fifth Avenue and Twenty-ninth, where the ceremony was performed with Bruno Zirato as best man and Mrs Keith the only other witness. Caruso, straw boater in hand, wore magpie shoes with a charcoal-grey lounge suit and a gardenia buttonhole. He had tears in his eyes when the minister gave his blessing but became boisterious as they drove to the Famous Players Studio. There Jesse Lasky hastily presented the bride with a bouquet of roses (from an adjacent set!) and arranged a private run-through of *My Cousin* as a wedding present.

A scrum of reporters, photographers and well-wishers had already gathered at the Knickerbocker. Champagne was served by the magnum, but Caruso felt too 'emotionated' to give them a song. When the last photograph had been taken, he kissed his mother's portrait and whispered to his bride, 'I wish she could have been here.' Before leaving for a quiet drive, taking the kitchen elevator to dodge the crowds, he urged her to write to her father and ask his forgiveness.

It was a well-meant but quite futile gesture. Park Benjamin never spoke to Dorothy again. Within a short time he legalised Anna's presence in his house by formally adopting her as his daughter. Dorothy was unceremoniously disinherited. He had at once drawn up a new will, in which he bequeathed his town-house and $60,000 to Anna, who was to become his sole heiress and beneficiary after the death of his widow. Caruso settled his own account rather less dramatically. In his ledger for 20 August 1918 he simply wrote in a neat clear hand: 'Expenses for my marriage ... $50.00.'

They took a six-room suite adjoining his previous apartment which would now accommodate Zirato and Mario, the studio, office, a lounge for visitors, a wardrobe-room and a small dining-room where he could snack lightly with his accompanist Fucito, during practice hours. The new private suite had three bedrooms and a large salon. Two rooms were also hopefully set aside for future occupation by a baby and nanny. A place of honour in the salon, into which Caruso had moved his showcases, was occupied by a very special wedding gift, the black and gold Chinese lacquer phonograph from the Victor Company, together with a gold disc of 'La donna è mobile', his very first recording for them.

Dorothy soon occupied herself with furnishing but had some awkward early moments trying to adjust to those two huge suites, which sometimes overspilled. She would later recall being summoned to Caruso's studio one afternoon when just about to take a bath. She forgot to turn off the taps and flooded the apartment. He pulled fierce faces but soon forgave her for the ruined carpets. He had interrupted her bath to present a small gold case containing her very first chequebook with a deposit of $5000 'for petty cash'.

Even without the disputed half million dollars, she discovered that life had suddenly become both opulent and nerve-rackingly public. Her husband encouraged her to open accounts at Tiffany's and elsewhere, but obviously preferred accompanying her on shopping sprees in which she would never have dared to indulge by herself. Soon after their marriage he took her to Joseph's on Fifth Avenue, where she selected a modest moleskin jacket. Laughing uproariously, he bought the entire selection of sables, ermine and chinchilla coats paraded by the manne-quins. Before long her wardrobes were bursting with over one hundred gowns, wraps and topcoats, together with all the accessories. He also bought jewels on almost a maharajah's scale, starting with his wedding present to her, a magnificent necklace of two hundred stones. A wall safe was specially installed in their bedroom.

One day, after lunching with him at the Casino in Central Park, she happened to admire the upholstery and bodywork of an open Packard. They drove in the park for a while in their little green Lancia, with the Irish chauffeur, Fitzgerald, at the wheel. Outside the Knickerbocker stood the Packard surroun-ded by a crowd of onlookers eagerly exploring its wonders. Caruso opened the door with a deep bow and solemnly invited his wife to take her first outing. He had bought it from the owner for $12,000 while she left him alone in the restaurant for a few minutes.

He took as much pride in her clothes as in his own and used to fuss over her while she dressed, often suggesting last-minute changes. Her new wardrobe and jewel-cases gave her much-needed confidence, but his encouragement helped even more after so many years with her father. Within a fortnight of her marriage, smiling and elegant but inwardly nervous, she made her first public début at the Sheepshead Bay race-track on

Long Island. Caruso wore a sporty boater, but his cheeks had such deep fissures that he might have passed as the middle-aged father of the plumpish young woman by his side. However, his eyes sparkled as usual and he responded like a rampant charge of electricity to the cheering audience of 100,000 people. The recital ended with 'The Star-Spangled Banner', rendered phonetically. This was a benefit performance for the New York Police Reserves, who later showed their appreciation by giving him an honorary captaincy. As Commissioner Enright pinned on the silver badge, Caruso asked solemnly whether he now had the authority to arrest people. Enright nodded. 'Then I must go to the Metropolitan right away and take Mr Gatti,' he laughed, gleefully rubbing his badge.

A few days after the police concert, Dorothy accompanied him to Central Park, where he inaugurated the free open-air recitals organised by Mayor John F. Hylan. She had become acutely nervous when a motor-cycle police escort flanked their car all the way from the Knickerbocker. She clutched his hand as they mounted the dais, where the Mayor presented her with a bouquet of roses, tied with red, white and blue ribbons. She managed a gracious smile although still terrified until Caruso sang 'Hover Dere', in which she and the rest of the vast crowd joined.

While preparing *Samson et Dalila* for the next Metropolitan season he performed at several Liberty Loan drives, one of which raised $4 million. It stimulated a journalist to estimate that his voice had sold bonds to the value of over $20 million since 1914. 'Doro' had tried to make him slow down but was herself the first to collapse after a severe attack of influenza.

On 9 November a rumour flashed through the city that the Armistice had been signed. Delirious New Yorkers surged into the streets. Hundreds converged on the Knickerbocker and called for Caruso to come out on a flag-bedecked balcony and sing the Allied national anthems. Dorothy impulsively bought the hotel florist's entire stock and tossed hundreds of red roses, white carnations and blue violets from the balcony.

Armistice night coincided with the opening of the opera season, but even Samson could not hold back the waves of hysteria that swept the house. An elaborate tableau was staged after Act One, with the flags of the victorious Allies held aloft by each country's representative in the company, led by Caruso and Louise Homer. As no Englishman happened to be singing that night, an Armenian baritone was hastily recruited to carry the Union Jack.

Next evening Dorothy made her first appearance at the Metropolitan escorted to a box by one of her uncles. 'I wore white velvet, diamonds and chinchilla and was in a daze,' she wrote afterwards. Very conscious of the glinting lorgnettes, she escaped to Caruso's dressing-room after the second act of *La Forza del Destino*. He took her in his arms and whispered tenderly, 'Do you enjoy, my Doro?' A day or two later she found him in tears at his desk. He was writing a letter of condolence to Jean de Reszke, whose only son, skylarking in a field a few hours after the Armistice, had stepped on a land-mine which blew off his head.

Caruso's kindness was often misplaced. Early in 1919 he received a surprise visit from the son-in-law of his old teacher, Vergine. Punzo had by now lost hair and voice but still boasted of past successes. Finally he broke down and confessed that he and his wife were almost destitute. Caruso confided privately to Dorothy that his former fellow pupil was as 'proud and stupid' as ever but nevertheless engaged him at a generous salary to assist Mario and help as dresser and make-up man. He also made himself useful as a masseur. With his strong build he could lift and manipulate Caruso far more easily than the slender valet.

Doro showed Punzo the same consideration and courtesy as to the rest of the staff. Mario adored her and was path-etically grateful when she promised to help reunite him with his Brunetta. She also treated Zirato with admirable tact, although often itching to take over when he laboriously typed out letters with two fingers. She appreciated his unstinted devotion to her husband and soon became a very close friend of his vivacious fiancée and future wife, Nina Morgana, a soprano who frequently partnered Caruso at concerts.

She shared her husband's affection for one of his favourite retainers named Schol, a German Jewish gnome with a shock of white hair. He was an umbrella-maker by trade and leader of the Metropolitan claque. He worshipped Caruso and regularly waited to escort him to his car and say good-night. Caruso always stopped at the stage-door for a cheerful word and sent messages or a hamper of kosher delicacies if little Schol missed an appearance through illness.

Caruso could be just as capable of unthinking cruelty. Dorothy had soon become aware of his idiosyncrasies about personal hygiene, but was shocked by his brutality towards a certain French tenor who had sent them seats for one of his concerts. Caruso seldom went to hear others sing, but had yielded on this occasion to humour her. Just before curtain-rise the Frenchman entered their box to welcome them. Caruso turned away in distaste. 'Go and brush your teeth,' he snapped. 'Your breath is intolerable.'

He was also abnormally possessive and sternly forbade his wife to put on rouge or mascara, although he did not object to other women using them. One night he refused to let her wear a new black velvet gown at the opera. 'It shows half your back,' he shouted. Next day he made amends with a bracelet from Tiffany's.

She recalled a more serious argument while they were dining out with friends after a performance in Atlanta. The night was warm and the restaurant band played so melodiously under the stars that he felt homesick for Naples. He jumped excitedly to his feet and asked her to dance. As nobody else had yet taken the floor, she begged to be excused. He laughed and trotted off with their hostess. The husband, a fat jolly man with a drink or three under his belt, then coaxed Dorothy to dance with him. Caruso glared at them as they waltzed past. He was already waiting with her wrap when she returned breathlessly to the table. Back at the hotel all his jealous rage boiled over as he accused her of making him a public figure of ridicule. He went on raving and swearing until she burst into tears.

Immediately he begged her forgiveness, beating his head against the wall until the blood ran. Over breakfast, wearing a shamefaced look and a plaster over his temple, he kissed her hand and sighed, 'I wish you to become very fatty so no one else look at you.'

Such outbursts were rare. She recognised the signs of irritation when his neuralgic headaches threatened or some critic had dared to write an unflattering notice. She would massage his temples or softly play the piano as he reclined on the sofa dressed in one of his brocaded jackets with silk trousers and a shirt open at the throat. They spent many tranquil evenings alone. He inspected his coins and stamps while she worked on her embroidery or pasted his press clippings (only the favourable ones!) into the big albums. By midnight he would be ravenous again and used to telephone the hotel chef to send up a plateful of chicken sandwiches, which he devoured before retiring for his normal eight hours. They dined once or twice a week at Del Pezzo's or Pane's, where she now forked her spaghetti like a good Italian and without the heresy of cutting it.

They gave several intimate dinner-parties in their private suite. 'Toto' Scotti was usually present, often with the Kreislers and Geraldine Farrar. George M. Cohan always managed to sparkle on crackers and milk, but John McCormack was the star turn at every gathering. One of his most hilarious party-pieces was to re-enact the scene when some stage-hand, infuriated by Chaliapin's autocratic behaviour, lifted the giant basso in full armour on his mule for his entrance in *Don Quixote* and then stuck a pin in its haunches, giving him a very rough ride indeed.

Chaliapin would dine with them whenever he passed through New York en route for a concert tour. He once took Caruso aside to warn him gravely against risking his voice and health by adding too many dramatic roles to his repertoire. Caruso thanked him without mentioning that he was secretly studying the score of Halévy's *La Juive*. Eléazar, the tragic

Jewish goldsmith, had set his imagination on fire, but it was an even more powerful challenge than Samson, and he would not discuss it with anyone except Dorothy.

He rarely allowed shop-talk at his dinner table and discouraged guests from repeating newspaper gossip in his presence. When someone once asked if McCormack actually paid more income tax than himself, as a columnist had reported, he would not be drawn. Next day, however, he sent a note to the Irishman: 'Congratulations, my friend, but see that it doesn't happen again.' In fact his earnings for 1918, despite numerous unpaid benefit performances, resulted in a tax demand for $153,933.70, well beyond anything McCormack had so far faced.

On New Year's Day, 1919, Caruso gave a party that cost even more than that enormous income tax bill. He had long felt guilty about his modest $50 wedding, which had brought an avalanche of gifts. He persuaded Dorothy that a little retroactive hospitality would not only thank their friends but give her an opportunity to shake hands over a glass of wine with the musicians, stage-hands and others who had helped him at the Metropolitan, apart from members of New York's Italian colony and a number of devoted opera-goers. Dorothy's brother and her half sisters would obviously be invited and some of her old friends with whom she had lost touch during her father's stern régime. They could not of course forget dear little Schol or the hotel barber or Frank, their regular waiter in the dining-room. The list grew by the hour until Dorothy, more and more bewildered, gave up all attempt to control the numbers.

A thousand invitations went out and three thousand people invaded the Armenonville Suite at the Knickerbocker. Gate-crashers were far outnumbered by those whom Caruso had good-naturedly invited without troubling to send formal cards. Guests danced to two orchestras until 3 a.m., refreshed by a lavish buffet and the finest imported champagne. After shaking hands continuously for five hours, the host and hostess fled to their own suite for chicken sandwiches and a chilled bottle which had materialised with Mario, that ever-thoughtful wraith in grey alpaca.

That season was perhaps the most testing in Caruso's entire career. Despite Chaliapin's warnings and his own fatigue, he added several performances of *Samson et Dalila* and *Le Prophète* to his normal repertoire. He also continued to give concerts which sometimes demanded the tightest of schedules. Early in March 1919, after singing at Ann Arbor, Michigan, he received a wire from Otto Kahn ordering him to return immediately to New York for a League of Nations rally concert. He had less than half an hour to rush from Grand Central and go on stage to sing 'the Star-Spangled Banner'. It inspired him to do a caricature of President Wilson for *La Follia*. Not long afterwards he was amused to see the original sketch in a shop window, priced at $75. 'Better we stop singing and draw,' he chuckled to Dorothy. But he never regretted turning down an offer of $100,000 a year from Joseph Pulitzer to do cartoons exclusively for his newspaper group. The commitment to draw free caricatures for Marziale Sisca remained sacred.

A week after the League of Nations concert, Dorothy was received into the Catholic faith, which enabled them to be remarried in St Patrick's Cathedral. Zirato and Dorothy's aunt, Mrs Walter Benjamin, acted as witnesses. Caruso had exerted no pressure but was obviously delighted by her decision, which may have been prompted by a recent consultation with her doctor. He was overjoyed to hear that he might soon become a father, although it was still too early for definite confirmation. Moreover, he was far too superstitious to announce the exciting news so far in advance, even to their closest friends.

Gatti-Casazza had been hugging a secret of his own. Rarely given to sentimental gestures, he now seized the opportunity to celebrate Caruso's silver jubilee on the operatic stage. With the approval of Otto Kahn and publicity-minded Billy Guard, he chose Saturday, 22 March, the end of the season, when the tenor would also be making his five hundred and fiftieth appearance at the Metropolitan. Caruso received the news with some dismay. He could not refuse to cooperate but hoped that the ceremony, if any, would be simple and not an occasion for speech-making, which always embarrassed him, particularly if he had to reply in English. He made only one condition: all proceeds would go to the Metropolitan's Emergency Fund.

He did not hear until afterwards of a vicious squabble backstage. The gala programme offered no difficulties. With Scotti and other members of the company he would give excerpts from *L'Elisir d'Amore*, *Le Prophète* and, inevitably, *I Pagliacci*. James M. Beck had agreed to deliver an official address after the performance, when Police Commissioner Enright would present the guest of honour with the City of New York's flag. This angered Mayor Hylan, who announced that it would only be handed over if Beck, a hated political opponent, withdrew. It took all Kahn's diplomacy to make the necessary adjustment.

All was sweetness and light on the stage, where Caruso sat on a gold chair near the footlights. Behind him stood a table laden with gifts. The thirty-five Diamond Horseshoe box-holders presented a parchment scroll and Gatti-Casazza bestowed a gold medal, but Caruso was rather more 'emotionated' by his loving cup from the chorus, a silver vase from the orchestra and an exquisite platinum and diamond watch which Geraldine Farrar offered on behalf of her fellow singers and sealed with an affectionate kiss. He was already in tears when, grasping the municipal flag, he made his brief thank-you speech, agonisingly mastered after several hours of coaching from Dorothy. Otto Kahn was also much moved when he addressed him on behalf of the board, but could not deny himself a touch of heavy Wall Street humour: 'You have managed even to find a generous thought, a pleasant gesture, and a gracious word in going through the painful process of paying an income tax into six figures.' He was applauded, however, for his tribute to 'the most glorious and perfect voice of a generation and one which, for having heard, posterity will envy us. But in your case, we admire the voice, the art, and the man.'

261

This jubilee celebration helped to comfort Caruso for his disastrous film début. The picture had opened at the Rivoli in New York with resounding studio publicity, but the star failed completely to register as a silent comedian. Box-office receipts slumped so dismally that Lasky had to refund rentals to scores of complaining exhibitors all over the country. Adolph Zukor cut his losses and cancelled all booking contracts for *A Splendid Romance*, which was never shown. 'I can't even remember the name of it, and please don't try and remind me,' Lasky lamented years later.*

After the Metropolitan season Caruso immediately began an eight-week concert tour at $7000 upwards a performance, often at two-day intervals. He soon paid the price in crippling headaches. Poor Mario would often stand by helplessly while his master tried on a dozen collars, discarding each in turn as too tight or too loose until he was satisfied. Sometimes he had to force himself to go on stage after tiring journeys to fulfil engagements in Atlanta, Nashville, St Louis, Kansas City, Chicago and Milwaukee. Postponements or cancellations were unthinkable nightmares. Special trains ran from surrounding towns, and posters announced that heavy cash deposits had been made by the promoters to guarantee refunds in the event of his non-appearance. He was billed everywhere as 'the most glorious voice of this generation'. Each performance became an automatic sell-out, with an unprecedented local rush for $100 dress suits. ('Caruso will be correctly attired and we feel certain you desire to be as well dressed,' one Denver outfitter reminded his customers.)

The tour ended on 22 May 1919 in Springfield, Massachusetts. Two days later he sailed for Naples with Dorothy and

* He was partially consoled by purchasing Dorothy's biography of her husband for $100,000 and persuading MGM a few years later to film it as *The Great Caruso*, with Mario Lanza in the star role. It broke all records at the Radio City Music Hall and almost every picture theatre throughout the world, despite numerous melodramatic inaccuracies, including Caruso's boyish romance with Dorothy after making his New York début and his wholly fictitious death scene.

Mario. It had been a year of strain, both professionally and personally, but now he was overjoyed by the prospect of becoming a father. Dorothy could expect a normal pregnancy and, complications apart, would have her baby in December. Caruso was bursting to break the news to his stepmother and Giovanni, whom he had invited to Signa to meet his wife. Martino had already been instructed to have the villa looking its best for what promised to be not only a late honeymoon but an emotional family reunion after two long years of separation.

They had booked passage on the *Giuseppe Verdi*, which seemed to him a happy augury. Without U-boats in prospect he had not troubled to consult his astrologer, who might possibly have warned him of other alarming portents. Aboard ship he felt completely relaxed and delighted Dorothy with his lyrical descriptions of the Villa Bellosguardo. She had argued against his decision to sing in Mexico City, even for $7000 a performance, before the Metropolitan season opened in November, but he laughed off her fears. He also pooh-poohed alarmist reports of a civil war in Mexico, but took the precaution of making the impresario deposit a large sum in advance. As for his health, he promised solemnly to take his ease until September apart from giving a little study to *La Juive*.

Not long after their arrival in Signa, an earthquake tremor shook the walls of the Villa Bellosguardo and brought down several of its ornate ceilings. A violent hailstorm made the watchdogs howl and rattle their chains, adding to Dorothy's terror. It was the first of her many shocks during that 'honeymoon' summer.

Chapter Nineteen

Dorothy was entranced by the views from their hilltop balustrades. The Arno threaded across Tuscany with Florence, forty miles distant, often glinting through the heat haze. In the shady park they walked hand in hand under stately cypresses while Caruso paused at intervals to discourse on some of the statues lining the main drive. He took far more pride, however, in a series of medallions adorning each door of the large salon and showing him in costume as Canio, Radamès and other familiar roles.

His sketchbooks had always included many self-caricatures, but in recent years he had also taken to casting bronzes of his own head. One of them stood on his white piano at the Knickerbocker, where visitors could not possibly miss it. This narcissism was paralleled, perhaps coincidentally, by a growing sensitiveness to any criticism of his voice. But he had a worthier and more practical reason for starting on yet another head that summer in Signa. It was modelled on the sketches he had drawn of Eléazar's features while experimenting with make-up, particularly on the beard and false nose. He spent at least three hours daily on the score of the five-act *La Juive*, which had developed into an almost obsessive personal challenge.

There seemed no valid reason for anxiety at this stage of his career. His performance level might be more variable than in his vintage, but his top notes and vocalisation still offered incomparable largesse in all the showpiece operas. Concert audiences were even easier to satisfy with the bravura arias and a silver shower of Neapolitan ballads for encores. But dollars and applause, while equally welcome, now meant less to him than a compulsion to silence both his own doubts and the occasional note of critical dissent. It had already driven him to master Samson, but the more complex subtleties of Eléazar had become the supreme test, both vocally and dramatically.

La Juive had not been heard at the Metropolitan for thirty years. Various previous attempts to revive the opera in German, with largely Wagnerian casts, had failed. Caruso resolved to sing it in French and prove himself superior to Gilbert-Louis Duprez, one of the few successful interpreters in that language. Unlike his own legendary countryman, Mario, who had disliked playing a character that denied him the chance to display his handsome profile, he had no such inhibitions about Halévy's devout Jew. He cut deeper and more ageing lines into the clay model, on which he would gaze with almost self-hypnotic absorption while singing Eléazar's moving 'Rachel! Quand du Seigneur' from Act Four. He also practised the most minute changes of inflexion until his accompanist slumped wearily over the keyboard. All textual difficulties in phrasing and pronunciation were meticulously entered into his note-book even while he was out for a drive.

Emerging from the studio in a sweat-drenched shirt, he would often apologise to Dorothy for his neglect. He fussed tenderly over her although as yet she showed no visible signs of pregnancy. She was made to rest quite unnecessarily, but did not object, much preferring the cool peace of her flower-filled room to meeting their house-guests. She could not follow their Neapolitan dialect and felt stupid when they blinked at her stilted Italian.

Caruso's stepmother had time for nobody but her Enrico, whom she often spoon-fed from her own plate to remind him of some childhood delicacy. Between long prayer sessions in the chapel she would fan herself in her favourite high-backed chair while listening to his records with a blissfully withdrawn smile. She treated Giovanni with contempt and once brought him so sharply to order that he snatched off his straw hat and bit a piece out of it in sheer impotent fury. Now fat and moon-faced he was very conscious of his status and liked to recall how he had started his brother's career by taking over as his military proxy in Rieti. He was polite to Dorothy only in Caruso's presence.

She wrote later of noisy meals in the vast banqueting-hall

where everyone smacked rubbery lips over pyramids of oily spaghetti and swilled the local wine. Her sensibilities had soon been shocked by the roughness of the men, who often sat down to table in soiled vests and afterwards belched or scratched their groins while the plump wives, with bosoms heaving under black satin, taunted each other and intrigued ceaselessly. She soon persuaded her husband to join her in a light poultry and fish diet, which Mario served them personally. It was yet another reason for isolating her from his relatives. They made it plain that this uppish foreigner had somehow seduced their idol.

Louise Saer, Mimmi's governess, was a comfort. She could at least speak English, although inclined to dry up completely in the vicinity of Caruso, whose mock-fierce teasing always panicked her. Dorothy took at once to the mousy little woman but thought she was spoiling Mimmi. Now nearly fifteen, big-boned and already sprouting bristles on his upper lip, he looked ridiculous in a sailor-suit with short pants, but he amused Dorothy with his small talk delivered in most careful English. Fofò, on the other hand, seemed far less agreeable. Surly and undersized, he lounged about in his army private's uniform, eating chocolate or taking his father's big hairless Newfoundland, Beppo, on solitary walks. His temper was not improved by Caruso's chatter about the coming baby, who, he predicted confidently, would be a beautiful American like her mother.

'I was often lonely at Signa, though never alone,' Dorothy recalled. She was relieved when they drove off to Florence for some shopping and afterwards ate delicious codfish in a quiet restaurant. But even these expeditions became less pleasant when food riots broke out and shops were looted by mobs of unemployed. The newspapers now carried daily reports of strikes by workers clamouring for jobs, higher wages and cheaper food. There was constant mention of a former newspaper editor, one Benito Mussolini, who had organised a militia of ex-soldiers to campaign for a tax on war profits and other reforms. But far more alarming than this grandly styled *Fasci di Combattimento*, which nobody took too seriously, was a

'Bolshevik' threat to seize factories and break up all the large estates.

Even little Signa awoke from centuries of peaceful dozing. Towards the end of July a crowd of labourers raided a local farm, killing off all the cattle and burning crops. Caruso's relations with his peasant-farmers had been so cordial that he imagined himself immune from any similar outrage. He was over optimistic. One morning several hundred peasants, many from beyond Signa, advanced on the Villa Bellosguardo. On being turned back they uprooted the huge gates and drove up the avenue in their farm waggons, waving red flags and singing revolutionary choruses.

Caruso kept his temper when their spokesman shouted angrily that whole families starved while his stores were bursting with grain, wine and olive oil. He questioned their authority to 'requisition', but by this time they had already broken down the cellar doors and were helping themselves. Some were eyeing his paintings and furniture so meaningly that he steered them from the salon and invited them to take any food they required. Once their waggons were loaded they drove his three cars out of the garage. He protested that he and his wife were shortly leaving and needed only enough victuals to last a fortnight and a car to take them as far as Genoa. A few days later their leader reappeared with a jingling pouch which, he explained sheepishly, contained the Signor Commendatore's share from the sale of his oil and grain. Caruso refused the money but found it difficult to look too severe.

Their disturbed 'holiday' had its compensations. He had finally mastered the score of *La Juive* and was now impatient to return to New York and discuss details with Gatti-Casazza. Meantime it had been decided, thanks to Dorothy's arguments, that Mimmi should travel back with them and complete his education in America. She also convinced her husband that he no longer had any right to oppose Mario's marriage. He grumbled but gave the valet three day's leave to marry before sailing time, reminding him fiercely, 'No babies,' a quite remarkable prohibition from an expectant father! To underline

267

his displeasure he refused to meet Brunetta, who was to be kept away from the Knickerbocker and not attempt to interfere in any way with her husband's duties.

Mario departed thankfully and was waiting at the dock in Genoa when his master went aboard with Dorothy and Mimmi. Brunetta remained in Mario's cabin throughout the voyage, miserably seasick and terrified of Caruso's displeasure, although Dorothy assured her that he was far too soft-hearted to stay angry for very long.

She knew him. Before departing for Mexico City with Zirato, Mario, Punzo and his accompanist, Fucito, Caruso suddenly enquired about Brunetta, who would be left alone and friendless in New York for two long months. Dorothy informed him that she had already been found part-time work. Instead of being relieved, he objected furiously to any 'member of my household' working outside. He quickly decided that Brunetta should help his wife prepare the baby's layette and generally make herself useful. He also rented a large room with bath at the hotel for the couple and quietly doubled Mario's salary.

With the baby due in three months, Dorothy could not of course accompany him to Mexico. She wept when he left, but was comforted by a tender note sent from Pennsylvania Station and delivered by special messenger. He would write or wire almost every day, declaring his longing for 'Doro mia' and his unbearable loneliness without her, appending the fullest bulletins on his own headaches, throat ailments and 'blod pression'. No doubt his 'maind' was full of her and the baby, as he said, but he could easily have refused an engagement which involved separation from his wife bearing their first child, quite apart from the obvious risks to his lungs in a high altitude. Plainly he had not relished facing several weeks in New York before the next Metropolitan season and looked forward to his first visit to Mexico. He also knew that Latin American audiences had always idolised him and bought huge numbers of his records.

He seemed in high spirits while he studied his notes on *La Juive* as the train headed for the border. It was flattering to be met at Saltillo by an armoured car and fifty soldiers who would escort him and his entourage through bandit country. He scoffed at Pancho Villa's rumoured presence in the area and was far more disturbed by the bumpy roads and his poor-quality meals en route to Mexico City. However, he enjoyed his first shot of tequila and could not fault the enormous house rented for him with a hundred servants. 'Is a little cold but rada comfy,' he reported jauntily to Dorothy, but was soon horrified to discover bugs in his elegant four-poster.

He made his first appearance in *L'Elisir d'Amore* on 29 September. It met with desultory applause until 'Una furtiva lagrima', which won an ovation noisier than anything he had experienced in Italy or the United States. He complained privately of a poor supporting cast, but his own performance put the success of the season beyond all doubt. The demand for tickets became so hysterical that an extra presentation of *Carmen* was arranged for the following Sunday afternoon in the El Toreo bull-ring. He accepted a fee of $15,000, which the promoters easily recouped as 22,000 people paid for tickets, although many soon had cause for regret.

During Act One a rainstorm flooded the arena, rattling a forest of upturned umbrellas. Soon the singers could neither hear the orchestra nor make themselves audible. By the end of the second act several refused to continue, but the spectators advanced so menacingly to the stage that the manager begged Caruso and the others to brave the weather. They sang with mackintoshes over their costumes.

More thunderstorms disturbed a performance of *Un Ballo in Maschera* in the same arena a week later. The changeable weather and the altitude soon affected his throat. 'My heart jomping so strong, I think I want to fly to you,' he wrote to New York. 'When I came bak I will bring you a plumber and let him put a ring which will enchain your leg at mine.' Often he lay prostrate with headaches and missed the electric pad which used to give him relief. He grew testy with Punzo, who had mislaid the key to one of his trunks but made amends by cooking him a splendid dinner of spaghetti with butter and several baby lamb cutlets. Fucito also became ill, and Zirato displeased him by flirting harmlessly with the languorous señoritas, as he reported back rather self-righteously to Dorothy. He continued to send her a litany of disturbed nights, breathlessness and neuralgic pains. Nevertheless his singing drew almost uncontrollable applause even from patrons paying treble the normal ticket prices. To take curtain calls for *Martha* and *I Pagliacci* he would scramble back on stage almost knee-high in bouquets. On gala nights he was cheered all the way back to his dressing-room by members of the chorus and stagehands who lined up four deep.

He was lionised whenever he appeared, but still complained bitterly to Dorothy about having to pay $1860 for his first fortnight's board and lodging, and *extra for towels*. Although solicitous over her health, he was curiously insensitive when she reported being troubled by obscene and threatening letters from some anonymous pest. He made light of it, having accustomed himself to nuisances of this kind, but did not seem to appreciate their possible effect on a sensitive woman alone in New York and with childbirth only a few weeks ahead. He discounted any real danger and assured her that jealousy and malice had to be expected in their position.

Early in November 1919 he breezed gaily into New York flourishing the gold medal presented to him by the municipal council of Mexico City after his farewell performance. He could now think of little else but the baby and his forthcoming début in *La Juive*. He studied Eléazar every night before retiring and went to remarkable lengths to perfect his interpretation. Fucito would play the score through each day while he hummed, repeated difficult passages and made extensive notes. To authenticate Eléazar's gestures he enlisted the help of a Yiddish Theatre actor and also visited a synagogue, where he studied the cantor's vocal inflections.

He had given long hours to make-up and constantly applied wax to nose and cheeks until his face took on almost a Rembrandtesque texture. The salon and studio were littered with books on fifteenth-century Paris and costume plates exhibiting distinguished actors as Shylock. As the opening approached he became more and more fastidious about detail and, at almost the last minute, begged one of his Jewish friends to procure him a prayer-shawl from a rabbi, who demonstrated exactly how it should be worn. He even made sure that his fingers were spread in precisely the right fashion for Eléazar's blessing of his friends in the Passover night scene.

Rehearsals for *La Juive* convinced the management that only complete nervous collapse could prevent an outstanding performance. Caruso had never sung with more intensity nor identified himself quite so passionately with any of his previous roles. Artur Bodanzky, the conductor, was soon caught up in the excitement and directed the orchestra like a Toscanini but without that Maestro's irritability. He humoured Caruso over finicky objections and helped Rosa Ponselle to overcome her own growing panic. Only a few months earlier she had made her Metropolitan bow with Caruso in *La Forza del Destino*, a fearsome trial for a twenty-one-year-old who had so recently been part of a singing-sister act in vaudeville. Now she was giving Rachel a dramatic interpretation that made the most case-hardened veterans clap at rehearsals.

The season opened on Monday, 17 November 1919, with *Tosca*, immaculately sung by Caruso, Geraldine Farrar and Scotti. The Diamond Horseshoe was in even more resplendent rig for a gala performance the following night in honour of the Prince of Wales, then winding up his four-day visit to New York. He had survived the usual ticker-tape snowstorm in an open car with Grover Whalen, mounted to the roof of the fifty-eight-storey Woolworth Building and received the Freedom of the City from Mayor John F. Hylan, who was, however, too scared of his Irish supporters to show the British heir apparent more than formal courtesy. Unlike his grandfather, King Edward VII, the Prince had little taste for opera and plainly preferred the Ziegfeld Follies to the delights in store for him at the Metropolitan. However, he smiled dutifully on

271

being escorted by Otto Kahn to J. Pierpont Morgan's box, where he sat between Lord Grey and Admiral Halsey, soon joined there by General Pershing. The programme began with excerpts from *Oberon* and *Samson et Dalila*. The Prince applauded politely, but only showed some animation when Caruso, with Florence Easton and Amato in support, gave Act One from *I Pagliacci*. The tenor took several solo curtain calls and bowed to the royal box with hands folded across his clown's costume.

Caruso spent the next five days rehearsing *La Juive*, for which New York seemed to be holding its breath. Billy Guard had filled the newspapers with advance pictures of the tenor as Eléazar, and gossip promised such a dynamic performance that the scalpers were feverishly buying back tickets for resale. The long box-office queues had already added to Caruso's nervousness, but he was more agitated than usual after putting on his make-up on the night of the performance. He complained that the false beard tickled him beyond endurance and his wax nose made breathing difficult.

He had scarcely eaten that day. He sipped a small glassful of whisky, diluted with mineral water, in his dressing-room and then cleansed his palate with half an apple. The obligatory two phials of salt solution were tucked into the pockets of his flowing robe which Punzo continually smoothed out while his master puffed cigarettes at some risk to his whiskers. He was sweating profusely and became even more agitated on being told, unwisely, that Bonci was out front.

His Eléazar hypnotized the jam-packed audience from his very first entrance to the pealing tenseness of the aria 'Rachel! Quand du Seigneur'. Everyone in the auditorium—Bonci, critics, dowagers and galleryites alike—stood up to applaud for several minutes. Writing long afterwards of Caruso's performance that night, Irving Kolodin recorded, 'It was without doubt the most striking artistic triumph of his career. ... It was particularly impressive as the accomplishment of a singer whose position in the esteem of the public was inviolate.'

Caruso repeated the heavy part another half dozen times

272

before that year ended, and also sang faultlessly in *Samson* and other operas. Georgina Iselin had no difficulty that season in renting off her Diamond Horseshoe box for $10,000. Caruso missed three appearances through bronchitis, but Miss Iselin's tenant had an unexpected bonus on Friday, 19 December, when, after an ovation for *L'Elisir*, the whole gallery rose and shouted in unison, 'Viva pappà! Viva pappà!' The stalls and box-holders soon joined in.

He had become a father the previous night. The entire Knickerbocker staff had celebrated and applauded when Caruso dipped a fingertip into the champagne to dab his baby's lips. She was named Gloria and baptised in their suite some weeks later. He doted on his 'Puschina', often tiptoeing into her nursery to assure himself that she had not smothered. Ethel Barrymore used to recall an occasion when she arrived at the hotel to collect her children from a party given by Dorothy for her nephews, nieces and their friends. As the guests were still sitting around in their paper hats and enjoying second helpings of ice-cream, she wandered into an adjoining room. Caruso was marching up and down with Gloria cradled in his arms while he crooned a Neapolitan lullaby.

The baby's arrival seemed to invigorate him. His temper also improved. On his daily promenades he strutted the sidewalks with the old bouncy step, plainly declaring himself the proudest father in New York City. He was always delighted when strangers stopped to enquire about 'Miss Caruso'. Backstage visitors were made welcome and he now showed more patience with acquaintances who called at the Knickerbocker without fixing an appointment through Zirato, already harassed by the tenor's heavy advance bookings.

As soon as the season ended he arranged to do several out-of-town concerts before starting an engagement in Havana that May. On returning to New York for a breather between concerts he faced a mountain of invitations, fan letters and the usual pleas for press interviews, including one on his forty-seventh birthday. He flashed his teeth for the photographers and boasted of never having had a toothache in his life. ('Samson's strength was in his hair. Mine is in my teeth.') Among his visitors in late March was Georges Carpentier, the dimpled boxer with the unexpected choirboy profile, who had just arrived to make a film and fight Battling Levinsky and Jack Dempsey.

Caruso could not refuse to meet him when the Frenchman explained winningly that, despite a bad sea-crossing, he desired to pay instant homage to the world's greatest singer. Although Caruso knew nothing about prize-fighting and had always refused invitations to visit Madison Square Garden except for the circus, he chatted pleasantly for half an hour before steering Carpentier into his private suite to meet Dorothy and admire the baby.

The spring series of concerts was enlivened by an emotional reunion with Tetrazzini, who partnered him zestfully at an Italian Dollar Loan Rally in the Lexington Opera House. He had waived his now routine $7000 fee, but felt more than rewarded when, after singing Tosti's 'A Vucchella' (one of Victor's top-selling records), a countryman jumped excitedly to his feet and immediately bought bonds to the value of $50,000.

Before departing for Cuba he had to give a special farewell performance of La Juive at the Metropolitan. This was followed in Atlanta by appearances in the same opera as well as in Samson et Dalila. Common sense dictated rest after eight months of almost uninterrupted singing, sometimes four times in a single week, but Caruso had no manager to exert a restraining hand, and neither Dorothy nor Zirato could discipline him. Impresarios and charity promoters were also far too ticket-conscious to give him respite. Moreover, to justify inflated box-office prices he had to be generous with encores and sometimes force himself to go on when feeling below his best. The crushing concert itinerary, exposing him to night trains and quick changes of temperature, was an added hazard for one prone to bronchial wheezes.

He had become a poor health risk. He continued to smoke to excess and ate too much oily food, which often led to intestinal poisoning. His lack of exercise did not improve his digestion. He would take a cab rather than walk a couple of hundred yards. He was also uxorious and probably an over-enthusiastic bedmate for an attractive and adoring young woman twenty years his junior. With the exception of his collection and the weekly caricatures for *La Follia*, he had no hobbies to relieve professional strains now intensified by roles like Samson and Eléazar.

He had always relished applause, but fees on an ever mount-ing scale were making it even more difficult for him to abandon an almost nonstop schedule. Like most self-made men raised in poverty, he would never feel securely rich. A sudden pile of bills gave him nightmares of impending bankruptcy, and in his letters to Dorothy he grumbled constantly at being over-charged. His ménage was of course luxurious even on an assured income of at least $400,000 a year. He now maintained fourteen rooms at the Knickerbocker and also had to meet heavy running costs at the Villa Bellosguardo. His New York staff was vast; Gloria's nanny, the valets, dresser, wig-maker, accompanists, Fitzgerald, the chauffeur, and his wife, Dorothy's Italian maid, Enrichetta, and the quite indispensable Zirato. The two boys, Fofò and Mimmi, were denied nothing, and their mother continued to receive her regular monthly allowance like the scores of other pensioners on his list. His earnings from the Metropolitan, recordings and concert engagements were more than adequate to cover even such a living scale, quite apart from income tax and the princely style in which he travelled, but it was still almost impossible for a man of his background and temperament to resist an offer to sing in Cuba for the highest guaranteed terms of his career; $10,000 for each evening performance and $5000 at matinées.

Nevertheless, but for the certainty of being sued for breach of contract by Adolfo Bracale, the impresario, he might have abandoned that engagement at the eleventh hour. While in Atlanta and just before departing for Havana early in May 1920 he read a newspaper report that the Knickerbocker Hotel was being sold and would be converted into an office block. As it had been his home for the past twelve years, he was not only distressed on sentimental grounds but indignant at being kept completely in the dark by the management, ignoring the fact that their business negotiations had to be conducted in secrecy. He at once cabled to Dorothy, who had rented a summer house at Easthampton on Long Island, where, attended by a staff of ten, she was vacationing with Gloria and Romeyn's family. She was instructed to return immediately to New York, transfer all their furniture to the Canessa Galleries and make provisional arrangements to lease an apartment in the Biltmore Hotel. The Knickerbocker manager, now most agitated and contrite, assured her that there was no immediate urgency to move, but Caruso could not overlook what he considered the blackest treachery.

To add to his irritability, the Cuban engagement soon became an inferno of tropical heat and nervous prostration. He bitterly resented paying $70 a day, without meals, for his apartment at the Hotel Sevilla, where he tossed sleeplessly in sweat-drenched sheets, which, as usual, had to be of pure linen and changed daily. Mario scoured Havana for extra supplies and also had to calm down his master, who was suffering from his very first toothache.

The heat had affected the others. Mario developed mysterious shooting pains in his right hand, Zirato chose an inconvenient time to start a strict diet, and Fucito's headaches caused him to make one or two rare mistakes which Caruso would normally have overlooked. Instead, he scolded the sensitive accompanist. This started a tiff exacerbated by Punzo, who had a Neapolitan taste for intrigue and habitually plotted against Mario and the others to win his master's favour. Bracale, the impresario, was meantime wrangling with Ricordi's representative over the copyright in Verdi's *La Forza del Destino*. It had to be dropped from the repertoire and *Aïda* hurriedly substituted, which did not improve Caruso's temper.

He sang Radamès on the night of 8 June, unaware that Zirato was sweating nervously in the wings over an Associated

Press release which had just come through. It reported the robbery of jewels worth over $250,000 from Caruso's summer-house at Easthampton. Among the missing pieces was the diamond necklace he had given Dorothy as a wedding present. Zirato broke the news to him as soon as he came off stage. He was shocked but quickly cabled to his wife: 'Thanks God you and baby safe. Lots of jewels will come.'

Dorothy had finally decided that the Vanderbilt Hotel on Park Avenue, south of Grand Central Station, would be more convenient for the opera house than the Biltmore. She reserved the luxurious top-floor suite, with penthouse, and planned to have it redecorated and their furniture installed by the time Caruso arrived back from Havana. She had then returned to Long Island with the safe containing her jewels. One night, not long afterwards, she was awakened by the alarm bell. The safe had been removed, emptied and dumped in the grounds. The house soon swarmed with detectives, including several investigators hired by the three insurance companies involved. They suspected an 'inside job', which gave Caruso so much anxiety that he ordered Dorothy to hire an Italian private detective as Gloria's bodyguard.

He was naturally impatient to return to America, but five more weeks of singing still lay ahead of him. However, he had begun to acclimatise to the sticky heat and won ovations for his performances, although not quite on the Mexico City scale. The supporting company and orchestra were below standard, and audiences, starved of Caruso, for whom they had long been clamouring, expected rather too much for their overpriced tickets. He and the management had received several abusive letters and anonymous threats from people who complained angrily that only the rich could afford to pay a minimum of $35 for their seats.

He was given much local hospitality but did not enjoy his one and only visit to the Casino, where he lost $300 at roulette in a few minutes. Crowds cheered him whenever he appeared on the streets, and all the local music stores played his records day and night. It helped to comfort him for some cool press

277

notices for his *Martha*, which a few critics thought overrated by comparison with their Spanish favourites. He won them over with *L'Elisir*, but the real acclaim was reserved for 'E lucevan le stelle' and 'Vesti la giubba'. He sang these arias with such emotion that the tears ran down his face. The audience sobbed with him.

Aïda again proved unfortunate. He was in his dressing-room at the Nacional, changing for the second scene of Act Two, when the theatre was rocked by an explosion. A bomb had been thrown at the stage from the gallery. Damage was slight, apart from débris in the side boxes and the collapse of some triumphal arches on the stage. But panic threatened and thirty people were injured before the police and firemen could clear the theatre. Caruso had volunteered to help with the casualties, but it was feared that other explosions might follow. Still wearing his Radamès costume, he was whisked out to a car and driven back to his hotel. Reports soon circulated that the long Black Hand had reached out to Havana to settle their old score with him. Others accused the local anarchists, but, more probably, some irate opera-goer had simply decided to demonstrate against the ticket profiteers.

Bracale still had every reason to congratulate himself. All performances were sold out and the season would yield him such an enormous profit that he became desperate to extend Caruso's engagement to Caracas and Lima, where he also ran opera houses. He guaranteed a stupendous $200,000, which tempted Caruso to try to persuade Dorothy to join him in South America. He pointed out that the fee would cover two years' American and Italian income tax and still leave enough over to take things more easy. For the first time he hinted at possible retirement ('If something arrive to me after this season of Lima, we can give a good-bye to the theatre and we will be alright without selling any bonds'), but this could have been an oblique manœuvre to win her over.

Bracale also kept up the pressure, offering her de luxe return passage with or without Gloria and her nanny, but Dorothy, normally so docile in all professional matters, now took a very firm stand. She refused to leave her seven-month-old baby or expose her to near-equatorial temperatures. She was equally apprehensive of the health risks to her husband and pleaded with him to relax for a few weeks at Easthampton. She reminded him of the gardens, a delightful lake and, above all, a small studio where he would be able to practice or shut himself off if Gloria, Mimmi or Romeyn's children became tiresome. He surrendered without too much of a struggle. Bracale was disappointed but withdrew gracefully. Before Caruso sailed at the end of June, Bracale gave him a gold nugget with an inscription recording his escape from the bomb outrage. He asked him to present it to Dorothy with his compliments, no doubt hoping that she might yet be persuaded to sanction a South American tour and hinting that his offer would stand open more or less indefinitely.

En route for Long Island, Caruso kept a long-standing concert engagement in New Orleans and then travelled on to Atlantic City, where the Victor Company was holding a convention. Although weary, he could not refuse Calvin Child's plea to sing for the delegates in the Ambassador Hotel ballroom, but had wired Dorothy to join him with the 'Puschina'. On 4 July, after a brief stop-over in New York to inspect their new hotel apartment, they departed at last for the welcome refuge on Long Island.

He expressed no regret for turning down Bracale's $200,000. He cooed blissfully over Gloria, whom he helped to feed at ten every night, but did not neglect Mimmi, who seemed a little apprehensive of entering the Culver Military Academy in the fall. They frolicked together in the woods and Caruso coaxed him to take piano lessons from Fucito. But the strain of Havana was still being felt. Although careful not to alarm Dorothy, Caruso wrote privately to Zirato in New York complaining of shooting pains all over his body. His brother-in-law, Romeyn, persuaded him to play a little tennis and do some gentle boating, but he gave up fishing after toppling into the lake in the excitement of landing his first perch. That was on Dorothy's birthday, 6 August, when he gave her a handsome emerald-cut diamond at breakfast. (Only a few of her jewels were ever recovered, and the insurance companies paid out later on the various claims.)

That afternoon Mario had handed Mrs Caruso an anonymous letter demanding $50,000 within six days, failing which the writer threatened to kill her, her husband and their baby. Caruso laughed it off as a hoax, but the Italian bodyguard was put on full alert and Fitzgerald, the chauffeur, now carried his revolver at all times. Although it turned out to be a damp squib Caruso had a week of sleepless nights.

He had been booked by the Metropolitan Bureau for a series of concerts in Canada and various American cities before the opening of the opera season that November. He would be paid $86,000 for the eleven appearances. Already tanned a cigar-leaf brown, he was unusually relaxed as he went over his forthcoming programme with Fucito and grumbled fairly good-humouredly at having to break off in mid-August for a single performance at Ocean Grove. However, he stepped briskly on to the stage of the huge Auditorium and beamed as the crowd gave him a welcoming cheer. He had included Rodolfo's Narrative in his recital and could not resist an unrehearsed topical touch. As he sang 'Your lovely eyes have robbed me of all my jewels', he winked at the audience and displayed empty palms.

On 12 September he moved formally into the Vanderbilt. He would miss Scotti as a near neighbour and also their old corner table at the Knickerbocker, but was partially consoled by Frank, their waiter for so many years, whom he had engaged as butler. Surprisingly for a man of Caruso's ingrained superstition, he saw nothing ominous in the fate of Alfred Gwynne Vanderbilt, for whom the luxurious suite had been originally designed. He had drowned when the *Lusitania* was torpedoed.

Chapter Twenty

A few days before departing for Montreal, Caruso made what would be his farewell appearance at the Victor studios in Camden, New Jersey. He recorded nine songs, including the 'Rachel!' aria from *La Juive*, and ended the sessions on 16 September 1920. He had complained of a slight head cold, which may have affected his high notes in the Crucifixus from Rossini's 'Messe Solennelle', his last disc of all, but discographers had long noticed certain signs of deterioration.★

He opened at the Mount Royal Arena in Montreal on the 27th and was enthusiastically received by an audience of ten thousand. He had an effusive press, yet was enraged by a single local critic who dared to dissent. His Toronto audience seemed more subdued but still demanded their money's worth in encores. After a fidgety night's sleep he rose at dawn to catch his train for Chicago, where he sang in the Medinah Temple before taking the next hops to St Paul and Denver.

Insomnia, aggravated by long train journeys and the first ticklings of a cough, made him more irritable. He rarely gave fewer than eleven songs at a performance and also had to sit through local luncheons and submit to interviews in Omaha, Tulsa, Fort Worth, Houston and every other city on that whistle-stop itinerary. He had lost his usual bonhomie towards reporters. By the time he reached Norfolk, Virginia, for his last concert he was talking gloomily of retiring from

★ H. J. Drummond, in a masterly summing-up in *The Gramophone* (March 1935), mentions that Caruso's record of 'M'appari' in 1917 was more dramatically sung than eleven years before, 'but the more frequent breathing gives a sort of staccato effect to this rendering and robs it of the smooth flowing legato of the earlier one. . . . Subsequently (after 1918), there was no recovery, though of course some records were better than others, but to the very end, where the music was slow enough to allow him plenty of time, Caruso's voice still retained much of that peculiar beauty which makes it so unlike all other tenor voices.'

a professional world that concealed so many painful thorns among the bouquets. This had been brought on by a backbiting newspaper attack on Tetrazzini's love life.

Towards the end of October he arrived back in New York weary in body and spirit. He was distressed by the sudden death of Pane, the old restaurateur, and also brooded inordinately on his next income tax assessment. However, the challenge of *La Juive*, with which the Metropolitan would open its season, helped to distract him. As he had not sung Eléazar for seven months he began a strenuous series of coaching sessions with Fucito and gave a performance up to his previous high level.

Two nights later the thirty-year-old tenor Beniamino Gigli made his New York début in Boito's *Mefistofele*. He won praise for a lyrical tone as light as a viola, although critics considered him 'provincial' in manner and short on acting talent. His Rodolfo, with Alda and Scotti in support, was so alluring that many rated him equally with the young Caruso, but he displeased some of the Metropolitan veterans by advancing to the footlights to take a bow in mid-opera when the gallery yelled 'Bella, bella, bella!' after a mellifluously sung aria.*

Caruso did not seem put out by the newcomer's triumph and sent him a generous note of congratulation on his début, although nettled by his own indifferent notices for one or two patchy performances. He became angry enough after one particularly sharp criticism to send in his notice of resignation. 'Mr Gatti' rushed in panic to the Vanderbilt and succeeded in pacifying him, but he was only reassured by the unanimous chorus of approval for his Samson on the 3rd of December, despite a most unpleasant experience in the last act, when part of a pillar descended on him as he was pulling down the Temple.

* When Gigli made his first record at the HMV studios in Milan in October 1918, he listened to Caruso's disc of 'Com è gentil' from *Don Pasquale* 'with humility and awe'. Throughout his career he had to endure reviews like that for a performance of *Martha*, of which a critic wrote: 'No one except Caruso ever surpassed his effort.'

Next day he caught a chill while out driving in Central Park with Dorothy. The cough worsened, but his doctor surprisingly passed him fit to sing in *I Pagliacci* on the 8th. He smoked a last cigarette before going on stage to the familiar roar of welcome, but his voice broke in 'Vesti la giubba'. He seemed to stumble, then staggered blindly to the wings, where he fell into Zirato's arms. He lay semi-conscious on the dressing-room sofa and complained of acute pain in his left side. His doctor, whom Dorothy disliked, minimised the attack as a symptom of 'intercostal neuralgia'. He calmly strapped up his ribs and allowed him to go on for the second act. The curtain fell to sympathetic applause.

On the 11th, apparently recovered, Caruso drove over to the Brooklyn Academy of Music for a Saturday-night performance of *L'Elisir*. At 7.45, already made up as Nemorino, he had a fit of coughing. He gargled and was alarmed to see blood-stains in the wash-basin. His wife begged him not to go on, but was shooed out to take her seat before curtain-up. However, she called the doctor, who arrived when Caruso was already on stage. He stood in the wings with Zirato, now ashen-faced and trembling.

Caruso gave a little cough during the first scene but came in on cue. Dorothy and others in the front stalls were horrified to see scarlet drops on Nemorino's smock. He continued singing while his mouth slobbered blood. At intervals he dabbed his lips with the towels which Zirato passed frantically to members of the chorus. He dropped the bloodstained towels, one by one, into the well at the centre of the stage and struggled through until the end of the act. In the dressing-room he was examined by his doctor, who briskly diagnosed a small burst vein at the tip of the tongue. As soon as the haemorrhage began to stop, Caruso raised himself from the sofa and declared himself fit to go on for the second act. Billy Guard and Zirato, tearfully supported by Dorothy, entreated him to abandon the performance. The issue was settled by Herbert T. Swan, the house manager, who went before the curtain to inform the audience that Caruso had volunteered to continue if they wished him to do so. He was answered by an explosive 'No' from the patrons, many of them in tears.

He was silent on the way back to the Vanderbilt, where Gatti-Casazza already awaited them. Instead of taking to his bed, Caruso paid his usual visit to Gloria's nursery and then asked 'Mr Gatti', Zirato and his fiancée to stay for supper. He managed a few jokes, but for the first time in many years did not light a cigarette. He spent Sunday quietly and tried out his voice cautiously with Fucito. On the following night, relieved by the absence of haemorrhage, he overrode Dorothy and sang *La Forza del Destino* at the Metropolitan. The house gave him a standing ovation before and after the performance but considerately abstained from shouting for encores.

The medical diagnosis of 'intercostal neuralgia' seemed to have been vindicated. With his ribs encased in plaster he sang an almost flawless Samson on 16 December. Five days later and just before his scheduled reappearance in *L'Elisir* he was again attacked by agonising pain in his left flank and had to cancel the performance. To discourage public alarm, Guard announced an attack of lumbago.

He picked up rapidly. Once pain-free he began rehearsing Eléazar for the Christmas Eve performance, brushing aside his wife's fears. Although he ate little, he was more cheerful and joked with the hotel barber while Fucito softly played over parts of the score. He ran through scales, seemingly without difficulty, and chuckled as his 'Puschina' stared wide-eyed at the sparkling Christmas tree in Alfred Gwynne Vanderbilt's red-brocaded salon. He had made his usual extravagant tour of Tiffany's for cigarette cases, watches and necklaces. To take his mind off the nagging ache in his side he filled dozens of boxes with the gold coins which would be presented, as usual, to the Metropolitan staff on Christmas Day. Dorothy says she was not allowed to open a vast carton containing his special gift to her: a luxurious chinchilla coat.

On Friday evening, 24 December, he left in good time for the opera house and made up carefully with Punzo's help while Mario hovered anxiously, alarmed by his master's drawn features. Sharp at eight the curtain went up for his 607th Metropolitan performance. He sang and acted with authority, now partnered by Florence Easton as Rachel, but Artur Bodanzky had scented danger from the pit. In the intermission he hurried to the tenor's dressing-room and was dismayed to see him holding his side and wincing. He sat stiffly upright in a chair, his eyes screwed up in agony. The Maestro tactfully proposed making certain adjustments to shorten the performance, but Caruso would not hear of it. In the car he slumped wearily and with half-closed eyes on the way back to the Vanderbilt, where Dorothy had arranged supper for several friends. He forced himself to play jovial host, but his face looked bloodless and he could swallow only a small cupful of soup.

By the next afternoon his wife had most of the coin boxes ready for presentation on the Metropolitan stage. They planned to leave as soon as Caruso had bathed and dressed. Suddenly she heard a piercing scream. Mario and Zirato rushed out of the room and found the tenor doubled up in his bath, whimpering with terror. Doctors were called, soon followed by a consultant, who gravely diagnosed acute pleurisy. A severe attack of bronchial pneumonia ensued. Various operations were performed with so many intermittent crises that the New York newspapers maintained a permanent squad in the suite to send out daily bulletins. Day and night nurses attended under the supervision of a corps of specialists, who removed part of a rib to gain access to the infected pleural cavity. It meant the almost certain end of Caruso's career, but this was naturally kept from him.

He rallied at times, tinkling his gold bell for his wife and little Gloria, but by mid-February 1921, after yet more surgery, he lasped into a coma. He was so near death that one night the last rites were administered. With Dorothy's hand in his, he gasped out a plea to take farewell of his friends. Zirato led in Scotti, Lucrezia Bori, Ponselle and Amato, who could not hold back their tears as they embraced him. Fucito sat in the studio hunched over the piano and drumming a sad tattoo on the closed lid. Mimmi arrived from Culver and was led to his father's bedside. Caruso grasped his hand feebly but could not speak.

He lingered between life and death for a week, during which his forty-eighth birthday passed almost unnoticed. He was too ill even to hear Dorothy's whispered greeting as she bent over his bed to kiss him. The lamp burned day and night before the fifteenth-century marble Madonna of Pompeii in the salon, where only the most intimate friends were admitted. They left flowers or little keepsakes and mumbled comfort to Dorothy.

Throughout those critical days the churches in New York and many other cities were jammed with people praying for his recovery. A continuous procession of admirers came to the Vanderbilt to enquire about his condition, many leaving cards, messages, holy medals and rosaries. One lady wrote to offer comfort, declaring fervently, 'I am a Protestant but I have a heart.' Caruso's bootblack stopped every day with a bunch of pansies on the way to his stand. He was followed one morning by six burly Italian labourers who asked for the latest bulletin before going off to lay new pipes under the road. Dorothy was saturated with quack remedies, like compresses of horse radish and castor oil, but felt more confidence in a report from the astrologer Evangeline Adams, who predicted emphatically that her husband would survive this crisis.

To everyone's amazement he began to rally and firmly assured his doctors, 'I will not die.' The crush of callers now became so unmanageable that old Schol was recruited to preside at a table in the corridor outside the apartment. He was overjoyed to be near his idol and dealt firmly with nuisances like the fanatic who claimed that he was Jesus Christ sent to raise the tenor from his tomb. Schol handled the visitors' book with the dignity of court chamberlain. He was greeted affectionately by celebrated singers like Scotti, Geraldine Farrar, McCormack and Tetrazzini.

Caruso seemed to have recovered his spirits but could not help murmuring bitterly to Scotti, 'They might have waited for me to die,' when told that Gigli had replaced him in

Andrea Chénier. However, he expressed sympathy when Gigli went down with tracheal catarrh and had to be replaced twice in a month. It was not the last of the Metropolitan's troubles in that nightmarish season. Sembrich contracted diphtheria, and an outbreak of influenza placed Farrar among others on the sick list.

Caruso's condition was slowly improving, although his doctors had noted a contraction of the left lung, which meant a long convalescence. However, by the end of April he was taking daily drives in Central Park accompanied by Dorothy and a nurse. He could walk only a few yards and his face was gaunt, but he raised his hat genially to the crowds who gathered to congratulate him on his recovery. He assured reporters that he would undoubtedly be back in New York after a few weeks in the Italian sun.

With all bills paid, including many thousands of dollars for medical expenses, he checked the final preparations for his journey but panicked when his right hand became so numb that it was difficult even to hold a pen between the fingers for signing cheques. However, he put on a buoyant show to take leave of Gatti-Casazza and other friends at the Metropolitan. Seasoned troupers all, they concealed their dismay when he walked through the doors. He smiled, but his eyes were cushioned with pain and his step had lost all its old spring. The porters, cleaners and stagehands pumped his left hand and lied cheerfully about his healthy appearance. The Padrone, with whom he had so often argued and shared so many nights of glory, embraced him fondly and announced that he would not fail to visit him in Sorrento within a few weeks, when they would discuss plans for his return to the Metropolitan.

At the last minute Caruso ominously decided not to take his big case of music scores, which was already packed. He also closed the piano lid with such a look of sadness that Fucito turned away to avoid blubbering. Fortunately, everyone was busily engaged in packing the thirty-eight trunks, several of them filled with his coins, bronzes, ceramics and other treasures intended for the Villa Bellosguardo. Gloria had a separate

287

trunk to herself for her little phonograph, records and favourite toys.

The Carusos and their entire entourage, except Zirato and Fucito, sailed from Brooklyn on 28 May. Punzo grew so feverish for his first glimpse of Vesuvius that he fell over his feet more often than usual, but Mario and his wife remained as calm and efficient as ever. Gloria's nanny and Dorothy's two personal maids completed the party. Everyone was in sparkling spirits, and Caruso posed gaily for the photographers at the ship's rail. He kept doffing his straw hat to hundreds of cheering well-wishers as the *Presidente Wilson* at last cast anchor. Among those to wave farewell from the pier was Schol, who soon afterwards departed for his native Munich. He had a presentiment that he would never see Caruso again and could not face life in America without him.

Huge crowds lined the quay at Algiers to wish Caruso godspeed on the last stage of the voyage. He looked so invigorated by the sea air when the steamer docked in Naples on 10 June that the reporters saw no reason to doubt that he would be sailing back to New York in October, as he said, for his next season at the Metropolitan.

The whole of the first floor at the Hotel Vittoria in Sorrento had been engaged. It overlooked the sunlit bay, and from the terrace he could see Naples and dream of soon being strong enough to drive out once again for lunch at Posilipo. Before long he was bathing and encouraging baby Gloria to splash about. He gained weight and quickly took on a healthy-looking tan, but he was still worried by the loss of power in his right hand and plunged it daily into a tub of hot mud. His temper had improved. With characteristic thoughtfulness he introduced Punzo to visitors from Naples as his 'personal assistant' rather than expose the valet-dresser to local humiliation. He also told Dorothy that he had made secret provision for a fund to keep Punzo and his wife from want in case he failed to recover.

He began taking short strolls around Sorrento, where children thrust small bunches of flowers into his hands while the local folk greeted him respectfully but did not pester him.

He braced himself to visit the Sanctuary of the Madonna of Pompeii, his patron saint, and left an offering of 10,000 lire for his recovery. It had been a tiring day, but he stopped for a few kindly words with a young Neapolitan singer who pleaded for an audition. Caruso laughed and told him to come to the hotel next morning.

In her book Dorothy recalled that the youth duly appeared, clutching a song sheet. He had chosen 'M'apparì' from *Martha* and began singing to Caruso's piano accompaniment. It was quickly apparent that he had no voice, but Caruso made allowances for nervousness and encouraged him to persevere. Finally, he said, 'No, no, try it like this.' From her bedroom his wife was astonished to hear him sing the aria with all the old sweetness. She rushed deliriously into the salon. 'There stood Enrico. As he finished the song he flung out his arms. His face was transfigured. "Doro, I can sing! I can sing! I have not lost my voice. I can sing!"'

Gatti-Casazza came to visit him early in July and was delighted by his cheerful face, although warning him not to hurry back to New York or pay too much heed to offers, including one from a London impresario to sing at the Albert Hall for a fee of 1000 guineas. Caruso promised to take care but could not resist making excursions to Capri, which overtaxed his strength. By the middle of that month he was again experiencing the dreaded ache in his side, yet still felt cheerful enough to send off a postcard to the Metropolitan treasurer: 'Salutations to all the boys. Feeling fine. Expect to be over the top soon.' On 27 July he wrote chirpily to Fucito: 'I have a voice that will last twenty years. Whatever I want to do I do with great vigour.' The following day he collapsed in considerable pain and was soon running a high temperature. Two famous surgeons were hastily summoned. They decided that a kidney would have to be removed at their clinic in Rome, but thought the operation could safely be delayed for a week. Caruso's temperature soon shot up so alarmingly that his wife telephoned Giovanni to come at once from Naples and send for Fofò. The stricken man's screams of agony then decided them

289

to leave Sorrento without delay. They planned to stay overnight in Naples and take a special train to Rome.

On Sunday, 31 July, a day of stifling heat, they checked into the Hotel Vesuvio, where Caruso, obviously in great pain, was put to bed. The local doctor seemed so overwhelmed by the celebrity of his patient that he fumbled hopelessly with his syringe until Dorothy snatched it from him and injected the merciful dose of morphine. Other doctors were summoned. They discovered an abscess in the region of the left kidney, but refused to take the responsibility to operate, arguing that it would mean certain death.

Caruso lingered for some hours, half drugged but with waking moments of agony. Just before nine o'clock on the morning of 2 August 1921, a doctor took his flickering pulse and glanced helplessly at Dorothy, who had knelt beside the bed throughout the night. Caruso made a desperate effort to speak. She leaned forward and heard him gasp, 'Doro, I can't get my breath.' In a few seconds the doctor closed the unseeing eyes.

The body was embalmed and laid out in the hotel salon between four towering candles. Hour after hour people filed through the improvised *chapelle ardente* while messages of condolence flooded in, none more touching or welcome to the widow than a simple wire from Germany: 'I am coming. Schol.' The King of Italy gave orders that, for the first time, the Royal Basilica of San Francisco di Paola would be opened for a commoner's funeral service. 'I alone in all the city could not feel the weight and glory of this solemn honour,' Dorothy wrote later. 'There had been many Kings, but only one Caruso.'

On the day of the funeral the flags of New York flew at half mast. The façade of the Metropolitan would be draped in black throughout that month. Queen Mary sent a wreath from England, and on Brighton Pier the bandmaster interrupted a concert to play a gramophone record of 'Vesti la giubba', while the holidaymakers all stood up, the men with heads bared. In Naples every shop had closed in mourning. The tenor's coffin, a crystal casket enclosed in wood, was transferred from the Hotel Vesuvio to a hearse covered with wreaths and drawn by six black horses. The procession moved slowly along Santa Lucia with 100,000 people lining the route, a cordon of troops having difficulty in holding back the crowds gathered in the hot sunshine at the Piazza del Plebiscito and outside the San Carlo Opera House. After the requiem mass, with a choir of two hundred singing in final tribute, the coffin was taken to a temporary chapel in the Del Planto cemetery nestling among the cypresses above Naples.

The glass casket was later removed to a new chapel. Scotti was in America when he heard of Caruso's death. 'It takes away half my life,' he said brokenly. 'I'd have done anything to save him.' With Tito Schipa and other friends he made arrangements to have the embalmed body dressed in new clothes every year. This came to an end in April 1927, when the widow, who had long objected to making a public display of her husband's body, had it laid under a slab of white granite and the mausoleum locked up. The authorities did not object after a disgraceful episode earlier that year when a party of cameramen, masquerading as tourists, had rampaged for hours round the casket with their paraphernalia.

Caruso's more fanatical admirers went to the other extreme. When some of his treasures and personal effects were sold in New York in March 1923, a member of the public solemnly demanded that everyone present should 'stand for a few minutes in silent prayer for the great Italian-American whose collections are about to be sold'. Hiram Parke looked startled, but agreed before proceeding with the auction.

Caruso's estate was valued at some $9 million (£1,800,000), the largest ever left by an opera singer. Half was held in trust for Gloria, the remainder being divided equally between his widow, his two sons and Giovanni. Mrs Caruso remarried twice. Both marriages were dissolved, and in each case she resumed her first husband's name. 'I don't think these failures were anyone's fault,' she later wrote in her edition of Caruso's letters. 'Death had not ended my marriage to Enrico.' Among all the relics, she most cherished his Canio costume, but would never again set foot in any opera house. She died in December 1955.

Caruso's unique voice did not pass to his descendants. Mimmi survived his elder brother and for a time studied hard in Los Angeles with the hope of taking up grand opera. Gloria was coached in Venice by her father's old friend Tanara, but eventually also abandoned thoughts of a professional career. She married and has raised her family in the United States.

The estate has continued to benefit from the posthumous sale of Caruso records. During his career he was paid nearly $2 million in royalties from the Victor Company alone, but even this enormous sum has been exceeded since his death. To date over fifty million of his records have been sold, and they continue to sell several thousands a year, thanks to electrically re-recorded titles with new orchestral accompaniment from the late twenties onwards.*

In December 1932, Tetrazzini visited the London offices of the Gramophone Company in Oxford Street to hear a re-recording of 'M'appari'. She found it impossible not to join in and sang until the very end. She then picked up the disc, kissed it and said brokenly, 'There can never be another Caruso.'

As the legendary Mario, Donzelli and other celebrated tenors antedated the birth of the gramophone, comparisons with Caruso can only be academic or highly speculative. Such distinguished successors as Gigli, Martinelli and Jussi Björling won immense followings without, in the opinion of most critics, challenging Caruso's all-round supremacy in the full glory of his vintage years. It is of course possible that a singer yet unborn, or perhaps already taking solos in some church

* A new release by RCA Victor, tied in with *The Great Caruso* film, quickly sold a million copies. Ironically, Lanza's treacly ballad, 'Be My Love' has outsold even Caruso's best-known titles.

choir, will replace Caruso as 'the greatest tenor of all time'. Even so, he may find it more difficult to win such universal affection as the bubbly, warm-hearted little Neapolitan whose voice soared and sobbed from the first wheezy phonographs to bring a new magic into countless lives.

Bibliography

Special acknowledgement is due to previous books on Caruso, notably his widow's *Wings of Song* (Hutchinson, 1928) and *Enrico Caruso: His Life and Death* (Simon & Schuster, New York, 1945, and T. Werner Laurie, London, 1946); Pierre Key and Bruno Zirato's *Enrico Caruso* (Little, Brown, Boston, 1922, and Hurst & Blackett, London, 1923); T. R. Ybarra's *Caruso* (Cresset Press, 1954); and Francis Robinson's *Caruso: His Life in Pictures* (Bramhall House, New York, 1957 and Thames & Hudson, London, 1958).

Other sources consulted or quoted are listed below,

Adami, Giuseppe, *Letters of Giacomo Puccini*, tr. Ena Makin (Lippincott, 1931; Harrap, 1941).

Alda, Frances, *Men, Women and Tenors* (Houghton Mifflin, Boston, 1937).

Barrymore, Ethel, *Memories* (Hulton Press, London, 1955).

Brockway and Weinstock, *The Opera, 1600–1941* (Simon & Schuster, New York, 1941).

Burke, Billie, *With a feather on my nose* (Peter Davies, London, 1950).

Burke, Thomas, *Nights in London* (Allen & Unwin, London, 1918).

Calvé, Emma, *My Life* (D. Appleton, New York, 1922).

Carner, Mosco, *Puccini* (Duckworth, London, 1958).

Caruso, Enrico, *How to Sing* (John Church Co., London, 1902).

Chaliapin, Fedor, *Man and Mask* (Gollancz, London, 1932).

Chaplin, Charles, *My Autobiography* (The Bodley Head, London, 1964).

Cohan, George M., *Twenty Years on Broadway* (Harper, New York, 1925).

Cortesi, Salvatore, *My Thirty Years of Friendships* (Harper, New York, 1927).

Daspuro, Nicola, *Enrico Caruso* (Ediciones Coli, Mexico, 1943).

Farrar, Geraldine, *Such Sweet Compulsion* (Greystone Press, New York, 1938).

Fiorentino, Dante del, *Immortal Bohemian* (Prentice-Hall, New York, 1952; Gollancz, London, 1952).

Flint, Mary H. *Impressions of Caruso and his Art* (J. P. Paret, New York, 1917).

Foxall, Raymond, *John McCormack* (Robert Hale, London, 1963).

Fucito, Salvatore, *Caruso and the Art of Singing* (George Allen & Unwin, London, 1922).

Gaisberg, F. W., *Music on Record* (Robert Hale, London, 1946).

Gara, Eugenio, *Caruso, Storia di un Emigrante* (Rizzoli, Milan, 1947).

Garden, Mary and Biancolli, L. L., *Mary Garden's Story* (Michael Joseph, London, 1952).

Gatti-Casazza, Giulio, *Memories of the Opera* (Scribner's, New York, 1941).

Gelatt, Roland, *The Fabulous Phonograph* (Lippincott, New York, 1955).

Gigli, Beniamino, *Memoirs* (Cassell, London, 1957).

Guinness Book of Records (Guinness Superlatives, London, 1971).

Gunsbourg, Raoul, *Cent ans de Souvenirs* (Monaco, 1959).

Hetherington, John, *Melba* (Faber, London, 1967).

Huneker, James, *Bedouins* (Scribner's, New York, 1920).

Jackson, Stanley, *The Savoy* (Frederick Muller, London, 1964).

Kahn, Otto, *Reflections of a Financier* (Hodder & Stoughton, London, 1921).

Krehbiel, H. E., *Chapters of Opera* (Henry Holt, New York, 1909).

——, *More Chapters of Opera* (Henry Holt, New York, 1919).

Kolodin, Irving, *The Metropolitan Opera*, 1883–1939 (Oxford University Press, 1940).

——, *The Metropolitan Opera*, 1883–1950 (Knopf, New York, 1953).

Lara, Isidore de, *Many Tales of Many Cities* (Hutchinson, London, 1952).

Lasky, Jesse L., *I Blew my own Horn* (Gollancz, London, 1957).

Ledner, Emil, *Erinnerungen an Caruso* (Steegmann, Hanover & Leipzig, 1922).

Lehmann, Lotte, *Midway in my Song* (Bobbs Merrill, New York, 1938).

Leiser, Clara, *Jean de Reszke* (Gerald Howe, London, 1933).

Mackenzie, Compton, *My Record of Music* (Hutchinson, London, 1955).

——, *Gramophone Nights* (Heinemann, London, 1923).

——, *A Musical Chair* (Chatto & Windus, London, 1939).

Marconi, Degna, *My Father, Marconi* (Frederick Muller, London, 1962).

McCormack, Lily, *I Hear you calling me* (W. H. Allen, London, 1950).

Melba, Nellie, *Melodies and Memories* (Thornton Butterworth, 1925).

Merkling, Frank, Freeman, John W., and Fitzgerald, G., *The Golden Horseshoe* (Secker & Warburg, London, 1965).

Nijinsky, Romola, *Nijinsky* (Gollancz, London, 1933).

Rosenthal, Harold, *Two Centuries of Opera at Covent Garden* (Putnam, New York, 1958).

Rushmore, Robert *The Singing Voice* (Hamish Hamilton, London, 1971).

Seligman, Vincent, *Puccini among friends* (Macmillan, London, 1938).

Sheean, Vincent, *Oscar Hammerstein* (Simon & Schuster, New York, 1956)

Sitwell, Osbert, *Great Morning* (Macmillan, London, 1948).

Taubman, Howard, *The Maestro* (Simon & Schuster, New York, 1951).

Waters, E. N. *Victor Herbert* (Macmillan, New York, 1955),

Wechsberg, Joseph, *Red Plush and Black Velvet* (Weidenfeld & Nicolson, London, 1962).

Winter, William, *The Life of David Belasco* (Moffat, Yard, New York, 1918).

Among numerous newspaper and magazine files consulted I am specially indebted to Pierre Key's articles in the London *Daily Telegraph*, which appeared between June and September 1920; to the *Reader's Digest* for Elizabeth Rosewald's 'The Day I Met Caruso' (August 1959) and 'Unforgettable Caruso' by Bruno Zirato (August 1971); and articles in *The Gramophone*, dated January 1934, March 1935, March 1937, September 1939 and January 1944.

Index

Adams, Evangeline, 230, 286.

Alda, Frances, 116–17, 146, 174–8, 195, 236, 282.

Amato, Pasquale, 116, 120, 195, 223, 240, 272, 285.

Arimondi, Vittorio, 58–60, 69–71, 100, 113, 116, 120.

Astor, Mrs William B., 103–4.

Astruc, Gabriel, 113.

Bard, Wilkie, 207.

Barrymore, Ethel, 235, 273.

Barrymore, Lionel, 235.

Barthélemy, Richard, 118–19, 123, 125, 136, 165, 169, 231.

Battistini, Mattia, 58–62, 69, 190.

Beck, James M., 261.

Belasco, David, 159–60, 196, 199.

Bellezza, Maestro Vincenzo, 237.

Bellincioni, Gemma, 18, 54, 56, 64–5.

Bellosguardo, Villa, 132–4, 144–6, 160, 172, 212, 252, 263–7.

Benjamin, Dorothy, *see* Caruso, Dorothy *and* Caruso, Enrico.

Benjamin, Park, 245–53.

Benjamin, Romeyn, 245–6, 276.

Benjamin, Mrs Walter R., 246, 260.

Bernays, Edward L., 207.

Bernhardt, Sarah, 153, 236.

Black Hand Gang, 182–3, 278.

Bodanzky, Maestro Artur, 271, 285.

Boito, Arrigo, 49, 54, 67–8, 74–5, 79, 81, 137, 282.

Bonci, Alessandro, 49, 55, 62, 73–4, 87–8, 90–1, 100, 114, 140, 154, 159, 166, 168, 173, 206.

Borgatti, Giuseppe, 55, 73–4, 77, 80.

Bori, Lucrezia, 214, 222, 285.

Bracale, Adolfo, 275–6, 278–9.

Bronzetti, Father, 7–9, 22, 33.

Burke, Billie, 181–2.

Calvé, Emma, 18, 28, 86, 90, 93, 104, 128–9, 155.

Campanini, Maestro Cleofonte, 59, 120, 126, 159, 161, 164–5, 168, 193.

Canessa (Amedeo) Galleries, 211, 239, 252, 276.

Carbonetti, Federico, 78.

Carelli, Emma, 76.

Carpentier, Georges, 274.

Caruso, Anna (mother), 3–11.

Caruso, Assunta (sister), 5, 6, 9, 11–12, 40, 67, 201, 225.

Caruso, Dorothy (wife), 240–92. *See also* Caruso, Enrico.

Caruso, Enrico,
  birth, childhood and choirboy years, 3–12.
  first singing lessons, 13–14, 21.
  military service, 22–3.
  operatic débuts, 24–30.
  success in Salerno, 31–8.
  meets Ada Giachetti, 41.
  wins Puccini's favour, 42–3.
  birth of first son, 54.
  triumphs in *Fedora*, 56–7.
  engagements in Russia, 58–62.
  La Scala début. 'Scenes' with Toscanini. Meets Chaliapin, 75–80.
  fiasco at San Carlo, 84–5.

Caruso, Enrico, *contd.*

partners Melba at Monte Carlo and Covent Garden, 86–96.

first gramophone records, 91–2.

contract with Metropolitan, New York, and first season, 104–10.

recording with the Victor Company, 108, 125, 138, 157, 166–7, 177, 189.

taste for clowning on stage, 116–17, 207, 277, 280.

technique and artistic preparation, 118–19, 226–7.

birth of second son, 120.

idiosyncrasies of dress and toilette, 132–3, 207.

Villa Bellosguardo, 113–14, 264–266.

San Francisco earthquake, 141–3.

Central Park Zoo scandal, 149–51.

Ada Giachetti deserts him, 170–3.

friendship with Tetrazzini, 58–62, 192–3, 292.

threatened by Black Hand Gang, 182–3.

first operation for throat trouble, 179.

affair with Elisa Ganelli, 197–8, 202.

slander action against Ada Giachetti, 202–4.

art, stamps and coin collecting, 211–13.

wartime activities, bond-raising, etc., 223 *et seq.*

courtship and marriage, 240–53.

film actor, 249–50, 262.

Metropolitan jubilee celebration, 260–2.

postwar troubles at Signa, 264–7.

visits Mexico, 268–70.

birth of Gloria, 273.

sings in Havana, 273–9.

Long Island jewel robbery, 277.

moves into Vanderbilt Hotel, 280.

illness and collapse, 282–6.

death in Naples, 290.

funeral scenes, 290–1.

estate, 291.

OPERAS AND MAIN REPERTOIRE (in order of first appearances):

L'Amico Francesco (Morelli).

Cavalleria Rusticana (Mascagni).

Faust (Gounod).

Rigoletto (Verdi).

La Gioconda (Ponchielli).

Manon Lescaut (Puccini).

La Traviata (Verdi).

Lucia di Lammermoor (Donizetti).

I Puritani (Bellini).

Carmen (Bizet).

La Favorita (Donizetti).

I Pagliacci (Leoncavallo).

La Bohème (Puccini).

La Navarraise (Massenet).

L'Arlésiana (Cilèa).

La Bohème (Leoncavallo).

Les Pecheurs de Perles (Bizet).

Fedora (Giordano).

Iris (Mascagni).

Mefistofele (Boito).

Aïda (Verdi).

Un Ballo in Maschera (Verdi).

Manon (Massenet).

La Tosca (Puccini).

Le Maschere (Mascagni).

L'Elisir d'Amore (Donizetti).

Germania (Franchetti).

Don Giovanni (Mozart).

Adrienne Lecourveur (Cilèa).

Les Huguenots (Meyerbeer).

Madama Butterfly (Puccini).

La Somnambula (Bellini).

Martha (Flotow).

Andrea Chénier (Giordano).
Il Trovatore (Verdi).
La Fanciulla del West (Puccini).
Julien (Charpentier).
Samson et Dalila (Saint-Saëns).
Lodoletta (Mascagni).
Le Prophète (Meyerbeer).
La Forza del Destion (Verdi).
La Juive (Halévy).

Caruso, Enrico Jr. (son, 'Mimmi'), 120, 134, 194, 217–18, 221–2, 230, 266–7, 275, 279, 285–6, 291–2.
Caruso, Giovanni (brother), 5, 9, 11–12, 14, 23, 35, 40, 144, 178, 221, 265, 291.
Caruso, Gloria (daughter), 273, 278–9, 284–8, 291–2.
Caruso, Marcellino (father), 3–11, 40, 66–7, 82–3, 85, 135, 169–70.
Caruso, Maria Castaldi (stepmother), 11–12, 14, 22–3, 28–9, 40, 66–7, 82–3, 85, 135, 170, 201, 265.
Caruso, Rodolfo (son, 'Fofò'), 54, 57, 63, 66, 81–2, 197, 218, 231, 248, 275, 291–2.
Cavalieri, Lina, 113–14, 126.
Central Park Zoo, 149–51.
Chaliapin, Fedor, 15, 79–80, 167–168, 190, 216–17, 258, 260.
Chaplin, Charles, 235–6.
Child, Calvin G., 108–9, 124–5, 157, 167, 177, 189, 219, 249, 279.
Cohan, George M., 235, 249, 258.
Conried, Heinrich, 98–100, 105–8, 135–6, 139, 143–4, 149, 152–60, 168–9.
Coquelin, Constant, 148, 211.
Covent Garden, *see* Caruso, Melba, Higgins.

Daspuro, Nicola, 19, 24, 40, 84–5.
Destinn, Emmy, 90, 125, 127–9, 145, 174, 195, 219, 232.
Diaghilev, Serge, 216, 232–3.
Dippel, Andréas, 169, 174–5.

Eames, Emma, 103–4, 136, 142, 145, 155, 157, 174.
Edward VII, King, 90–1, 114, 129, 145, 161, 171, 247.
Enright, Police Commissioner, 255, 261.

Farrar, Geraldine, 104, 111 *et seq.*, 152–3, 157, 165–6, 174, 176, 187, 219, 222–3, 229–30, 235, 238, 258, 261, 286.
Follia, La, 124, 208, 260, 275.
Fucito, Salvatore, 226–7, 253, 268, 270, 276, 279–80, 282, 284 *et seq.*, 287–9.

Gaisberg, Fred and Will, 91–2, 98, 108, 139.
Galli-Curci, Amelita, 225.
Ganelli, Elisa, 197–8, 202, 213, 248.
Garden, Mary, 106, 154, 165, 168, 174–6.
Gatti-Casazza, Giulio, 54–5, 74–81, 168–9, 174–7, 187–90, 199–200, 219, 221–4, 232–3, 260–1, 267, 282, 284, 287, 289.
Gest, Morris, 223, 235.
Giachetti, Ada, 36, 41 *et seq.* See *also* Caruso, Enrico.
Giachetti, Rina, 52–3, 57, 82, 85, 120, 123, 145–6, 172, 180, 197, 206, 218, 222.
Gigli, Beniamino, 206, 282, 286–7, 292.
Giraldoni, Eugenio, 117.
Goddard, Mrs Torrance, 248.
Goulet, Mrs Ogden, 137–8, 153, 249.

Grahame-White, Claude, 219.
Grassi, Peppo and Giuseppina, 32–8.
Grau, Maurice, 63–4, 88–9, 95, 97–8, 100, 104.
Gravina, 208–9.
Guard, William J., 151, 154–7, 165–6, 207, 229, 260, 272, 283–4.
Gunsbourg, Raoul, 57, 81, 86–8, 110–11, 113, 222–3.

Hammerstein, Oscar, 143, 151, 153 et seq., 168, 187 et seq.
Herbert, Victor, 137, 228, 233, 235.
Higgins, Harry V., 90–1, 93, 97, 120, 164.
Homer, Louise, 216, 256.
Humperdinck, Engelbert, 182.
Hylan, Mayor, 255, 261.

Kahn, Otto H., 104–5, 143, 152, 168, 178, 188, 195, 223–4, 260–1.
Keller, Helen, 236.
Kessler, George A., 130–1.
Kreisler, Fritz, 64, 161, 192, 198, 238, 258.
Kruscheniska, Salomea, 69–70.
Kurz, Selma, 127, 148.

Lanza, Mario, 262 f., 292 f.
Lara, Isidore de, 18.
Lasky, Jesse L., 209, 223, 229, 249–50, 252, 262.
Ledner, Emil, 173, 180, 204.
Lehmann, Lotte, 180–1.
Leoncavallo, ˜ ᵃˣᵉᵣo, 20, 23, 34, 39, 50–1, 62, 78, 98, 113.
Lombardi, Maestro Vincenzo, 30–9, 118, 210.
Lorello, Enrico (secretary), 31, 33, 37, 67 et seq., 82, 99, 132.
Lucia, Fernando de, 18, 20, 25, 32, 34, 36, 49, 55, 61–2, 70, 84, 90.

Mackenzie, Sir Compton, quoted, 138.
Marchi, Emilio de, 68, 70, 72–3, 80, 83.
Mario, Cavaliere di Candia (tenor), 17, 28, 49, 238, 265, 292.
Mario (Caruso's valet), 196 et seq., 223, 238 et seq., 253, 256, 259, 263, 266–8, 276, 280, 285, 288.
Martin, Riccardo, 210.
Martinelli, Giovanni, 206, 292.
Martini (valet and major domo), 132–3 et passim.
Mascagni, Pietro, 19–20, 23, 63, 77–8, 96, 118, 221.
Masini, Angelo, 18, 23, 58, 60–2, 101, 126.
McCormack, John, 127, 164–6, 187, 190–2, 206, 212, 231, 235, 258–9, 286.
McNamara, Ed, 209.
Melba, Nellie, 61, 81, 86 et seq., 111 et seq., 120, 125–9, 139, 146, 157, 161, 164, 215–6.
Metropolitan Opera House, see Caruso, Grau, Conried, Gatti-Casazza, Farrar.
Meuricoffre, Francesco, 6, 10–12, 23.
Missiano, Eduardo, 13–14, 24, 144–145.
Mocchi, Walter, 224–5, 237.
Morelli, Mario, 24–5.
Morgana, Nina, 257.
Mugnone, Maestro Leopoldo, 31–41, 67 et seq., 70, 73–4, 144, 226, 231.

Nagliotti, Major, 22–3.
Nicholas II, Tsar, 60, 62–3, 66, 84, 247.
Nijinsky, Vaslav, 201, 232–3.
Niola, Dr Raffaele, 9, 11.

Pagani's Restaurant, London, 96–7, 118, 128, 146, 198.
Patti, Adelina, 102, 164.
Plancon, Pol, 141–2.
Ponselle, Rosa, 271, 285.
Puccini, Giacomo, 19–20, 23, 27, 37, 41–5, 61, 63, 68–70, 74, 76, 78, 81–2, 91, 96, 99, 110–11, 125–6, 128, 134, 146–7, 157–9, 198–9, 206, 221, 226, 231.
Punzo (valet), 14–15, 21, 23, 40, 256, 268–9, 272, 276, 284, 288.

Réjane, 195.
Renaud, Maurice, 81, 87, 105, 113, 159, 172, 187.
Reszke, Edouard de, 104, 115, 125.
Reszke, Jean de, 17, 21, 61–2, 69, 86–90, 101, 104, 106–8, 114–15, 126, 140, 159, 195, 256.
Ricordi, Giulio, 18–20, 41–2, 44, 51, 55.
Ricordi, Tito, 68, 120, 125, 198.
Rodewald, Elizabeth, 234.
Roosevelt, President Theodore, 139, 141, 143.
Ruffo, Titta, 83–4, 111, 116, 126, 148, 214, 219.

Saer, Louise, 134, 194, 218, 221, 230, 266.
Sammarco, Mario, 80, 120, 215, 225.
San Carlo, Naples, see Caruso, Gatti-Casazza, Toscanini, Chaliapin, Daspuro.
San Francisco earthquake, 141–3.
Savoy Hotel, London, 118, 130–1, 146, 160, 162.
Schenck, Joseph, 249–50.
Schipa, Tito, 291.
Schol (Metropolitan claque), 257, 259, 286, 288, 290.
Scotti, Antonio, 31, 55, 64–5, 70,

73–4, 81, 90–1, 94 *et seq.*, 107, 124–6, 128–9, 139, 141–2, 147, 152–3, 174, 219–21, 258, 280, 282, 286, 291.
Segurola, Andrés de, 167.
Seligman, Sybil, 128, 159, 161–2, 198, 218.
Sembrich, Marcella, 102, 107, 125, 142, 153, 174, 287.
Simonelli, Pasquale, 99–100, 106, 110, 124.
Sisca, Marziale, 124, 260.
Sitwell, Sir Osbert, *quoted*, 215–16.
Sonzogno, Eduardo, 18–20, 34, 40–1, 45, 49 *et seq.*, 57, 63, 68.
Sperco, Constant J., 239.
Stagno, Roberto, 18, 23, 56, 102.

Tamagno, Francesco, 13, 17–19, 21, 23, 28, 37, 49, 55, 60, 62, 69, 78, 84, 86, 93, 104, 140, 209.
Tanara, Maestro Fernando, 240, 292.
Tetrazzini, Eva (Signora Campanini), 59, 98.
Tetrazzini, Luisa, 59 *et seq.*, 64, 69, 70, 88, 91, 105, 154, 163 *et seq.*, 172–3, 187–8, 191–3, 210, 213, 274, 281, 286, 292.
Tonello, Father, 169–71.
Toscanini, Arturo, 16, 31, 35, 49, 54–5, 74–80, 83, 91, 100–1, 119, 169, 174–8, 196, 199–200, 219, 222–4, 226.
Tosti, Sir Paolo, 17–18, 54–5, 68, 91, 95–7, 116, 118, 161, 170–1, 196, 198, 215–16, 231.

Vanderbilt, Alfred Gwynne, 280, 284.
Vanderbilt, Mrs Cornelius, 103, 136–7, 200.
Verdi, Giuseppe, 15–20, 23, 54–5, 60, 62, 67, 70, 78, 92, 101, 108.

Vergine, Maestro Guglielmo, 13–14, 17, 21–4, 26–8, 32, 40, 45, 51, 66–7.

Vigna, Maestro Arturo, 107, 112–13, 158, 168.

Voghera, Maestro Tullio, 169–70, 226.

Wales, Prince of (Duke of Windsor), 216, 271–2.

Whitney, Mrs W. Payne, 108.

Wilhelm II, Kaiser, 148, 173, 231, 247.

Zenatello, Giovanni, 159, 206.

Zezza, Baron, 12–13.

Zirato, Bruno (private secretary), 239 *et seq.*, 252–3, 256–7, 260, 268, 270, 273–9, 282–5, 288.

Zucchi, Francesco, 25–31, 33–4, 66.

Zukor, Adolph, 262.